AF430911

اَلْحِزْبُ الْأَعْظَمُ

Al-Hizbul A'zam

NEW REVISED TRANSLATION

Compiled by

Shaikh Ali ibn Sultaan Muhammad Al-Qaari

(rahmatullahi alayh)

Title: Al Hizbul A'zam

Author: Shaikh Ali ibn Sultaan Muhammad Al-Qaari *(rahmatullahi alayh)*

Translation revised by
Jamiatul Ulama (KZN)
Ta'limi Board
4 Third Avenue
P.O.Box 26024
Isipingo Beach
4115
South Africa

First Edition: Rabiul Awwal 1435 / February 2014
Second Edition: Safar 1436 / December 2014
Third Edition: Zul Hijjah 1439 / August 2018

Published by:
Islamic Book Store
302 Saad Residency
Sahin Park Bardoli
Surat Gujarat
India
Pin – 394601
Ph. 0091 9979353876

Contents

Introduction to the revised edition

All praise is due to Allah Ta'ala, The Supreme Master of the worlds. Countless Durood and Salaam be upon our beloved Nabi, Sayyiduna wa Mawlana Muhammad ﷺ.

Just as the Qur-aan-e-Majeed is a living mu'jizah (miracle) of our beloved Nabi Muhammad ﷺ, so too are the mubaarak duas of Rasulullah ﷺ. Every dua that Nabi ﷺ made is applicable to every period of time and will be applicable till the day of Qiyaamah.

The great Muhaddith, Mullah A'li Qaari (*rahmatullahi alayh*), most excellently compiled the duas mentioned in the Qur-aan-e-Kareem as well as the duas and supplications of our beloved Nabi Muhammad ﷺ, in his booklet titled Al- Hizbul A'zam. These include the duas that Nabi ﷺ made at the Ka'bah Shareef, in the Hateem, the duas made on the occasion of Haj, in Mina, Arafaat and Muzdalifa, the duas that Nabi ﷺ made at the time of Tahajjud and in the different battles and expeditions that took place in the twenty-three year period of his Nubuwwat. Each dua was divinely inspired by Allah Ta'ala and will remain a balm for ailing hearts till the day of Qiyaamah.

These duas are a means of protection for all Muslims against the harms of this world and the next. It is mentioned in a Hadith,

"Dua is the essence of ibaadah." How wonderful it would be to invoke, beg, plead and ask from Allah Ta'ala in the very words of His beloved Nabi ﷺ. Undoubtedly the words of Nabi ﷺ will have its own noor (light) and barkat (blessings), as compared to making dua in our own words.

This book is excellently divided into seven sections, thus making it easier for the reader to recite one section per day. Many of our Akaabir (elders) would instruct their students and mureeds to recite one section daily as part of their ma'moolaat (daily practices). This masterpiece has indeed gained great acceptance in the court of Allah Ta'ala. People all over the world recite these duas daily and gain great solace from these Prophetic Duas. Hadhrat Shaikhul Hadeeth, Moulana Muhammad Zakariyya (rahmatullahi alayh) in particular, was very punctual on its recitation.

Hadhrat Moulana Badr-e-Aalam Saahib *(rahmatullahi alayh)*, of Madinah Munawwarah, was among the very first people to translate these duas into the Urdu language, thus making it easier for the general public to understand the meanings of the duas of Rasulullah ﷺ. These duas were subsequently translated into many other languages.

In 1968, Sayed Aqeel Muhammad Saahib, with the encouragement and duas of Moulana Sayed Aftaab Ahmed, the son of the late Moulana Badr-e-Aalaam Saahib *(rahmatullahi alayh)*, took up the courage to translate these duas into English. *Al-hamdulillah,* this translation was widely accepted in many parts of the world.

May Allah Ta'ala bless Bhai Ahmed Yaqoob Laher of Johannesburg as well as the Ulama of the Waterval Islamic Institute for having arranged for its printing.

However, as the years progressed and literacy levels dropped, the need arose once again to simplify the language and bring it close to spoken English, as many of the words that are used in the said translation are not commonly spoken anymore. Therefore, with the *fadhal* of Allah Ta'ala and the duas of our elders, especially Hadhrat Mufti Ebraheem Salehjee Saahib *(daamat barakaatuhu)*, the Jamiatul Ulama (KZN) Ta'limi Board made an attempt to simplify the English to make it easier for the readers. Our Mashaaikh have emphasised that we ponder over the meanings of these duas when reciting them, rather than just reciting them parrot fashion. References have also been added in accordance to the book prepared by Moulana Abu Bakr Patni of Dhabel.

The 40 durood and salaam has now also been included at the end of the kitaab. May Allah Ta'ala accept this translation and make it a means of *hidaayat* for the *ummah* as well as *Sadaqah-e-Jaariyah* for us all. *Aameen.*

The readers are humbly requested that should they come across any errors then they should please inform the publishers. *Insha Allah,* these corrections will be made in the new edition. This will also be in keeping with the spirit of the Hadith *"Deen is to advise one another."*

Introduction by the author, Mullah Ali Qari (rahmatullahi alayh)

الحمد لله الذى دعانا للايمان و هدانا بالقران......

This servant, Mullah Ali ibn Sultaan Muhammad Al-Qaari (may Allah Ta'ala conceal his faults), had seen many *saalikeen* (seekers of the love of Allah Ta'ala) who were linked to our noble and reliable scholars reciting their wazaaif (daily recitations) with much enthusiasm. However, I found that some of them were reading Dua-e-Sayfi and Arbaeen-e-Ismi, etc. I even saw some people reading Dua-e-Qa<u>dh</u>ah. However, the chain of narrators of these duas clearly shows that they have been fabricated.

This motivated me to compile the duas mentioned in the reliable books of Hadith, similar to what Allamah Jazari *(rahimahullah)* compiled in "Hisn-e-Haseen" and Allamah Nawawi *(rahimahullah)* compiled in his Azkaar. Likewise Allamah Suyuuti *(rahimahullah)* had also compiled 'Al Kalimut Tayyib', 'Aljami'een and Ad-Durar while Allamah Sakhaawi *(rahimahullah)* compiled 'Alqawlul Badee'.

In the first part of this book I have recorded the duas mentioned in the Quraan-e-Kareem and I have ended the book with the narrations of durood upon Nabi-e-Kareem ﷺ. I am hopeful that I will also enjoy the benefits of these duas because the one who initiates a good act is rewarded as if he had done it himself. I make dua to Allah Ta'ala that He accept this work, keep my intention pure and sublime and that He keeps these duas always on the lips of the people.

I have named this compilation Al-Hizbul 'Azam wal Wirdul Afkham. I chose this name because these duas are all linked to our beloved Nabi Muhammad ﷺ. Hence, please take full care of its words, ponder deeply over its meanings and practice on its contents. This compilation of duas will become a means of your success and a saviour from all kinds of harms.

Nabi ﷺ did not leave out any good habit or excellent practice for which he did not make dua for and there were no evil habits or bad practices from which he did not seek protection.

How wonderful it would be if every day we read this entire compilation, or at least every week, or even once a month. If this also is not possible, then at least once a year and if this also is not possible, then in your entire lifetime if you manage to read it at least once only, this too is commendable.

If you get a chance to read these duas in Arafaat then add the following to it; 100 times Fourth Kalimah, 100 times Surah Ikhlaas, 100 times Third Kalimah.

Do not forget to also recite the *labbaik* in between the deep sighs of your duas so that your invocations may be quickly accepted.

① اَعُوْذُ بِاللهِ مِنَ الشَّيْطَانِ الرَّجِيْمِ

1. I seek protection in Allah from shaytaan the accursed.

② بِسْمِ اللهِ الرَّحْمٰنِ الرَّحِيْمِ

2. In the name of Allah, the most Compassionate the most Merciful.

③ اَلْحَمْدُ لِلّٰهِ رَبِّ الْعٰلَمِيْنَ ۙ الرَّحْمٰنِ

3. All praise is due to Allah, the Cherisher of the worlds, Most Compassionate Most Merciful,

الرَّحِيْمِ ۙ مٰلِكِ يَوْمِ الدِّيْنِ ۙ اِيَّاكَ نَعْبُدُ وَاِيَّاكَ

Master of the Day of Judgment. You alone we worship and You alone

3. Faatiha

نَسْتَعِيْنُ ۞ اِهْدِنَا الصِّرَاطَ الْمُسْتَقِيْمَ ۞ صِرَاطَ

we ask for help. Guide us to the straight path, the path

الَّذِيْنَ اَنْعَمْتَ عَلَيْهِمْ ۞ غَيْرِ الْمَغْضُوْبِ

of those whom You have favoured. Not of those whom You became angered with

عَلَيْهِمْ وَلَا الضَّآلِّيْنَ ۞ اٰمِيْنَ

nor (of those) who went astray. *Aameen.*

۞ اَعُوْذُ بِاللهِ اَنْ اَكُوْنَ مِنَ الْجٰهِلِيْنَ

4. I seek Allah's protection that I be from the ignorant ones.

۞ رَبَّنَا تَقَبَّلْ مِنَّا اِنَّكَ اَنْتَ السَّمِيْعُ

5. O Allah! Accept from us (our good actions), verily You are all Hearing

| 4. Baqarah # 67 | 5. Baqarah # 127, 128 |

الْعَلِيْمُ وَتُبْ عَلَيْنَا اِنَّكَ اَنْتَ التَّوَّابُ

and all Knowing. Accept our *taubah* (repentance). Verily You are Most Forgiving,

الرَّحِيْمُ

Most Merciful.

۶ رَبَّنَآ اٰتِنَا فِى الدُّنْيَا حَسَنَةً وَّ فِى الْاٰخِرَةِ

6. O Allah! Grant us the good of this world and the good of the Hereafter

حَسَنَةً وَّ قِنَا عَذَابَ النَّارِ

and save us from the punishment of the fire.

۷ رَبَّنَآ اَفْرِغْ عَلَيْنَا صَبْرًا وَّثَبِّتْ اَقْدَامَنَا

7. O Allah! Infuse *sabr* (patience) in us, keep our feet firm

6. Baqarah # 201	7. Baqarah # 250

وَانْصُرْنَا عَلَى الْقَوْمِ الْكَٰفِرِيْنَ

and help us against the disbelievers.

۝۸ سَمِعْنَا وَاَطَعْنَا غُفْرَانَكَ رَبَّنَا وَاِلَيْكَ

8. We have heard and obeyed. We seek Your forgiveness, O Allah, and to You

الْمَصِيْرُ ۚ رَبَّنَا لَا تُؤَاخِذْنَآ اِنْ نَّسِيْنَآ اَوْ

is our return. O Allah! Do not punish us for the sins we committed by mistake or

اَخْطَأْنَا رَبَّنَا وَلَا تَحْمِلْ عَلَيْنَآ اِصْرًا كَمَا

in error. Do not burden us with such heavy duties as had been

حَمَلْتَهٗ عَلَى الَّذِيْنَ مِنْ قَبْلِنَا رَبَّنَا وَلَا تُحَمِّلْنَا

placed on the people before us. O Allah! Do not burden us

8. Baqarah # 285, 286

مَا لَا طَاقَةَ لَنَا بِهٖ وَاعْفُ عَنَّا وَاغْفِرْ لَنَا

with that which is beyond our ability. Overlook our sins, Forgive us

وَارْحَمْنَا اَنْتَ مَوْلٰنَا فَانْصُرْنَا عَلَى الْقَوْمِ

and have mercy on us. You are our Master so help us against the

الْكٰفِرِيْنَ

disbelievers.

رَبَّنَا لَا تُزِغْ قُلُوْبَنَا بَعْدَ اِذْ هَدَيْتَنَا ۝

9. O Allah! Do not let our hearts go astray after You have guided us, and grant us

وَهَبْ لَنَا مِنْ لَّدُنْكَ رَحْمَةً اِنَّكَ اَنْتَ الْوَهَّابُ

mercy from Your side. Verily You are The Great Giver of favours.

9. Aali-Imraan # 8, 9

O Allah! You will definitely gather all human beings on a Day in which there is no doubt. Verily

اللهَ لَا يُخْلِفُ الْمِيْعَادَ

Allah never breaks His promise.

رَبَّنَا اِنَّنَا اٰمَنَّا فَاغْفِرْ لَنَا ذُنُوْبَنَا وَقِنَا ﴿١٠﴾

10. O Allah! We have definitely believed in You, so please forgive our sins and save us from the

عَذَابَ النَّارِ

punishment of the fire.

11. (Say) O Allah! Owner of the kingdom, You give authority to whomsoever

10. Aali-Imraan # 16	11. Aali-Imraan # 26, 27

تَشَآءُ وَتَنْزِعُ الْمُلْكَ مِمَّنْ تَشَآءُ وَتُعِزُّ مَنْ

You wish and snatch it away from whomsoever You wish. You grant respect to whom

تَشَآءُ وَتُذِلُّ مَنْ تَشَآءُ بِيَدِكَ الْخَيْرُ اِنَّكَ عَلٰى

You please and You disgrace whom You wish. All good is in Your hands and surely You

كُلِّ شَىْءٍ قَدِيْرٌ ۚ تُوْلِجُ الَّيْلَ فِى النَّهَارِ وَتُوْلِجُ

have power over all things. You introduce the night into day

النَّهَارَ فِى الَّيْلِ وَتُخْرِجُ الْحَىَّ مِنَ الْمَيِّتِ

and the day into night. You take out the living from the dead

وَتُخْرِجُ الْمَيِّتَ مِنَ الْحَىِّ وَتَرْزُقُ مَنْ تَشَآءُ

and the dead from the living and You grant sustenance to whomsoever You wish

بِغَيْرِ حِسَابٍ

without any limit.

۞ رَبِّ هَبْ لِيْ مِنْ لَّدُنْكَ ذُرِّيَّةً طَيِّبَةً اِنَّكَ

12. O Allah! Bless me from Your side with a noble offspring. Verily You

سَمِيْعُ الدُّعَآءِ

hear our duas.

۞ رَبَّنَا اٰمَنَّا بِمَآ اَنْزَلْتَ وَاتَّبَعْنَا الرَّسُوْلَ

13. O Allah! We have believed in what You revealed and we obeyed the messenger

فَاكْتُبْنَا مَعَ الشَّاهِدِيْنَ

so enlist us among the witnesses.

| 12. Aali-Imraan # 38 | 13. Aali-Imraan # 53 |

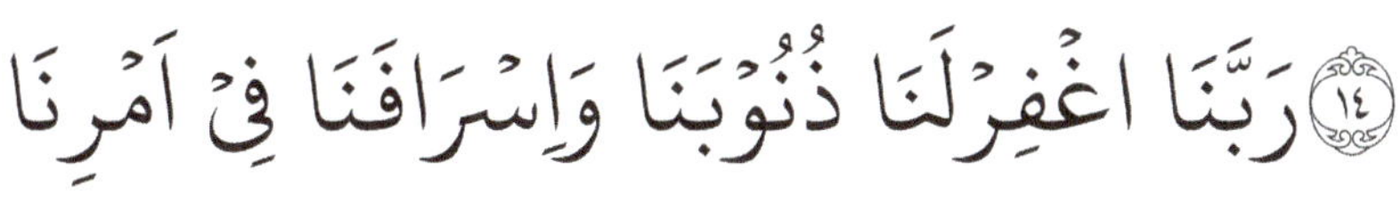

رَبَّنَا اغْفِرْلَنَا ذُنُوْبَنَا وَاِسْرَافَنَا فِيْ اَمْرِنَا ﴿١٤﴾

14. O Allah! Forgive our sins and forgive us for overstepping the mark,

وَثَبِّتْ اَقْدَامَنَا وَانْصُرْنَا عَلَى الْقَوْمِ

keep our feet firm and help us against the

الْكٰفِرِيْنَ

disbelievers.

رَبَّنَا مَا خَلَقْتَ هٰذَا بَاطِلًا سُبْحٰنَكَ فَقِنَا ﴿١٥﴾

15. O Allah! You have not created this (world) without any purpose. You are free from all blemishes so protect us

عَذَابَ النَّارِ ۗ رَبَّنَآ اِنَّكَ مَنْ تُدْخِلِ النَّارَ

from the fire of Hell. O Allah! Whoever You have admitted into Hell,

14. Aali-Imraan # 147	15. Aali-Imraan # 191 - 194

فَقَدْ اَخْزَيْتَهٗ وَمَا لِلظّٰلِمِيْنَ مِنْ اَنْصَارٍ ۗ رَبَّنَاۤ

really You have disgraced him and there are no helpers for the sinners. O Allah!

اِنَّنَا سَمِعْنَا مُنَادِيًا يُّنَادِيْ لِلْاِيْمٰنِ اَنْ اٰمِنُوْا

We heard a caller calling us to Imaan saying "Believe in

بِرَبِّكُمْ فَاٰمَنَّا ۗ رَبَّنَا فَاغْفِرْلَنَا ذُنُوْبَنَا وَكَفِّرْ

your Rabb!" so we believed. O Allah! Forgive our sins and pardon

عَنَّا سَيِّئَاتِنَا وَتَوَفَّنَا مَعَ الْاَبْرَارِ ۗ رَبَّنَا وَاٰتِنَا

our wrongs and when removing our souls include us among the righteous. O Allah! Grant us

مَا وَعَدْتَّنَا عَلٰى رُسُلِكَ وَلَا تُخْزِنَا يَوْمَ الْقِيٰمَةِ

what You have promised us through Your Messengers and do not disgrace us on the Day of Judgement.

اِنَّكَ لَا تُخْلِفُ الْمِيْعَادَ

Surely You never break Your promise.

رَبَّنَاۤ اَخْرِجْنَا مِنْ هٰذِهِ الْقَرْيَةِ الظَّالِمِ ۙ ⟨١٦⟩

16. O Allah! Remove us from this town whose inhabitants practise oppression

اَهْلُهَا وَاجْعَلْ لَّنَا مِنْ لَّدُنْكَ وَلِيًّا ۙ وَّاجْعَلْ لَّنَا

and make for us from Your side, friends

مِنْ لَّدُنْكَ نَصِيْرًا

and helpers.

رَبَّنَاۤ اَنْزِلْ عَلَيْنَا مَآئِدَةً مِّنَ السَّمَآءِ ⟨١٧⟩

17. O Allah! Send for us from the heavens a tray of food

| 16. Nisaa # 75 | 17. Maa'idah # 114 |

تَكُوْنُ لَنَا عِيْدًا لِّاَوَّلِنَا وَاٰخِرِنَا وَاٰيَةً مِّنْكَ

so that it becomes a day of rejoicing for the first and the last among us and a sign from You

وَارْزُقْنَا وَاَنْتَ خَيْرُ الرّٰزِقِيْنَ

and bless us with sustenance. You are the Best of Sustainers.

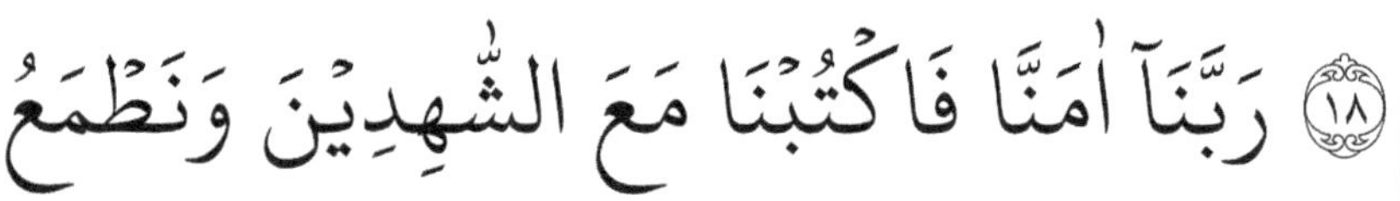

رَبَّنَاۤ اٰمَنَّا فَاكْتُبْنَا مَعَ الشّٰهِدِيْنَ وَنَطْمَعُ ۝١٨

18. O Allah! We have brought Imaan so enlist us among the witnesses. And we have hope

اَنْ يُّدْخِلَنَا رَبُّنَا مَعَ الْقَوْمِ الصّٰلِحِيْنَ

that our Rabb will include us among the righteous people.

رَبَّنَا لَا تَجْعَلْنَا مَعَ الْقَوْمِ الظّٰلِمِيْنَ ۝١٩

19. O Allah! Do not make us among those who commit oppression.

| 18. Maa'idah # 83, 84 | 19. A'araaf # 47 |

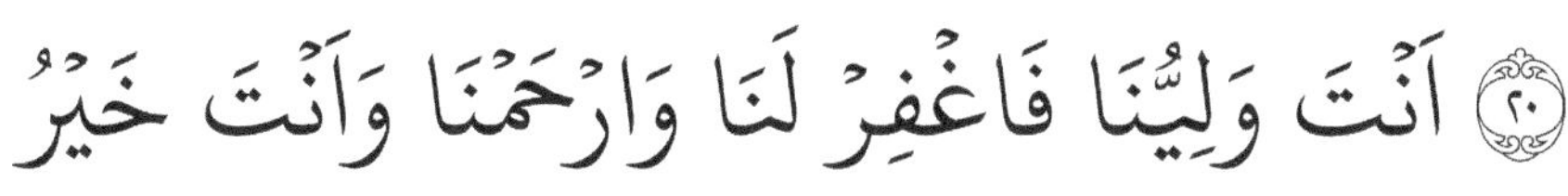

اَنْتَ وَلِيُّنَا فَاغْفِرْ لَنَا وَارْحَمْنَا وَاَنْتَ خَيْرُ ۝

20. You are our guardian, forgive us and have mercy on us and You are the Best

الْغٰفِرِيْنَ وَاكْتُبْ لَنَا فِيْ هٰذِهِ الدُّنْيَا حَسَنَةً

of forgivers. Destine good for us in this world

وَّفِي الْاٰخِرَةِ اِنَّا هُدْنَآ اِلَيْكَ

and the next. Truly we have turned to You.

رَبَّنَآ اِنَّكَ تَعْلَمُ مَا نُخْفِيْ وَمَا نُعْلِنُ وَمَا ۝

21. O Allah! You know what we do secretly and what we do openly. Nothing

يَخْفٰى عَلَى اللهِ مِنْ شَيْءٍ فِي الْاَرْضِ وَلَا فِي

in the earth nor in

| 20. A'araaf # 155, 156 | 21. Ibrahim # 38 |

السَّمَآءِ

the heavens is hidden from Allah Ta'ala.

رَبَّنَا ظَلَمْنَا اَنْفُسَنَا وَاِنْ لَّمْ تَغْفِرْ لَنَا ﴿٢٢﴾

22. O Allah! We have wronged ourselves and if You do not forgive us

وَتَرْحَمْنَا لَنَكُوْنَنَّ مِنَ الْخَاسِرِيْنَ

and have mercy on us, we shall certainly be from amongst the losers.

رَبَّنَا افْتَحْ بَيْنَنَا وَبَيْنَ قَوْمِنَا بِالْحَقِّ ﴿٢٣﴾

22. O Allah! Judge between us and our people with justice

وَاَنْتَ خَيْرُ الْفَاتِحِيْنَ

and You are the Best of judges.

22. A'araaf # 23	23. A'araaf # 89

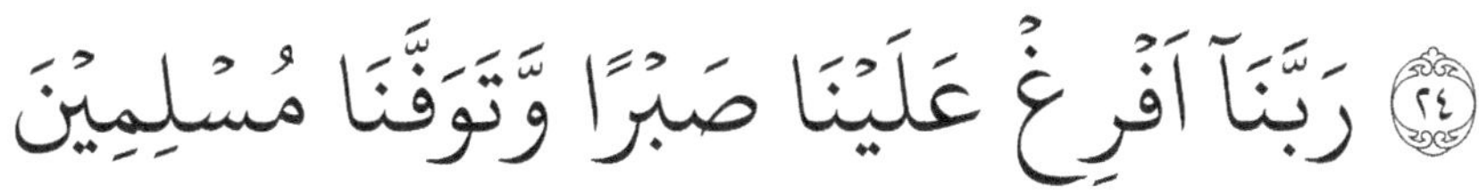

رَبَّنَآ اَفْرِغْ عَلَيْنَا صَبْرًا وَّتَوَفَّنَا مُسْلِمِيْنَ ۝

24. O Allah! Infuse patience in us and cause us to die as Muslims.

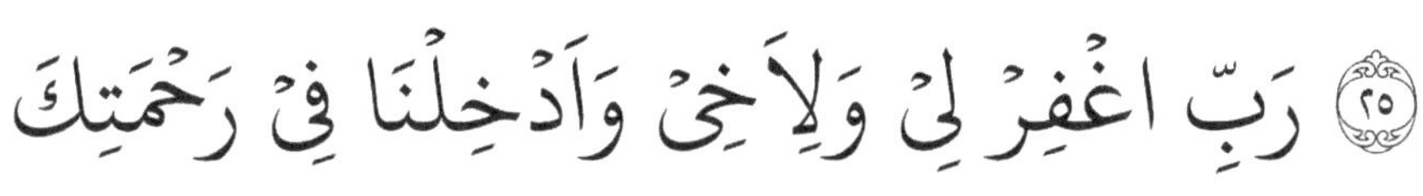

رَبِّ اغْفِرْ لِيْ وَلِاَخِيْ وَاَدْخِلْنَا فِيْ رَحْمَتِكَ ۝

25. O Allah! Forgive me and my brother and admit us into Your mercy.

وَاَنْتَ اَرْحَمُ الرّٰحِمِيْنَ

You arc Thc Most Merciful of those who show mercy.

عَلَى اللّٰهِ تَوَكَّلْنَا ۗ رَبَّنَا لَا تَجْعَلْنَا فِتْنَةً ۝

26. We place our trust in Allah. O Allah! Do not make us a victim

لِّلْقَوْمِ الظّٰلِمِيْنَ وَنَجِّنَا بِرَحْمَتِكَ مِنَ الْقَوْمِ

for the cruel ones and save us, by Your mercy, from the clutches of

| 24. A'araaf # 126 | 25. A'araaf # 151 | 26. Yunus # 85, 86 |

الْكَافِرِيْنَ

the disbelievers.

27. O Allah! I seek Your protection from asking for anything which I have no

بِهٖ عِلْمٌ وَاِلَّا تَغْفِرْ لِيْ وَتَرْحَمْنِيْ اَكُنْ مِّنَ

knowledge of and if You do not forgive me and have mercy on me, I shall

الْخٰسِرِيْنَ

become a loser.

28. O The Maker of the skies and the earth. You are my guardian in this world

27. Hood # 47	28. Yusuf # 101

وَالْاٰخِرَةِ تَوَفَّنِيْ مُسْلِمًا وَّاَلْحِقْنِيْ بِالصَّالِحِيْنَ

and the hereafter. Cause me to die as a Muslim and join me with the pious.

اِنَّ رَبِّيْ لَسَمِيْعُ الدُّعَآءِ رَبِّ اجْعَلْنِيْ مُقِيْمَ ۩

29. Verily, my Rabb hears all duas. O Allah! Make me

الصَّلٰوةِ وَمِنْ ذُرِّيَّتِيْ رَبَّنَا وَتَقَبَّلْ دُعَآءِ

and my children from those who establish salaah and accept my duas.

رَبَّنَا اغْفِرْ لِيْ وَلِوَالِدَيَّ وَلِلْمُؤْمِنِيْنَ يَوْمَ

O Allah! Forgive me, my parents and all the Muslims on the Day of

يَقُوْمُ الْحِسَابُ

Reckoning.

29. Ibrahim # 39-41

رَبِّ ارْحَمْهُمَا كَمَا رَبَّيَانِيْ صَغِيْرًا ۝

30. O Allah! Have mercy on them (my parents) as they (had mercy on me) when they brought me up in my childhood.

رَبِّ اَدْخِلْنِيْ مُدْخَلَ صِدْقٍ وَّاَخْرِجْنِيْ ۝

31. O Allah! Grant me a blessed entry (into Madinah) and

مُخْرَجَ صِدْقٍ وَّاجْعَلْ لِّيْ مِنْ لَّدُنْكَ سُلْطٰنًا

a blessed departure (from Makkah) and grant me from Your side the required strength

نَّصِيْرًا

which will assist me (against Your enemies).

رَبَّنَاۤ اٰتِنَا مِنْ لَّدُنْكَ رَحْمَةً وَّهَيِّئْ لَنَا مِنْ ۝

32. O Allah! Grant us Your mercy and make easy for us

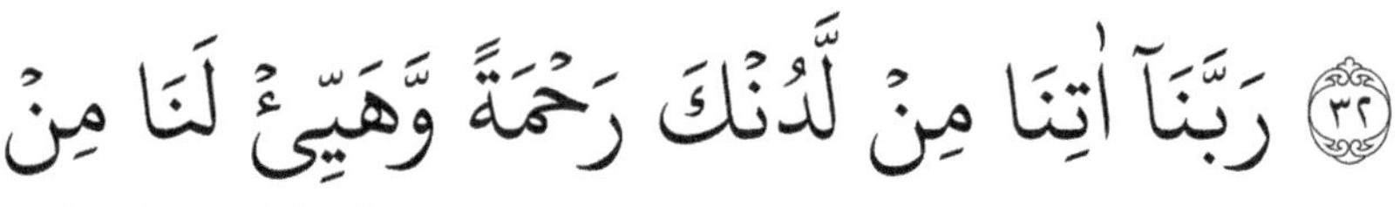

| 30. Bani Israaeel # 24 | 31. Bani Israaeel # 80 | 32. Kahaf # 10 |

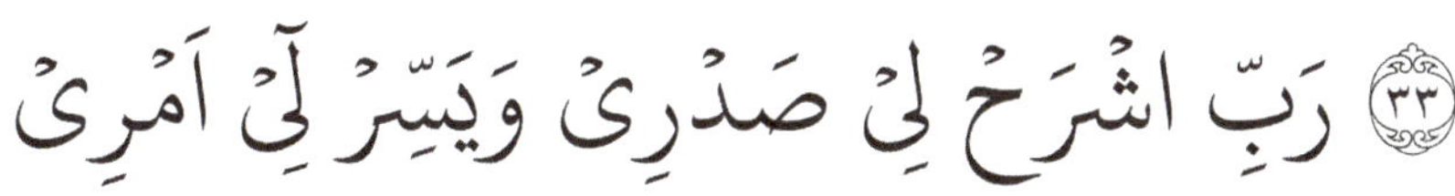

the fulfilment of our aims.

33. O Allah! Open up my heart and make my work easy for me.

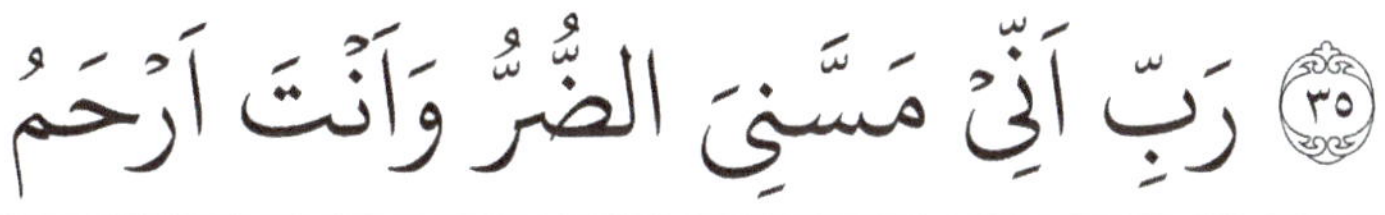

34. O Allah! Increase me in knowledge.

رَبِّ اَنِّيْ مَسَّنِيَ الضُّرُّ وَاَنْتَ اَرْحَمُ

35. O Allah! I have been overtaken by hardship and You are The Most Merciful

الرَّاحِمِيْنَ

of those who show mercy.

| 33. Taahaa # 25,26 | 34. Taahaa # 114 | 35. Ambiyaa # 83 |

لَآ اِلٰهَ اِلَّا اَنْتَ سُبْحٰنَكَ اِنِّیْ كُنْتُ مِنَ ﴿٣٦﴾

36. There is no god besides You, You are Pure from all faults, definitely I am from the

الظّٰلِمِیْنَ

sinners.

رَبِّ لَا تَذَرْنِیْ فَرْدًا وَّاَنْتَ خَیْرُ الْوٰرِثِیْنَ ﴿٣٧﴾

37. O Allah! Do not leave me alone; and You are the Best Successor.

رَبِّ احْكُمْ بِالْحَقِّ وَرَبُّنَا الرَّحْمٰنُ ﴿٣٨﴾

38. O Allah! Judge with truth and justice. And our Rabb is extremely kind,

الْمُسْتَعَانُ عَلٰی مَا تَصِفُوْنَ

we seek His help against what you forge.

36. Ambiyaa # 87	37. Ambiyaa # 89	38. Ambiyaa # 112

39. O Allah! Make my landing a blessed one (from Hadhrat Nuh's عَلَيْهِٱلسَّلَامُ ark). You are the best of those who bring people safely to

الْمُنْزِلِيْنَ

land.

40. O Allah! Do not make me from the sinning people.

رَبِّ اَعُوْذُ بِكَ مِنْ هَمَزٰتِ الشَّيٰطِيْنِ

41. O Allah! I seek Your protection against the insinuations of the devils and that they

وَاَعُوْذُ بِكَ رَبِّ اَنْ يَّحْضُرُوْنِ

(or anyone of his class) may approach me.

39. Muminoon # 29	40. Muminoon # 94	41. Mu'minoon # 97,98

﴿٤٢﴾ رَبَّنَا اٰمَنَّا فَاغْفِرْ لَنَا وَارْحَمْنَا وَاَنْتَ خَيْرُ

42. O Allah! We have believed, forgive us and have mercy on us and You are the best of those who show

الرّٰحِمِيْنَ

Mercy.

﴿٤٣﴾ رَبِّ اغْفِرْ وَارْحَمْ وَاَنْتَ خَيْرُ الرّٰحِمِيْنَ

43. O Allah! Forgive us and have mercy upon us. Verily You are the best of those who show Mercy.

﴿٤٤﴾ رَبَّنَا اصْرِفْ عَنَّا عَذَابَ جَهَنَّمَ اِنَّ عَذَابَهَا

44. O Allah! Turn away the punishment of Hell from us. Verily its punishment

كَانَ غَرَامًا اِنَّهَا سَآءَتْ مُسْتَقَرًّا وَّمُقَامًا

is indeed dreadful. Undoubtedly it is an evil place for staying and resting.

| 42. Mu'minoon # 109 | 43. Mu'minoon # 118 | 44. Furqaan # 65,66 |

رَبَّنَا هَبْ لَنَا مِنْ اَزْوَاجِنَا وَذُرِّيّٰتِنَا قُرَّةَ

45. O Allah! Grant us such wives and children who will be a source of coolness (delight)

اَعْيُنٍ وَّاجْعَلْنَا لِلْمُتَّقِيْنَ اِمَامًا

to our eyes and make us leaders of pious people.

رَبِّ هَبْ لِيْ حُكْمًا وَّاَلْحِقْنِيْ بِالصّٰلِحِيْنَ

46. O Allah! Bless me with wisdom and join me with the pious.

وَاجْعَلْ لِّيْ لِسَانَ صِدْقٍ فِى الْاٰخِرِيْنَ وَاجْعَلْنِيْ

Grant me a reputation of truthfulness in generations to come. Make me

مِنْ وَّرَثَةِ جَنَّةِ النَّعِيْمِ وَاغْفِرْ لِاَبِيْ اِنَّهُ كَانَ

among those who will inherit the garden of bliss. Forgive my father

45. Furqaan # 74	46. Shu'araa # 117, 118

مِنَ الضَّآلِّيْنَ وَلَا تُخْزِنِيْ يَوْمَ يُبْعَثُوْنَ يَوْمَ

who had gone astray. Do not disgrace me on the Day of Qiyaamah, a day

لَا يَنْفَعُ مَالٌ وَّلَا بَنُوْنَ اِلَّا مَنْ اَتَى اللهَ بِقَلْبٍ

when wealth and children will be of no use except those who come to Allah with a

سَلِيْمٍ

pure heart.

٤٧ رَبِّ نَجِّنِيْ وَاَهْلِيْ مِمَّا يَعْمَلُوْنَ

47. O Allah! Save me and my family from what these people do. (i.e. from the effect of the people's misdeeds).

٤٨ رَبِّ اِنَّ قَوْمِيْ كَذَّبُوْنِ فَافْتَحْ بَيْنِيْ

48. O Allah! Verily my people have denied my teachings. You judge between me

47. Shu'araa # 169   48. Shu'araa # 117, 118

وَبَيْنَهُمْ فَتْحًا وَّنَجِّنِيْ وَمَنْ مَّعِيَ مِنَ

and them and save me and those believers

الْمُؤْمِنِيْنَ

who are with me.

رَبِّ اَوْزِعْنِيْ اَنْ اَشْكُرَ نِعْمَتَكَ الَّتِيْ ۞

49. O Allah! Enable me to become grateful for Your favour that You have bestowed

اَنْعَمْتَ عَلَيَّ وَعَلٰى وَالِدَيَّ وَاَنْ اَعْمَلَ صَالِحًا

on me and on my parents. and (grant me the ability) to do such actions that will

تَرْضٰهُ وَاَدْخِلْنِيْ بِرَحْمَتِكَ فِيْ عِبَادِكَ الصّٰلِحِيْنَ

please You. (Please) admit me, through your mercy, amongst Your pious servants.

49. Naml # 19

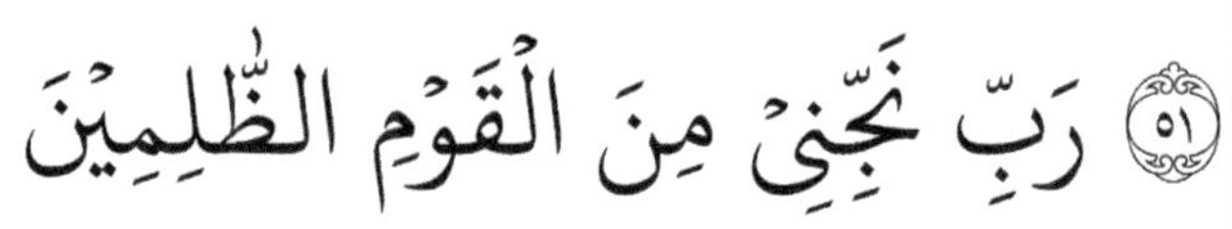

50. O Allah! I have oppressed myself, please forgive me.

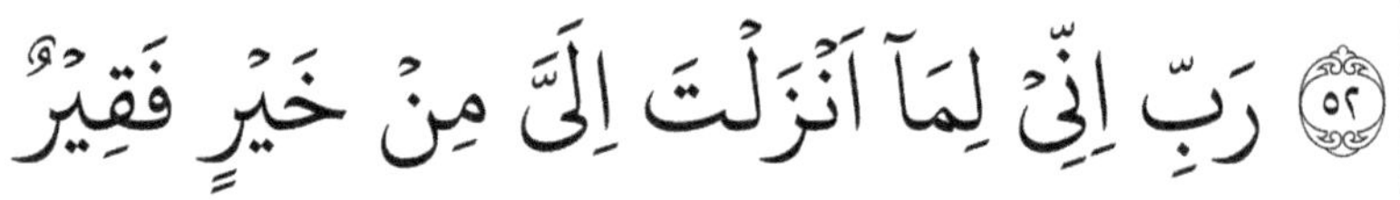

51. O Allah! Save me from the oppressive people.

52. O Allah! I am desperately in need of whatever good You have in store for me.

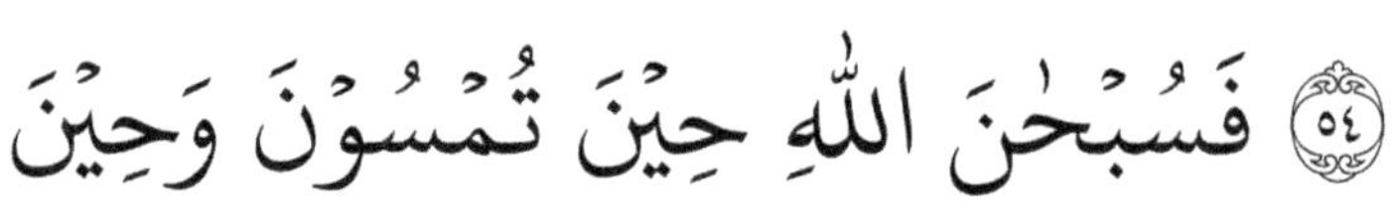

53. O Allah! Help me against people that cause corruption.

54. Glory be to Allah during the evening and the

تُصْبِحُوْنَ وَلَهُ الْحَمْدُ فِى السَّمٰوٰتِ وَالْاَرْضِ

morning. And for Him is all praise in the heavens and on earth

وَعَشِيًّا وَّحِيْنَ تُظْهِرُوْنَ يُخْرِجُ الْحَىَّ مِنَ

after sunset and at noon. He takes out the living from

الْمَيِّتِ وَيُخْرِجُ الْمَيِّتَ مِنَ الْحَىِّ وَيُحْيِ

the dead and the dead from the living and fills life

الْاَرْضَ بَعْدَ مَوْتِهَا وَكَذٰلِكَ تُخْرَجُوْنَ

into the earth after it is dead. And so will you be raised alive (on the Day of Judgoment).

﴿٥٥﴾ رَبِّ هَبْ لِيْ مِنَ الصّٰلِحِيْنَ

55. O Allah! Grant me pious children.

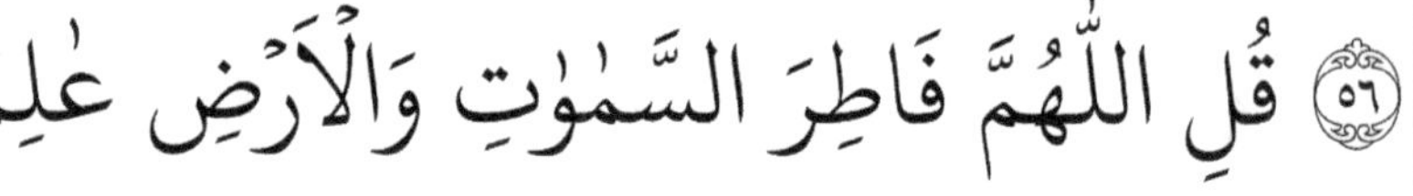

قُلِ اللّٰهُمَّ فَاطِرَ السَّمٰوٰتِ وَالْاَرْضِ عٰلِمَ ٥٦

56. Say O Allah! Creator of the heavens and the earth, The One Who knows whatever is

الْغَيْبِ وَالشَّهَدَةِ اَنْتَ تَحْكُمُ بَيْنَ عِبَادِكَ فِيْ

hidden or visible, You alone will decide between Your servants in

مَا كَانُوْا فِيْهِ يَخْتَلِفُوْنَ

matters on which they differ.

٥٧ رَبَّنَا وَسِعْتَ كُلَّ شَيْءٍ رَّحْمَةً وَّعِلْمًا فَاغْفِرْ

57. O Allah! Your mercy and knowledge encompasses everything, forgive

لِلَّذِيْنَ تَابُوْا وَاتَّبَعُوْا سَبِيْلَكَ وَقِهِمْ عَذَابَ

those who have repented and followed Your path and save them from the punishment

الْجَحِيمِ ۔ رَبَّنَا وَاَدْخِلْهُمْ جَنّٰتِ عَدْنِ الَّتِيْ

of Hell. O Allah! Admit them into the everlasting Jannah which

وَعَدْتَّهُمْ وَمَنْ صَلَحَ مِنْ اٰبَآئِهِمْ وَاَزْوَاجِهِمْ

You promised them, as well as their parents, wives and children who were pious.

وَذُرِّيّٰتِهِمْ اِنَّكَ اَنْتَ الْعَزِيْزُ الْحَكِيْمُ وَقِهِمُ

Verily You are Powerful and Wise. And save them

السَّيِّئَاتِ وَمَنْ تَقِ السَّيِّئَاتِ يَوْمَئِذٍ فَقَدْ

from evil deeds. And whomsoever you will save from evil, on that day, has truly

رَحِمْتَهٗ وَذٰلِكَ هُوَ الْفَوْزُ الْعَظِيْمُ

received Your mercy, and that is indeed a great success.

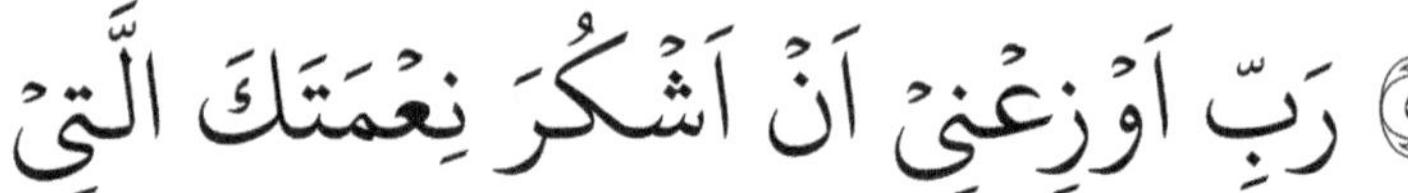

رَبِّ اَوْزِعْنِيْۤ اَنْ اَشْكُرَ نِعْمَتَكَ الَّتِيْۤ ۝٥٨

58. O Allah! Grant me the ability of making shukar (thanking) You for the bounties

اَنْعَمْتَ عَلَيَّ وَعَلٰى وَالِدَيَّ وَاَنْ اَعْمَلَ صَالِحًا

You have showered upon me and my parents and (grant me the ability) to do such actions

تَرْضٰهُ وَاَصْلِحْ لِيْ فِيْ ذُرِّيَّتِيْ اِنِّيْ تُبْتُ اِلَيْكَ

which will please You and also reform my children. I truly repent before You

وَاِنِّيْ مِنَ الْمُسْلِمِيْنَ

and I am truly from the Muslims.

رَبَّنَا اغْفِرْ لَنَا وَلِاِخْوَانِنَا الَّذِيْنَ سَبَقُوْنَا ۝٥٩

59. O Allah! Forgive us and our Muslim brothers who preceded us

بِالْاِيْمَانِ وَلَا تَجْعَلْ فِيْ قُلُوْبِنَا غِلًّا لِّلَّذِيْنَ

in faith and do not leave any ill feelings in our hearts towards those

اٰمَنُوْا رَبَّنَآ اِنَّكَ رَءُوْفٌ رَّحِيْمٌ

who believe. O Allah! You are Most Kind and Merciful.

رَبَّنَا عَلَيْكَ تَوَكَّلْنَا وَاِلَيْكَ اَنَبْنَا وَاِلَيْكَ ۞٦٠

60. O Allah! On You have we placed our trust and towards You have we turned and towards You

الْمَصِيْرُ رَبَّنَا لَا تَجْعَلْنَا فِتْنَةً لِّلَّذِيْنَ كَفَرُوْا

is our return. O Allah! Do not make us a *fitnah* (victim) for the disbelievers

وَاغْفِرْ لَنَا رَبَّنَآ اِنَّكَ اَنْتَ الْعَزِيْزُ الْحَكِيْمُ

and forgive us. O Allah! Verily You are Powerful and Wise.

60. Mumtahina # 4,5

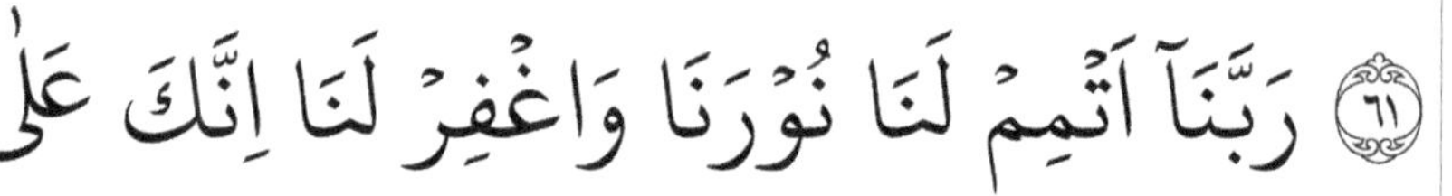

61. O Allah! Complete for us our *noor* (light) and forgive us. Verily You have

كُلِّ شَىْءٍ قَدِيْرٌ

power over all things.

62. O Allah! Forgive me, my parents, and those Muslims who have entered my house

مُؤْمِنًا وَّلِلْمُؤْمِنِيْنَ وَالْمُؤْمِنَاتِ

as well as all the believing men and women.

بِسْمِ اللهِ الرَّحْمٰنِ الرَّحِيْمِ

In the name of Allah, most Compassionate most Merciful.

| 61. Tahreem # 8 | 62. Nooh # 28 |

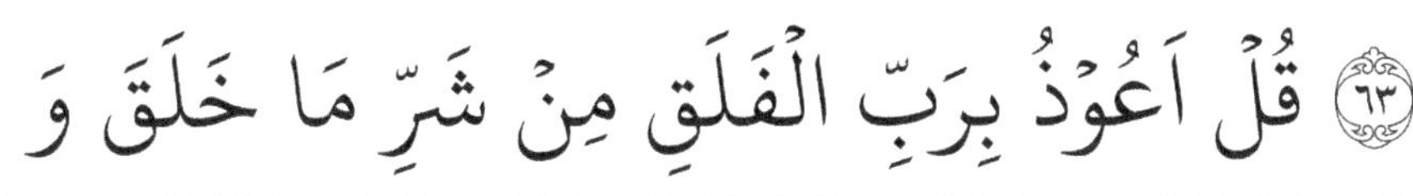

قُلْ اَعُوْذُ بِرَبِّ الْفَلَقِ مِنْ شَرِّ مَا خَلَقَ وَ ۝

63. Say: "I seek refuge in the Rabb of the daylight, from the evil of what He created,

مِنْ شَرِّ غَاسِقٍ اِذَا وَقَبَ وَ مِنْ شَرِّ النَّفّٰثٰتِ

from the evil of the darkness of night when it covers (all things), from the evil of those who blow

فِى الْعُقَدِ وَ مِنْ شَرِّ حَاسِدٍ اِذَا حَسَدَ

into knots and from the evil of the jealous one when his jealousy becomes active."

بِسْمِ اللهِ الرَّحْمٰنِ الرَّحِيْمِ

In the name of Allah, the most Compassionate the most Merciful.

قُلْ اَعُوْذُ بِرَبِّ النَّاسِ مَلِكِ النَّاسِ اِلٰهِ ۝

64. Say: "I seek refuge in the Rabb of mankind, the Ruler of mankind, Deity

| 63. Falaq | 64. Naas |

النَّاسِ مِنْ شَرِّ الْوَسْوَاسِ الْخَنَّاسِ الَّذِىْ

of mankind, from the evil of the devil, who withdraws (when Allah Ta'ala is remembered) and

يُوَسْوِسُ فِيْ صُدُوْرِ النَّاسِ مِنَ الْجِنَّةِ وَالنَّاسِ

who whispers evil thoughts into the hearts of men whether from jinn or man ."

٦٥ سُبْحٰنَكَ اللّٰهُمَّ وَتَحِيَّتُهُمْ فِيْهَا سَلٰمٌ

65. O Allah! You are Free from all blemishes. The greeting of the inmates of Jannah will be: "Salaam"

وَاٰخِرُ دَعْوٰىهُمْ اَنِ الْحَمْدُ لِلّٰهِ رَبِّ الْعٰلَمِيْنَ

and their final call will be: "All praise is due to Allah the Nourisher of the worlds."

٦٦ قَالَ اللّٰهُ تَعَالٰى : وَلِلّٰهِ الْاَسْمَآءُ الْحُسْنٰى

66. Allah Ta'ala has declared: "And for Allah are beautiful names

| 65. Yunus # 10 | 66. A'araaf # 180 |

فَادْعُوْهُ بِهَا

so call Him by those names."

۞ وَقَالَ النَّبِيُّ صَلَّى اللهُ عَلَيْهِ وَسَلَّمَ: اِنَّ لِلّٰهِ

67. Rasulullah ﷺ has said:

تَعَالٰى تِسْعَةً وَّتِسْعِيْنَ اِسْمًا مَنْ اَحْصٰهَا دَخَلَ

"There are 99 names of Allah. Whoever memories them, will enter

الْجَنَّةَ (وَفِيْ رِوَايَةٍ) مَنْ حَفِظَهَا

into Jannah." **(They are as follows)**

الرَّحِيْمُ	الرَّحْمٰنُ	هُوَ اللهُ الَّذِيْ لَآ اِلٰهَ اِلَّا هُوَ
The Most Merciful	The Most Kind	He is Allah besides whom none is worthy of worship

67. Tirmizi # 3507

الْمُهَيْمِنُ	الْمُؤْمِنُ	السَّلَامُ	الْقُدُّوسُ	الْمَلِكُ
The Guardian of all things	The Giver of protection	The Giver of peace	The Most Holy	The King
الْبَارِئُ	الْخَالِقُ	الْمُتَكَبِّرُ	الْجَبَّارُ	الْعَزِيزُ
The one who brings creation into being	The Creator	The Greatest in majesty	The Overpowering Rabb	The Mighty
الرَّزَّاقُ	الْوَهَّابُ	الْقَهَّارُ	الْغَفَّارُ	الْمُصَوِّرُ
The Sustainer	The Generous Giver	The Almighty Rabb	Exceedingly Forgiving	The Fashioner of shapes
الْخَافِضُ	الْبَاسِطُ	الْقَابِضُ	الْعَلِيمُ	الْفَتَّاحُ
The being that causes people to be lowered	The Being that grants increase	The Being that causes sustenance to shrink	The All Knowing	The Giver of decisions
الْبَصِيرُ	السَّمِيعُ	الْمُذِلُّ	الْمُعِزُّ	الرَّافِعُ
The One who sees all things	The One who hears all things	The Giver of dishonour	The Giver of honour	The being who exalts

الْحَلِيمُ	الْخَبِيرُ	اللَّطِيفُ	الْعَدْلُ	الْحَكَمُ
The Tolerant	The all Aware	The Knower of innermost secrets	The Just	The Maker of Judgments
الْكَبِيرُ	الْعَلِيُّ	الشَّكُورُ	الْغَفُورُ	الْعَظِيمُ
The Most Great	The Most High	The Highly Appreciative	The Forgiving	The Great
الْكَرِيمُ	الْجَلِيلُ	الْحَسِيبُ	الْمُقِيتُ	الْحَفِيظُ
The Benevolent	The Glorious	The Reckoner	The Distributor of due shares	The Protector
الْوَدُودُ	الْحَكِيمُ	الْوَاسِعُ	الْمُجِيبُ	الرَّقِيبُ
The Most Loving	The Most Wise	The Lenient	The Answerer	The Custodian
الْوَكِيلُ	الْحَقُّ	الشَّهِيدُ	الْبَاعِثُ	الْمَجِيدُ
The Guardian	The Absolute true in His being and existence	The Witnesser	The Resurrector of the dead	The glorious and exalted

الْمُحْصِى	الْحَمِيدُ	الْوَلِيُّ	الْمَتِينُ	الْقَوِيُّ
The All Knowing	The Praiseworthy	The Loving Patron and Supporter	The Invincible	The Almighty
الْحَيُّ	الْمُمِيتُ	الْمُحْيِ	الْمُعِيدُ	الْمُبْدِئُ
The Everlasting	The Giver of death	The Giver of life	The Recreator	The Originator
الْأَحَدُ	الْوَاحِدُ	الْمَاجِدُ	الْوَاجِدُ	الْقَيُّومُ
The Unequalled	The ONE	The All-Excellent	The Self sufficient	The Eternal Sustainer
الْمُؤَخِّرُ	الْمُقَدِّمُ	الْمُقْتَدِرُ	الْقَادِرُ	الصَّمَدُ
The One who causes retrogress	The One who causes progress	The prevailing	The All-Powerful	The Being Who is Free from want
الْوَالِي	الْبَاطِنُ	الظَّاهِرُ	الْأَخِرُ	الْأَوَّلُ
The one Who Exercises responsibility over all things	The Concealed	The Manifest	The Last	The First

الْمُتَعَالِ	الْبَرُّ	التَّوَّابُ	الْمُنْتَقِمُ	الْعَفُوُّ
The Being far above the attributes of all creation	The One Who is Kind	The Accepter of repentance	The One who takes retribution	The One Inclined to pardon sins

الرَّؤُوْفُ	مَالِكُ الْمُلْكِ	ذُوالْجَلَالِ وَالْاِكْرَامِ
The Most Kind	The Ruler of the kingdom	The Majestic and Kind

الْمُقْسِطُ	الْجَامِعُ	الْغَنِيُّ	الْمُغْنِي	الْمَانِعُ
The Just	The Assembler	The Being Who is Free from need	The Bestower	The Depriver

الضَّآرُّ	النَّافِعُ	النُّوْرُ	الْهَادِى	الْبَدِيْعُ
The One who can cause loss	The One who confers benefits	The Light	The One who grants guidance	The Deviser

الْبَاقِى	الْوَارِثُ	الرَّشِيْدُ	الصَّبُوْرُ	
The Eternal	The Supporter of all	The One who guides onto the path of virtue	The Most Forbearing	

وَاسْمُ اللهِ الْاَعْظَمُ الَّذِىْ اِذَا دُعِىَ بِهٖ ۶۸

68. The Greatest name (Ism-e-A'zam) of Allah, which when invoked

اَجَابَ وَاِذَا سُئِلَ بِهٖ اَعْطٰى: (لَآ اِلٰه اِلَّا اَنْتَ

surely leads to the acceptance of dua and one is granted whatever is asked for, (it is as follows)...... "There is no deity besides You.

سُبْحٰنَكَ اِنِّىْ كُنْتُ مِنَ الظّٰلِمِيْنَ)

You are free from all blemishes; Indeed I am from the sinners."

اَللّٰهُمَّ اِنِّىْ اَسْاَلُكَ بِاَنِّىْ اَشْهَدُ اَنَّكَ اَنْتَ اللهُ ۶۹

69. O Allah! I beg of You by saying that I bear witness that verily You are Allah.

لَآ اِلٰه اِلَّا اَنْتَ الْاَحَدُ الصَّمَدُ الَّذِىْ لَمْ يَلِدْ

There is no deity beside You. You are One and totally independent, Who was neither born from anyone

وَلَمْ يُوْلَدْ وَلَمْ يَكُنْ لَّهُ كُفُوًا اَحَدٌ

nor gave birth to anyone nor is there anyone equal to Him.

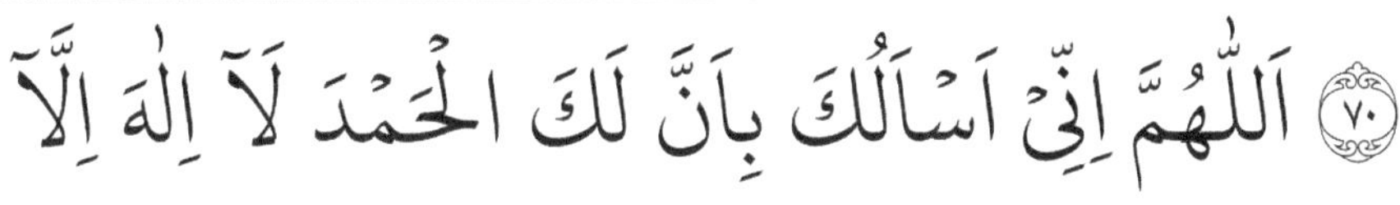

اَللّٰهُمَّ اِنِّيْ اَسْئَلُكَ بِاَنَّ لَكَ الْحَمْدَ لَاۤ اِلٰهَ اِلَّاۤ

70. O Allah! I beg of You by saying that all praise is for You. There is no god besides

اَنْتَ وَحْدَكَ لَا شَرِيْكَ لَكَ الْحَنَّانُ الْمَنَّانُ

You. You are One, You have no partner. You are Most Kind and Most Compassionate

بَدِيْعُ السَّمٰوَاتِ وَالْاَرْضِ يَاذَا الْجَلَالِ

The Creator of the heavens and the earth. O You Majestic

وَالْاِكْرَامِ يَا حَىُّ يَا قَيُّوْمُ

and Benevolent Rabb, the Everlasting, the Sustainer,

70. Ibnu Hibbaan # 890

71. O The Most Merciful of those who show mercy.

72. My Rabb is unblemished, Most High and The Most Generous Giver.

73. I seek refuge with the perfect words of Allah against the evil of what He

خَلَقَ

created.

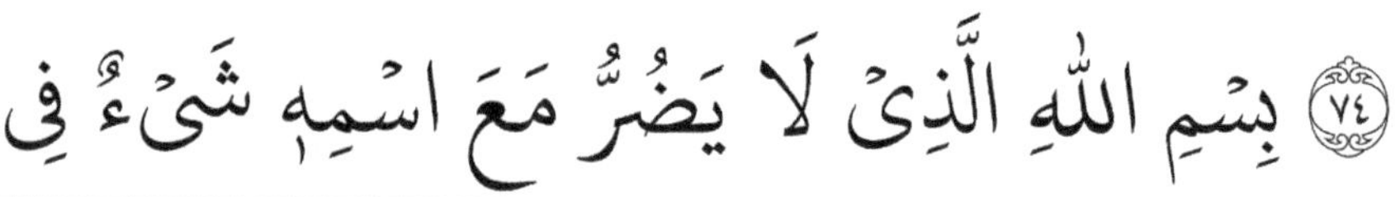

74. In the name of Allah whose name wards off the harm of all things in

| 71. Mustadrak # 1995 | 72. Mustadrak # 1835 | 73. Tirmizi # 3437 | 74. Tirmizi # 3388 |

الْاَرْضِ وَلَا فِي السَّمَآءِ وَهُوَ السَّمِيعُ الْعَلِيمُ

the earth and the heavens and He hears and knows everything.

﴿٧٥﴾ اَصْبَحْنَا وَاَصْبَحَ الْمُلْكُ لِلّٰهِ وَالْحَمْدُ لِلّٰهِ

75. Morning has come to us, and the entire kingdom, in a condition that it belongs solely to Allah. All Praise be to Allah.

لَآ اِلٰهَ اِلَّا اللّٰهُ وَحْدَهُ لَاشَرِيْكَ لَهُ لَهُ الْمُلْكُ

There is no god besides Allah. He is One and without any partner. For Him is the entire Kingdom

وَلَهُ الْحَمْدُ وَهُوَ عَلٰى كُلِّ شَيْءٍ قَدِيْرٌ ۰ رَبِّ

and praises and He has power over everything. O Allah!

اَسْاَلُكَ خَيْرَ مَا فِيْ هٰذَا الْيَوْمِ وَخَيْرَ مَا بَعْدَهُ

I beg of You for all the good which pertains to this day as well as the coming days

75. Muslim # 2723

وَاَعُوْذُبِكَ مِنْ شَرِّ مَا فِيْ هٰذَا الْيَوْمِ وَشَرِّ مَا

and I seek Your protection from all evil which pertains to this day as well as the

بَعْدَهٗ ۰ رَبِّ اَعُوْذُ بِكَ مِنَ الْكَسَلِ وَسُوْءِ

coming days. O Allah! I seek Your protection from laziness and extreme

الْكِبَرِ رَبِّ اَعُوْذُ بِكَ مِنْ عَذَابٍ فِي النَّارِ

old age. O Allah! I seek Your protection from the punishment of Jahannam

وَعَذَابٍ فِي الْقَبْرِ

and the punishment of the grave.

﴾٧٦﴿ اَللّٰهُمَّ فَاطِرَ السَّمٰوَاتِ وَالْاَرْضِ عَالِمَ

76. O Allah! The Creator of the heavens and the earth, who knows

76. Abu Dawood # 5067

الْغَيْبِ وَالشَّهَادَةِ رَبَّ كُلِّ شَىْءٍ وَّمَلِيْكَهٗٓ اَشْهَدُ

what is concealed and visible, the Rabb and Master of everything. I
bear witness

اَنْ لَّآ اِلٰهَ اِلَّآ اَنْتَ وَحْدَكَ لَاشَرِيْكَ لَكَ

that there is no deity besides You and You are One and without
any partner.

اَعُوْذُ بِكَ مِنْ شَرِّ نَفْسِىْ وَمِنْ شَرِّ الشَّيْطَانِ

I seek Your protection from the evil of my Nafs (carnal self) and
from the evil of Shaytaan

وَشَرَكِهٖ وَاَنْ اَقْتَرِفَ عَلٰى نَفْسِىْ سُوْءًا اَوْ اَجُرَّهٗ

and his traps and from committing evil or involving

اِلٰى مُسْلِمٍ

another Muslim in evil

اَللّٰهُمَّ اِنِّيْ اَصْبَحْتُ اُشْهِدُكَ وَاُشْهِدُ حَمَلَةَ ۷۷

77. O Allah! The morning has come to me whilst I make You my witness, and the angels that carry

عَرْشِكَ وَمَلَآئِكَتَكَ وَجَمِيْعَ خَلْقِكَ اَنَّكَ اَنْتَ

Your Throne, and all Your remainder angels and Your entire creation witnesses that indeed You are

اللهُ لَآ اِلٰهَ اِلَّا اَنْتَ وَاَنَّ مُحَمَّدًا عَبْدُكَ

Allah, there is no deity besides You and that Muhammad 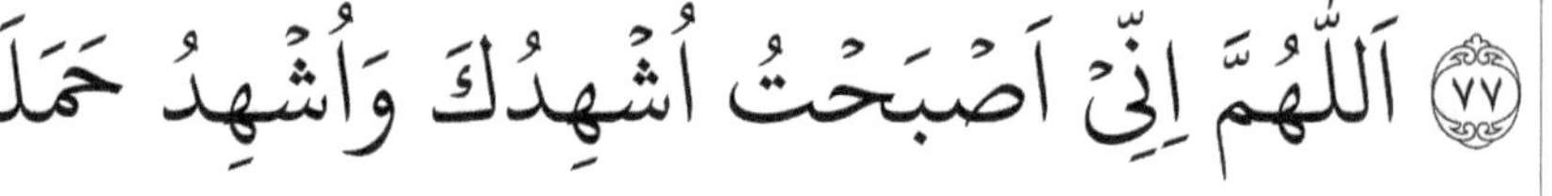 is Your servant

وَرَسُوْلُكَ

and Your messenger.

اَللّٰهُمَّ اِنِّيْ اَسْاَلُكَ الْعَافِيَةَ فِي الدُّنْيَا ۷۸

78. O Allah! I beg of You for aafiyat (safety & ease) in this world

| 77. Abu Dawood # 5069 | 78. Abu Dawood # 5074 |

وَالْاٰخِرَةِ. اَللّٰهُمَّ اِنِّیْ اَسْأَلُكَ الْعَفْوَ وَالْعَافِيَةَ فِیْ

and the Hereafter. O Allah, I beg of You for forgiveness and aafiyat (safety and ease) in

دِیْنِیْ وَدُنْیَاىَ وَاَهْلِیْ وَمَالِیْ

my Deen, my dunya, my family, and in my wealth.

اَللّٰهُمَّ اسْتُرْ عَوْرَاتِیْ وَاٰمِنْ رَوْعَاتِیْ اَللّٰهُمَّ

O Allah! Hide my faults and save me from fear and apprehension. O Allah!

احْفَظْنِیْ مِنْ بَیْنِ یَدَیَّ وَمِنْ خَلْفِیْ وَعَنْ

Protect me from in front of me and from behind me, on

یَّمِیْنِیْ وَعَنْ شِمَالِیْ وَمِنْ فَوْقِیْ وَاَعُوْذُ بِعَظَمَتِكَ

my right and on my left and above me. I seek protection in Your Grandeur

اَنْ اُغْتَالَ مِنْ تَحْتِيْ

that I may be destroyed by any disaster from beneath me.

﴿٧٩﴾ رَضِيْنَا بِاللهِ رَبًّا وَّبِالْاِسْلَامِ دِيْنًا

79. We are pleased with Allah as our Rabb, Islam as our religion and Hadhrat Muhammad ﷺ

وَّبِمُحَمَّدٍ صَلَّى اللهُ عَلَيْهِ وَسَلَّمَ رَسُوْلًا وَّنَبِيًّا

as our Rasul and Messenger.

﴿٨٠﴾ اَللّٰهُمَّ مَا اَصْبَحَ بِيْ مِنْ نِّعْمَةٍ اَوْ بِاَحَدٍ مِّنْ

80. O Allah! Whatever blessings and favours I or any of

خَلْقِكَ فَمِنْكَ وَحْدَكَ لَا شَرِيْكَ لَكَ فَلَكَ

Your creation have received this morning is exclusively from You and You have no partner.

79. Abu Dawood # 5072	80. Ibnu Hibbaan # 858

اَلْحَمْدُ وَلَكَ الشُّكُرُ

All praise and gratitude is due to You only.

اَللّٰهُمَّ عَافِنِيْ فِيْ بَدَنِيْ اَللّٰهُمَّ عَافِنِيْ فِيْ ﴿٨١﴾

81. O Allah! Grant me *aafiyat* (sound health) in my body,

سَمْعِيْ اَللّٰهُمَّ عَافِنِيْ فِيْ بَصَرِيْ لَآ اِلٰهَ اِلَّا

my hearing and my cyc-sight. There is no deity besides

اَنْتَ (ثَلَاثَ مَرَّاتٍ) اَللّٰهُمَّ اِنِّيْ اَعُوْذُ بِكَ مِنَ

You. (Read thrice). O Allah! I seek Your protection from

الْكُفْرِ وَالْفَقْرِ اَللّٰهُمَّ اِنِّيْ اَعُوْذُ بِكَ مِنْ

(kufr) disbelief and poverty. O Allah! I seek Your protection from

81. Abu Dawood # 5090

عَذَابِ الْقَبْرِ لَاۤ اِلٰهَ اِلَّاۤ اَنْتَ (ثَلَاثَ مَرَّاتٍ)

being punished in the grave. There is no deity besides You. (Read this dua thrice).

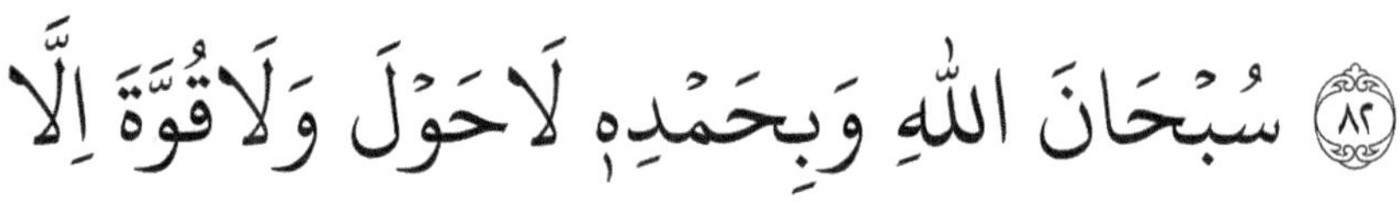

سُبْحَانَ اللهِ وَبِحَمْدِهٖ لَاحَوْلَ وَلَاقُوَّةَ اِلَّا

82. Allah Ta'ala is absolutely pure and all praises are due to Him. There is no power to do good nor to avoid evil except

بِاللهِ مَا شَآءَ اللهُ كَانَ وَمَا لَمْ يَشَاْ لَمْ يَكُنْ

with the help of Allah. Whatever Allah willed has happened and whatever He did not will could not happen.

اَعْلَمُ اَنَّ اللهَ عَلٰى كُلِّ شَىْءٍ قَدِيْرٌ وَاَنَّ اللهَ

I am convinced that Allah Ta'ala has power over everything and that Allah Ta'ala

قَدْ اَحَاطَ بِكُلِّ شَىْءٍ عِلْمًا

fully comprehends all things in His knowledge.

82. Abu Dawood # 5075

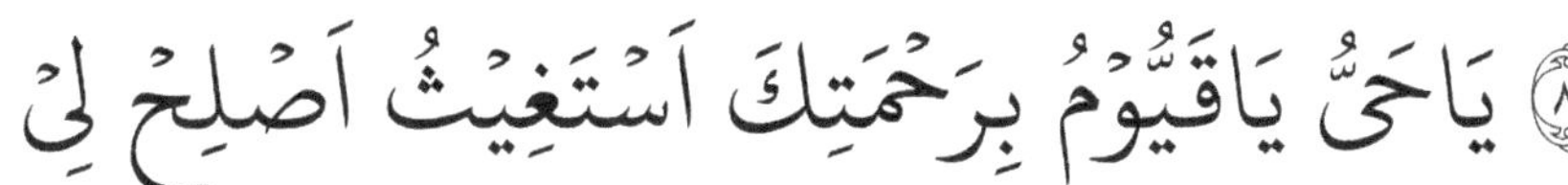

83. O Allah! The Everlasting The Sustainer, I passionately beg Your mercy. Correct

all my affairs for me and do not hand me over to myself even for a blink of an eye.

84. **Sayyidul Istighfaar:** for istighfaar the most comprehensive dua is the following:

O Allah, You are my Rabb, there is no god besides You. You have created me and I am

Your servant. As far as possible I try to abide by the covenants and promises (which I made to You).

اَعُوْذُ بِكَ مِنْ شَرِّ مَا صَنَعْتُ اَبُوْءُ لَكَ

I seek Your protection from the evil of my sins. I fully acknowledge the favours You

بِنِعْمَتِكَ عَلَيَّ وَاَبُوْءُ بِذَنْبِيْ فَاغْفِرْ لِيْ فَاِنَّهُ

have bestowed upon me and I confess to my mistakes. Please forgive me

لَا يَغْفِرُ الذُّنُوْبَ اِلَّا اَنْتَ

as none besides You can forgive sins.

٨٥ اَللّٰهُمَّ اَنْتَ اَحَقُّ مَنْ ذُكِرَ وَاَحَقُّ مَنْ عُبِدَ

85. O Allah! Of all the things that are remembered, You are most rightful to be remembered and of all things that are worshipped

وَاَنْصَرُ مَنِ ابْتُغِيَ وَاَرْءَفُ مَنْ مَّلَكَ وَاَجْوَدُ

You are the most worthy of being worshipped, of all the agencies from whom help is asked for, You are the Most Helpful. Of all

85. Mu'jamul Kabeer # 8027

مَنْ سُئِلَ وَاَوْسَعُ مَنْ اَعْطٰى ۙ اَللّٰهُمَّ اَنْتَ

those who are kind, You are the Most Kind. Of all those who are looked up to for favours You are the Most Generous and of all the

الْمَلِكُ لَاشَرِيْكَ لَكَ وَالْفَرْدُ لَانِدَّ لَكَ كُلُّ

givers You are the Most well-off. O Allah! You are the Supreme Ruler and You have no partner. You are unique with no

شَىْءٍ هَالِكٌ اِلَّا وَجْهَكَ لَنْ تُطَاعَ اِلَّا بِاِذْنِكَ

equivalent. All things are to be destroyed except Your Countenance. You cannot be obeyed except with Your permission.

وَلَنْ تُعْصٰى اِلَّا بِعِلْمِكَ تُطَاعُ فَتَشْكُرُ وَتُعْصٰى

You cannot be disobeyed except that it is within Your knowledge. If You are obeyed, it pleases You. If You are disobeyed,

فَتَغْفِرُ اَقْرَبُ شَهِيْدٍ وَاَدْنٰى حَفِيْظٍ حُلْتَ دُوْنَ

You forgive acts of disobedience. You are the nearest of all those who are present. The closest of protectors, You intervene between

النُّفُوسِ وَاَخَذْتَ بِالنَّوَاصِىْ وَكَتَبْتَ الْاٰثَارَ

the nafs and its evil desires. The hair of the foreheads is in Your hands. You have written down the actions of man (in the Loh-e-

وَنَسَخْتَ الْاٰجَالَ ۰ اَلْقُلُوْبُ لَكَ مُفْضِيَةٌ

Mahfooz), You have written down the lifespan of man. The (thoughts) of the hearts are known to You

وَالسِّرُّ عِنْدَكَ عَلَانِيَةٌ اَلْحَلَالُ مَا اَحْلَلْتَ

and all secrets are disclosed to You. Permissible are only those things which You have specified

وَالْحَرَامُ مَا حَرَّمْتَ وَالدِّيْنُ مَا شَرَعْتَ

and likewise prohibition is according to Your commandment. Deen is what You have ordained.

وَالْاَمْرُ مَا قَضَيْتَ اَلْخَلْقُ خَلْقُكَ وَالْعَبْدُ

The ruling is according to what You have decreed. All creation belongs to You, all slaves

عَبْدُكَ وَاَنْتَ اللهُ الرَّءُوْفُ الرَّحِيْمُ اَسْاَلُكَ

belong to You and You are Allah, The Kind, The Merciful. I beg You

بِنُوْرِ وَجْهِكَ الَّذِى اَشْرَقَتْ لَهُ السَّمٰوَاتُ

with the light of Your Countenance, which illuminates the heavens

وَالْاَرْضُ وَبِكُلِّ حَقٍّ هُوَ لَكَ وَبِحَقِّ السَّآئِلِيْنَ

and the earth, and with every right which You only possess and the right which You have allowed unto Your beggars

عَلَيْكَ اَنْ تُقِيْلَنِيْ فِيْ هٰذِهِ الْغَدَاةِ وَفِيْ هٰذِهِ

when they beg from You, that You forgive me this morning and

الْعَشِيَّةِ وَاَنْ تُجِيْرَنِيْ مِنَ النَّارِ بِقُدْرَتِكَ

evening and that You save me from the fire of Hell with Your power.

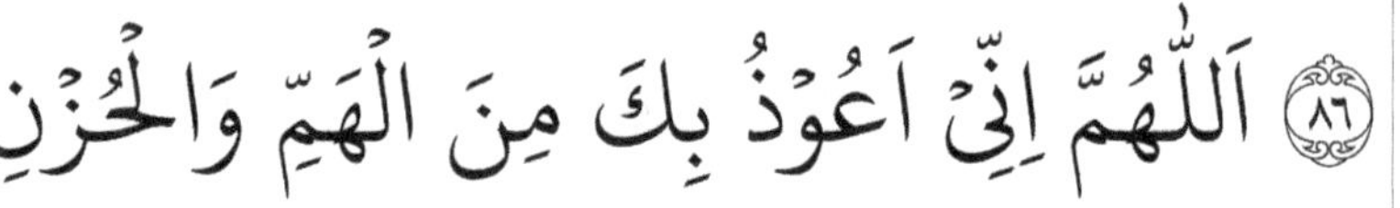

اَللّٰهُمَّ اِنِّيْ اَعُوْذُ بِكَ مِنَ الْهَمِّ وَالْحُزْنِ

86. O Allah! I seek Your protection from worry and grief,

وَاَعُوْذُ بِكَ مِنَ الْعَجْزِ وَالْكَسَلِ وَاَعُوْذُ بِكَ

I seek Your protection from weakness and laziness,

مِنَ الْجُبْنِ وَالْبُخْلِ وَاَعُوْذُ بِكَ مِنْ غَلَبَةِ

from cowardice and miserliness and from being overpowered by

الدَّيْنِ وَقَهْرِ الرِّجَالِ

debt and the oppression of men.

لَبَّيْكَ اَللّٰهُمَّ لَبَّيْكَ وَسَعْدَيْكَ وَالْخَيْرُ فِيْ

87. O Allah! I am present, I am present and ready to obey You. All good is in

| 86. Abu Dawood # 1555 | 87. Mustadrak # 1900 |

يَدَيْكَ وَمِنْكَ وَاِلَيْكَ اَللّٰهُمَّ مَا قُلْتُ مِنْ قَوْلٍ

Your hands, it is from You and it all leads towards You. O Allah! Whatever word I have uttered,

اَوْ حَلَفْتُ مِنْ حَلْفٍ اَوْ نَذَرْتُ مِنْ نَّذْرٍ

or promise I have made, or vow I have undertaken,

فَمَشِيْئَتُكَ بَيْنَ يَدَىْ ذٰلِكَ كُلِّهٖ مَا شِئْتَ كَانَ

it is all subject to Your will. Whatever You willed has happened

وَمَالَمْ تَشَاْ لَا يَكُوْنُ وَلَاحَوْلَ وَلَاقُوَّةَ اِلَّا بِكَ

and whatever You do not intend will never happen. There is no ability to avoid sins nor power to do good except with Your help.

اِنَّكَ عَلٰى كُلِّ شَىْءٍ قَدِيْرٌ۝ اَللّٰهُمَّ مَا صَلَّيْتُ

You have power over everything. O Allah! If I made dua for anyone,

مِنْ صَلٰوةٍ فَعَلٰى مَنْ صَلَّيْتَ وَمَالَعَنْتُ مِنْ لَعْنٍ

let it benefit that person whom You regard as deserving of it, and if I cursed anyone,

فَعَلٰى مَنْ لَعَنْتَ اَنْتَ وَلِيٍّ فِی الدُّنْیَا وَالْاٰخِرَةِ

let it affect him whom You regard as deserving of it. You are my Guardian in this world and the hereafter.

تَوَفَّنِیْ مُسْلِمًا وَّاَلْحِقْنِیْ بِالصَّالِحِیْنَ

Allow me to die as a Muslim and unite me with the pious.

اَللّٰهُمَّ اِنِّیْ اَسْاَلُكَ الرِّضَاءَ بَعْدَ الْقَضَاءِ وَبَرْدَ

O Allah! I beg of You to make me pleased with Your decisions, (I beg of You) a comfortable

الْعَیْشِ بَعْدَ الْمَوْتِ وَلَذَّةَ النَّظَرِ اِلٰی وَجْهِكَ

life after death, the extreme delight of seeing Your Countenance

وَشَوْقًا اِلٰى لِقَآئِكَ فِىْ غَيْرِ ضَرَّآءَ مُضِرَّةٍ وَّلَا

and a passion for meeting You in a condition where I am not in any difficult position nor

فِتْنَةٍ مُّضِلَّةٍ وَّاَعُوْذُ بِكَ اَنْ اَظْلِمَ اَوْ اُظْلَمَ اَوْ

any *fitnah* (trial) that would render me misguided. I seek Your protection from oppressing others or from being oppressed or

اَعْتَدِىَ اَوْ يُعْتَدٰى عَلَىَّ اَوْ اَكْسِبَ خَطِيْئَةً

that I should be unjust to anyone or others be unjust to me or that I should deliberately fall into such an error

اَوْ ذَنْبًا لَّا تَغْفِرُهُ اَللّٰهُمَّ زَيِّنَّا بِزِيْنَةِ الْاِيْمَانِ

or sin which You would not forgive. O Allah, beautify us with the beauty of Imaan

وَاجْعَلْنَا هُدَاةً مُّهْتَدِيْنَ ۰ اَللّٰهُمَّ فَاطِرَ

and make us among those who are rightly guided themselves, as well as a means of guidance for others. O Allah! The Creator of the

السَّمٰوَاتِ وَالْاَرْضِ عَالِمَ الْغَيْبِ وَالشَّهَادَةِ

heavens and the earth, The Knower of the unseen and the apparent,

ذَا الْجَلَالِ وَالْاِكْرَامِ فَاِنِّيْ اَعْهَدُ اِلَيْكَ فِيْ هٰذِهِ

Majestic and Caring, I make a promise with You in this

الْحَيَاةِ الدُّنْيَا وَاُشْهِدُكَ وَكَفٰى بِكَ شَهِيْدًا اَنِّيْ

worldly life and call upon You to bear witness — and You are a sufficient witness — that

اَشْهَدُ اَنْ لَّا اِلٰهَ اِلَّا اَنْتَ وَحْدَكَ لَا شَرِيْكَ لَكَ

I bear witness that there is no god besides You alone and You have no partner.

لَكَ الْمُلْكُ وَلَكَ الْحَمْدُ وَاَنْتَ عَلٰى كُلِّ شَىْءٍ

All power and praise belong to You. You have power over everything

قَدِيْرٌ وَّاَشْهَدُ اَنَّ مُحَمَّدًا صَلَّى اللهُ عَلَيهِ

and I bear witness that Hadhrat Muhammad ﷺ

وَسَلَّمَ عَبْدُكَ وَرَسُوْلُكَ وَاَشْهَدُ اَنَّ وَعْدَكَ حَقٌّ

is Your Servant and Messenger. I bear witness that Your promise
is true,

وَّلِقَآئِكَ حَقٌّ وَّالسَّاعَةَ اٰتِيَةٌ لَّارَيْبَ فِيْهَا

meeting You is true, the Hour (of Resurrection) is sure to come
without doubt

وَاَنَّكَ تَبْعَثُ مَنْ فِى الْقُبُوْرِ وَاَنَّكَ اِنْ تَكِلْنِيْ

You will bring alive those who are in their graves. If You entrust
me

اِلٰى نَفْسِيْ تَكِلْنِيْ اِلٰى ضَعْفٍ وَّعَوْرَةٍ وَّذَنْبٍ

to myself You will surely make me a victim to weakness, sin

وَّخَطِيْئَةٍ وَّاَنِّيْ لَا اَثِقُ اِلَّا بِرَحْمَتِكَ فَاغْفِرْ لِيْ

and faults. I have no reliance on anything except Your Kindness. Forgive

ذُنُوْبِيْ كُلَّهَا اِنَّهٗ لَا يَغْفِرُ الذُّنُوْبَ اِلَّا اَنْتَ

all my sins as none besides You can do so

وَتُبْ عَلَيَّ اِنَّكَ اَنْتَ التَّوَّابُ الرَّحِيْمُ

and accept my repentance as You are Most forgiving, Most Merciful.

(٨٨) اَللّٰهُمَّ اِنِّيْ اَسْاَلُكَ صِحَّةً فِيْ اِيْمَانٍ وَّاِيْمَانًا

88. O Allah! I beg of You that I be blessed with perfect Imaan, such Imaan

فِيْ حُسْنِ خُلُقٍ وَّنَجَاةً يَّتْبَعُهَا فَلَاحٌ وَّرَحْمَةً

which is accompanied by good manners, a prosperous life (in this world) followed by complete success (in the Hereafter). I beg of

88. Mu'jamul Awsat # 9333

مِنْكَ وَعَافِيَةً وَّمَغْفِرَةً مِّنْكَ وَرِضْوَانًا

Your mercy, peace and forgiveness and (I beg) for Your pleasure.

٨٩ اَللّٰهُمَّ اِنِّى اَعُوْذُ بِوَجْهِكَ الْكَرِيْمِ

89. O Allah! I beg of You through Your Noble countenance

وَبِكَلِمَاتِكَ التَّامَّةِ مِنْ شَرِّ مَآ اَنْتَ اٰخِذٌ

and Your perfect words for Your protection from the evil of all things which You are in

بِنَاصِيَتِهٖ ۰ اَللّٰهُمَّ اَنْتَ تَكْشِفُ الْمَغْرَمَ وَ

full control of. O Allah! Only You can remove debts and

الْمَأْثَمَ۰ اَللّٰهُمَّ لَا يُهْزَمُ جُنْدُكَ وَلَا يُخْلَفُ

only You can pardon sins. O Allah! Your army can never be defeated, Your promise can never be broken

89. Abu Dawood # 5052

وَعُدُكَ وَلَا يَنْفَعُ ذَا الْجَدِّ مِنْكَ الْجَدُّ

and the wealth of the wealthy cannot benefit them against Your punishment.

سُبْحَانَكَ وَبِحَمْدِكَ

You are Pure. All praises are due to You.

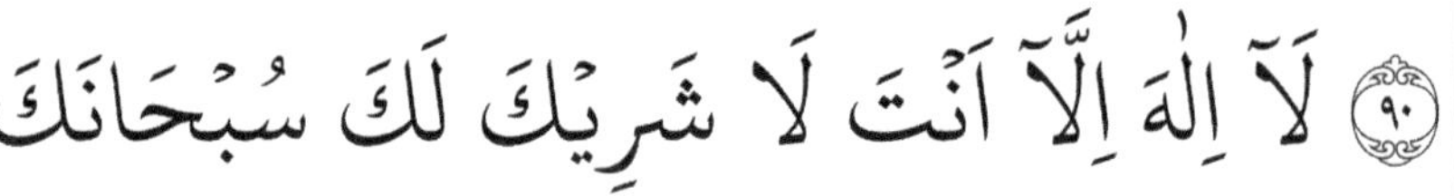

لَا اِلٰهَ اِلَّا اَنْتَ لَا شَرِيْكَ لَكَ سُبْحَانَكَ

90. There is no deity besides You. You have no partner. You are so pure.

اَللّٰهُمَّ اَسْتَغْفِرُكَ لِذَنْبِيْ وَاَسْأَلُكَ رَحْمَتَكَ

O Allah! I beg You to forgive my sins and I beg of You for Your mercy.

اَللّٰهُمَّ زِدْنِيْ عِلْمًا وَلَا تُزِغْ قَلْبِيْ بَعْدَ اِذْ

O Allah! Increase me in knowledge and do not turn my heart away (from You) after

90. Abu Dawood # 5061

هَدَيْتَنِيْ وَهَبْ لِيْ مِنْ لَّدُنْكَ رَحْمَةً اِنَّكَ اَنْتَ

having guided it and bless me with Your special mercy. Verily You are the

اَلْوَهَّابُ

Generous Giver.

(٩١) اَللّٰهُمَّ اغْفِرْلِيْ ذَنْبِيْ وَوَسِّعْ لِيْ فِيْ دَارِىْ

91. O Allah! Forgive my sins, grant me spaciousness in my home

وَبَارِكْ لِيْ فِيْ رِزْقِيْ

and bless me with *barakah* (blessings) in my sustenance.

(٩٢) اَللّٰهُمَّ اجْعَلْنِيْ مِنَ التَّوَّابِيْنَ وَاجْعَلْنِيْ مِنَ

92. O Allah! Make me from those who repent and make me from those who

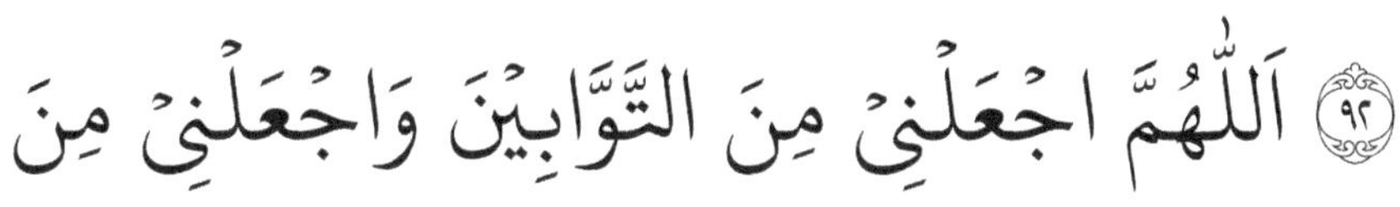

91. Amalul Yawmi Wal Laylah Pg. 35	92. Tirmizi # 55

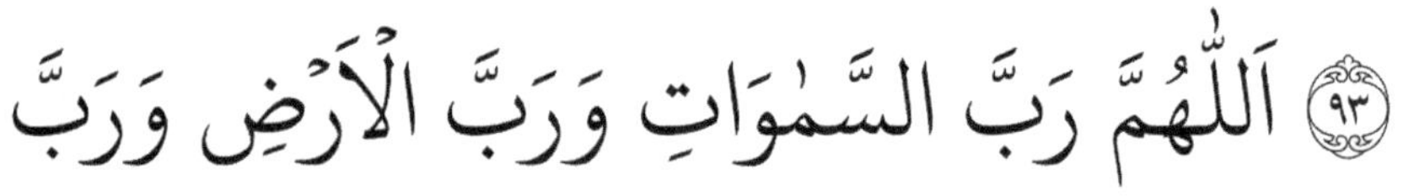

observe cleanliness.

اَللّٰهُمَّ رَبَّ السَّمٰوَاتِ وَرَبَّ الْاَرْضِ وَرَبَّ ⟨٩٣⟩

93. O Allah! The Rabb of the heavens, the earth and

الْعَرْشِ الْعَظِيْمِ رَبَّنَا وَرَبَّ كُلِّ شَىْءٍ فَالِقَ

the Great Throne (Arsh), My Rabb and The Rabb of all things, The One who causes trees to grow

الْحَبِّ وَالنَّوٰى وَمُنْزِلَ التَّوْرٰةِ وَالْاِنْجِيْلِ

by the splitting of a seed and a kernel, the Revealer of the Taurat, Injeel

وَالْفُرْقَانِ اَعُوْذُ بِكَ مِنْ شَرِّ كُلِّ شَىْءٍ اَنْتَ

and The Qur-aan Shareef, I seek Your protection from the evil of all things which You

93. Muslim # 2713

اٰخِذٌ بِنَاصِيَتِهٖ ۰ اَللّٰهُمَّ اَنْتَ الْاَوَّلُ فَلَيْسَ

are in full control of. O Allah! You are the First and nothing

قَبْلَكَ شَىْءٌ وَاَنْتَ الْاٰخِرُ فَلَيْسَ بَعْدَكَ شَىْءٌ

preceded You. You are the Last and nothing will come after you.

وَاَنْتَ الظَّاهِرُ فَلَيْسَ فَوْقَكَ شَىْءٌ وَاَنْتَ

You are Apparent and there is nothing above You. You are

الْبَاطِنُ فَلَيْسَ دُوْنَكَ شَىْءٌ اِقْضِ عَنَّا الدَّيْنَ

Concealed and nothing is beyond You. Pay out our debts

وَاَغْنِنَا مِنَ الْفَقْرِ

and free us from poverty.

اَللّٰهُمَّ رَبَّ السَّمٰوَاتِ السَّبْعِ وَمَا اَ ظَلَّتْ

94. O Allah! The Rabb of the seven heavens and whatever it has over shadowed,

وَرَبَّ الْاَرَضِيْنَ وَمَا اَقَلَّتْ وَرَبَّ الشَّيَاطِيْنِ

And the Rabb of the earths and whatever it holds, the Rabb of the devils

وَمَا اَضَلَّتْ كُنْ لِّيْ جَارًا مِّنْ شَرِّ خَلْقِكَ

and what ever evil they had spread, be a Protector for me against the evil of all Your creatures

اَجْمَعِيْنَ اَنْ يَّفْرُطَ عَلَيَّ اَحَدٌ مِّنْهُمْ اَوْ اَنْ

if they be unjust or

يَّطْغٰى عَزَّ جَارُكَ وَتَبَارَكَ اسْمُكَ

cruel to me. Your protection is indeed strong and Your name is full of blessings.

94. Targeeb wat Tarheeb # 5 (Vol. 2 Pg. 457)

اَللّٰهُمَّ لَكَ الْحَمْدُ اَنْتَ قَيِّمُ السَّمٰوَاتِ

95. O Allah! All praise is for You and You are the Sustainer of the heavens

وَالْاَرْضِ وَمَنْ فِيهِنَّ وَلَكَ الْحَمْدُ اَنْتَ مَلِكُ

and the earth and whatever is in them. All praise is for You and You are the Ruler of the

السَّمٰوَاتِ وَالْاَرْضِ وَمَنْ فِيهِنَّ وَلَكَ الْحَمْدُ

heavens and the earth and whatever is in them. All praise is for You and

اَنْتَ نُوْرُ السَّمٰوَاتِ وَالْاَرْضِ وَمَنْ فِيهِنَّ وَلَكَ

You are the (noor) light of the heavens and the earth and whatever is in them. All

الْحَمْدُ اَنْتَ الْحَقُّ وَوَعْدُكَ الْحَقُّ وَلِقَآؤُكَ

praise is for You and You are True, Your promise is true and our meeting You

حَقٌّ وَقَوْلُكَ حَقٌّ وَالْجَنَّةُ حَقٌّ وَالنَّارُ حَقٌّ

is a reality, Your word is true. Paradise is a reality. Hell is a reality

وَالنَّبِيُّوْنَ حَقٌّ وَمُحَمَّدٌ صَلَّى اللهُ عَلَيْهِ وَسَلَّمَ

and all the Ambiyaa are true. Muhammad ﷺ,

رَسُوْلُ اللهِ حَقٌّ وَالسَّاعَةُ حَقٌّ ۰ اَللّٰهُمَّ لَكَ

the Messenger of Allah is true and the Hour (of Resurrection) is a reality. O Allah!

اَسْلَمْتُ وَبِكَ اٰمَنْتُ وَعَلَيْكَ تَوَكَّلْتُ وَاِلَيْكَ

I have submitted before You in obedience. I have believed in You and I have placed my trust in You.

اَنَبْتُ وَبِكَ خَاصَمْتُ وَاِلَيْكَ حَاكَمْتُ وَاَنْتَ

I have turned my attention solely towards You. Wherever I have quarrelled (in support of right and justice) it was with Your help. I

رَبُّنَا وَاِلَيْكَ الْمَصِيْرُ فَاغْفِرْلِيْ مَا قَدَّمْتُ وَمَا

have turned towards You for judgment. You are our Rabb and to You is our ultimate return. Forgive all my sins, past and

اَخَّرْتُ وَمَا اَسْرَرْتُ وَمَا اَعْلَنْتُ وَمَا اَسْرَفْتُ

future, whether done secretly or openly and those sins where I have surpassed the limit (in sinning)

وَمَا اَنْتَ اَعْلَمُ بِهٖ مِنِّيْ اَنْتَ الْمُقَدِّمُ وَاَنْتَ

and You know more (what I have done) than I know. You are The first and

الْمُؤَخِّرُ لَآ اِلٰهَ اِلَّاۤ اَنْتَ وَلَاحَوْلَ وَلَا قُوَّةَ اِلَّا

The Last. There is no god besides You. There is no power to do good and no strength to refrain from evil except

بِاللّٰهِ

with the help of Allah.

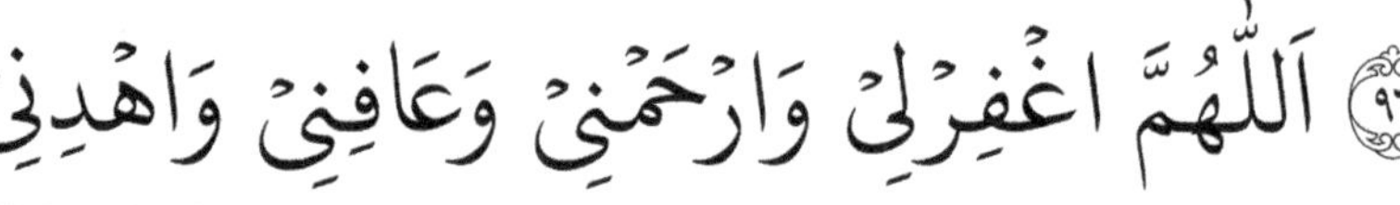

٩٦ اَللّٰهُمَّ اغْفِرْ لِيْ وَارْحَمْنِيْ وَعَافِنِيْ وَاهْدِنِيْ

96. O Allah! Forgive me, have mercy on me, grant me peace, guide me,

وَارْزُقْنِيْ وَاجْبُرْنِيْ وَارْفَعْنِيْ

grant me sustenance, take care of my needs and elevate me.

٩٧ رَبِّ اِنِّيْ لِمَاۤ اَنْزَلْتَ اِلَيَّ مِنْ خَيْرٍ فَقِيْرٌ

97. O Allah! I am in desperate need towards You for whatever good You may choose to grant me.

٩٨ اَللّٰهُمَّ رَبَّ جِبْرِيْلَ وَمِيْكَائِيْلَ

98. O Allah! Rabb of Jibraeel عَلَيْهِ السَّلَام, Mikaeel عَلَيْهِ السَّلَام,

وَاِسْرَافِيْلَ فَاطِرَ السَّمٰوَاتِ وَالْاَرْضِ عَالِمَ

and Israfeel عَلَيْهِ السَّلَام, The Creator of the heavens and the earth, The Knower

96. Abu Dawood # 850	97. Qasas # 24	98. Muslim # 770

الْغَيْبِ وَالشَّهَادَةِ اَنْتَ تَحْكُمُ بَيْنَ عِبَادِكَ

of the unseen and the visible. Certainly You will judge between Your servants (on the Day of Qiyaamah)

فِيْمَا كَانُوْا فِيْهِ يَخْتَلِفُوْنَ اِهْدِنِيْ لِمَا اخْتُلِفَ

in matters where they have differed. (O Allah) in these differences,

فِيْهِ مِنَ الْحَقِّ بِاِذْنِكَ اِنَّكَ تَهْدِىْ مَنْ تَشَآءُ

guide me to the truth, with Your command. Verily You guide whomsoever You wish.

اِلٰى صِرَاطٍ مُّسْتَقِيْمٍ

to the straight path.

ﭐ اَللّٰهُمَّ اهْدِنِىْ فِيْمَنْ هَدَيْتَ وَعَافِنِىْ فِيْمَنْ

1. O Allah! Guide me along with those whom you have guided, grant me ease along with those whom

عَافَيْتَ وَتَوَلَّنِىْ فِيْمَنْ تَوَلَّيْتَ وَبَارِكْ لِىْ فِيْمَآ

you have granted ease, support me along with those whom You have supported, grant me barakah (blessings) in what

اَعْطَيْتَ وَقِنِىْ شَرَّ مَا قَضَيْتَ فَاِنَّكَ تَقْضِىْ

You have given me, save me from the harm of what You have decreed. Verily You decide

وَلَا يُقْضٰى عَلَيْكَ اِنَّهٗ لَا يَذِلُّ مَنْ وَّالَيْتَ

and none decides against You. Whoever is under Your protection, cannot be disgraced.

1. Abu Dawood # 1425

وَلَا يَعِزُّ مَنْ عَادَيْتَ تَبَارَكْتَ رَبَّنَا وَتَعَالَيْتَ

and who is opposed by You cannot gain dignity. Our Rabb, You are full of blessings and Most High.

نَسْتَغْفِرُكَ وَنَتُوْبُ اِلَيْكَ

We beg forgiveness and repent before You and

وَصَلَّى اللهُ عَلَى النَّبِيِّ

may the blessings of Allah be showered upon Nabi صَلَّى ٱللَّهُ عَلَيْهِ وَسَلَّمَ.

اَللّٰهُمَّ اغْفِرْ لِيْ وَلِلْمُؤْمِنِيْنَ وَالْمُؤْمِنَاتِ ۝

2. O Allah! Forgive me and all the believing men and women,

وَالْمُسْلِمِيْنَ وَالْمُسْلِمَاتِ وَاَلِّفْ بَيْنَ

all the Muslim men and women, unite

2. Sunanul Kubraa lil Bayhaqi # 3143

قُلُوْبِهِمْ وَاَصْلِحْ ذَاتَ بَيْنِهِمْ وَانْصُرْهُمْ عَلٰى

their hearts, correct their mutual affairs and help them against

عَدُوِّكَ وَعَدُوِّهِمْ اَللّٰهُمَّ الْعَنِ الْكَفَرَةَ الَّذِيْنَ

Your enemy and their enemy. O Allah! Let Your curse fall on those Kuffaar (disbelievers)

يَصُدُّوْنَ عَنْ سَبِيْلِكَ وَيُكَذِّبُوْنَ رُسُلَكَ

who stop people from treading Your path, deny Your prophets

وَيُقَاتِلُوْنَ اَوْلِيَآءَكَ اَللّٰهُمَّ خَالِفْ بَيْنَ

and fight Your Awliyaa (friends). O Allah! Create rifts

كَلِمَتِهِمْ وَزَلْزِلْ اَقْدَامَهُمْ وَاَنْزِلْ بِهِمْ

in their ranks, shake their feet and send upon them

بَأْسَكَ الَّذِيْ لَا تَرُدُّهُ عَنِ الْقَوْمِ الْمُجْرِمِيْنَ

such a punishment which is not averted from sinners.

بِسْـــمِ اللهِ الرَّحْمٰنِ الرَّحِيْـــمِ

In the name of Allah, The most Compassionate, The most
Merciful.

اَللّٰهُمَّ اِنَّا نَسْتَعِيْنُكَ وَ نَسْتَغْفِرُكَ

3. O Allah! We seek Your help and we seek forgiveness from You

وَنَسْتَهْدِيْكَ وَنُؤْمِنُ بِكَ وَنَتُوْبُ اِلَيْكَ

and we seek Your guidance. We believe in You, O Allah! We repent
to You

وَنَتَوَكَّلُ عَلَيْكَ وَنُثْنِيْ عَلَيْكَ الْخَيْرَ كُلَّهُ

and we place our trust in You. We praise You for every kind of
favour (bestowed upon us).

وَنَشْكُرُكَ وَلَانَكْفُرُكَ وَ نَخْلَعُ وَنَتْرُكُ مَنْ

We express our thanks to You and we are not ungrateful to You. We stay away from the one who

يَّفْجُرُكَ اَللّٰهُمَّ اِيَّاكَ نَعْبُدُ وَلَكَ نُصَلِّ

disobeys You. O Allah! You alone do we worship and to You do we perform salaah

وَنَسْجُدُ وَاِلَيْكَ نَسْعٰى وَنَحْفِدُ

and make sajdah. It is towards You that we flee and we are quick in doing so.

وَنَرْجُوْا رَحْمَتَكَ وَنَخْشٰى عَذَابَكَ الْجِدَّ

We hope for Your mercy and fear Your severe punishment.

اِنَّ عَذَابَكَ الْجِدَّ بِالْكُفَّارِ مُلْحِقٌ

Verily, Your severe punishment is sure to overtake the disbelievers.

٤ اَللّٰهُمَّ اِنِّیْۤ اَعُوْذُ بِرِضَاكَ مِنْ سَخَطِكَ

4. O Allah! I seek refuge through Your pleasure from Your displeasure

وَبِمُعَافَاتِكَ مِنْ عُقُوْبَتِكَ وَاَعُوْذُ بِكَ مِنْكَ

and through Your forgiveness from Your punishment. I seek refuge from Yourself.

لَاۤ اُحْصِیْ ثَنَآءً عَلَیْكَ اَنْتَ كَمَاۤ اَثْنَیْتَ عَلٰى

I am unable to praise You sufficiently. You are as You have praised

نَفْسِكَ

Yourself.

٥ اَللّٰهُمَّ رَبَّ جِبْرِیْلَ وَمِیْكَاِئِیْلَ وَاِسْرَافِیْلَ

5. O Allah! The Rabb of Jibraeel عَلَیْهِالسَّلَامُ, Mikaeel عَلَیْهِالسَّلَامُ, Israfeel عَلَیْهِالسَّلَامُ

---

4. Muslim # 486 | 5. Mustadrak # 6610

وَمُحَمَّدٍ صَلَّى اللهُ عَلَيْهِ وَسَلَّمَ اَعُوْذُ بِكَ مِنَ

and Muhammad ﷺ, I seek Your protection from

النَّارِ

the Fire of Hell.

(٦) اَللّٰهُمَّ اِنِّى اَعُوْذُ بِكَ مِنْ اَنْ اَضِلَّ اَوْ اُضَلَّ

6. O Allah! I seek Your protection from being misled or that I should be misled by others and

اَوْ اَزِلَّ اَوْ اُزَلَّ اَوْ اَظْلِمَ اَوْ اُظْلَمَ اَوْ اَجْهَلَ اَوْ

from slipping or being made to slip by others, from oppressing others or from being oppressed, from acting ignorantly or that

يُجْهَلَ عَلَىَّ

anyone behaves ignorantly towards me.

6. Abu Dawood # 5094

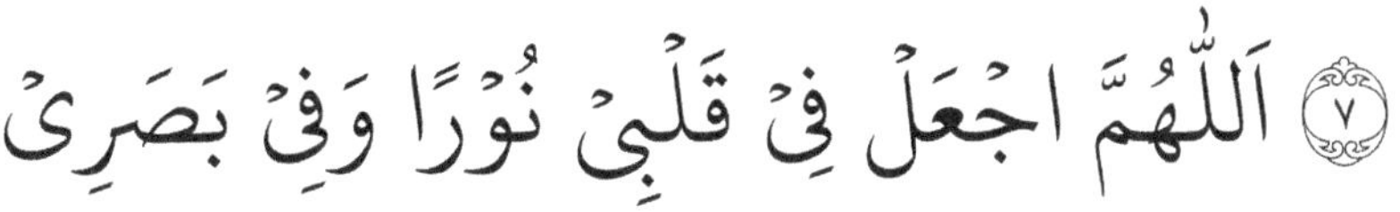

⑦ اَللّٰهُمَّ اجْعَلْ فِيْ قَلْبِيْ نُوْرًا وَفِيْ بَصَرِيْ

7. O Allah! Fill Your noor (light) into my heart, my eyes,

نُوْرًا وَفِيْ سَمْعِيْ نُوْرًا وَعَنْ يَّمِيْنِيْ نُوْرًا وَعَنْ

my ears, to my right,

شِمَالِيْ نُوْرًا وَمِنْ خَلْفِيْ نُوْرًا وَمِنْ اَمَامِيْ

to my left, behind me, in front of me,

نُوْرًا وَّاجْعَلْ مِنْ فَوْقِيْ نُوْرًا وَمِنْ تَحْتِيْ نُوْرًا

over me and beneath me

اَللّٰهُمَّ اَعْطِنِيْ نُوْرًا وَّاجْعَلْ لِّيْ نُوْرًا وَفِيْ عَصَبِيْ

O Allah! Bestow Your (Noor) light upon me and infuse it into my (muscle) nerves,

7. Muslim # 763

نُوْرًا وَفِىْ لَحْمِىْ نُوْرًا وَفِىْ دَمِىْ نُوْرًا وَ فِىْ

flesh, blood,

شَعْرِىْ نُوْرًا وَّ فِىْ بَشَرِىْ نُوْرًا وَفِىْ لِسَانِىْ نُوْرًا

hair, skin, tongue

وَاجْعَلْ فِىْ نَفْسِىْ نُوْرًا وَاَعْظِمْ لِىْ نُوْرًا

and soul. Grant it to me profusely

وَاجْعَلْنِىْ نُوْرًا

and make my entire being into Noor.

⑧ اَللّٰهُمَّ افْتَحْ لَنَا اَبْوَابَ رَحْمَتِكَ وَسَهِّل لَّنَا

8. O Allah! Open the gates of Your mercy for us and make easy for us

8. Ibnu Maajah # 772

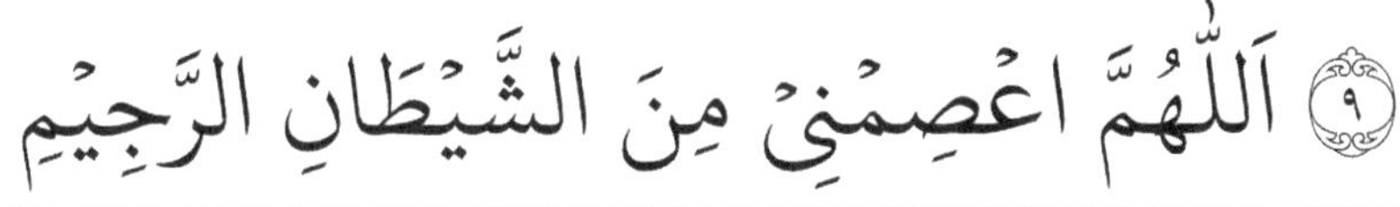

اَبْوَابَ رِزْقِكَ

the doors of Your sustenance.

اَللّٰهُمَّ اعْصِمْنِيْ مِنَ الشَّيْطَانِ الرَّجِيْمِ ⑨

9. O Allah! Save me from the accursed shaytaan.

اَللّٰهُمَّ اهْدِنِيْ لِاَحْسَنِ الْاَخْلَاقِ لَا يَهْدِىْ ⑩

10. O Allah! Grant me excellent character as You alone can guide me

لِاَحْسَنِهَا اِلَّا اَنْتَ وَاصْرِفْ عَنِّيْ سَيِّئَهَا لَا

to acquire this and remove from me all evil character

يَصْرِفُ عَنِّيْ سَيِّئَهَا اِلَّا اَنْتَ

which You alone can remove.

| 9. Ibnu Maajah # 773 | 10. Muslim # 771 |

اَللّٰهُمَّ بَاعِدْ بَيْنِيْ وَبَيْنَ خَطَايَاىَ كَمَا ⟨١١⟩

11. O Allah! Distance me from my sins like how

بَاعَدْتَّ بَيْنَ الْمَشْرِقِ وَالْمَغْرِبِ

You have distanced the east from the west.

اَللّٰهُمَّ اغْسِلْ خَطَايَاىَ بِالْمَآءِ وَالثَّلْجِ

O Allah! Wash away my sins with water, snow and hail.

وَالْبَرَدِ وَنَقِّنِيْ مِنَ الْخَطَايَا كَمَا نَقَّيْتَ الثَّوْبَ

Cleanse me of sins in the manner white clothing

الْاَبْيَضَ مِنَ الدَّنَسِ

is cleansed of dirt.

11. Bukhaari # 744

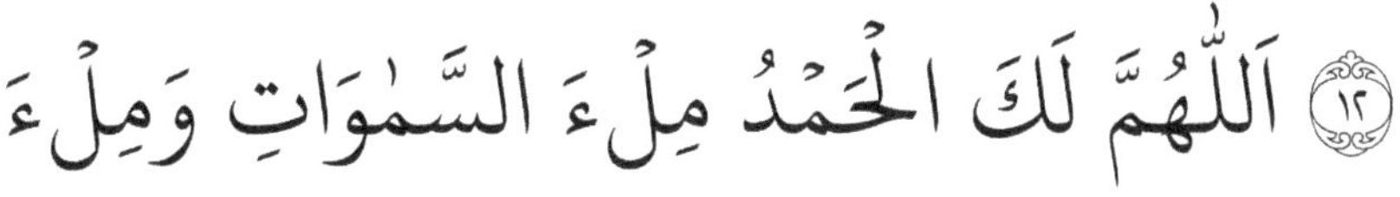

١٢ اَللّٰهُمَّ لَكَ الْحَمْدُ مِلْءَ السَّمٰوَاتِ وَمِلْءَ

12. O Allah! All praise be to You in quantities equal to the heavens and

الْاَرْضِ وَمِلْءَ مَا بَيْنَهُمَا وَمِلْءَ مَاشِئْتَ مِنْ

the earth, what is in-between them and whatever is beyond them

شَىْءٍ بَعْدُ اَنْتَ اَهْلُ الثَّنَآءِ وَالْكِبْرِيَآءِ

as You may wish. You alone deserve to be praised, glorified

وَالْمَجْدِ اَحَقُّ مَا قَالَ الْعَبْدُ وَكُلُّنَا لَكَ عَبْدٌ

and revered. Whatever Your slave has said is true, and we are all Your slaves.

لَاَمَانِعَ لِمَا اَعْطَيْتَ وَلَامُعْطِىَ لِمَا مَنَعْتَ

None can prevent what You bestow and none can bestow what You prevent.

12. Muslim # 477

وَلَا رَآدَّ لِمَا قَضَيْتَ وَلَا يَنْفَعُ ذَا الْجَدِّ مِنْكَ

None can reverse what You have decreed and the wealth of the wealthy in front of You (O Allah) is of no benefit

الْجَدُّ

to them.

﴿١٣﴾ اَللّٰهُمَّ اغْفِرْ لِيْ ذَنْبِيْ كُلَّهُ دِقَّهُ وَجِلَّهُ وَاَوَّلَهُ

13. O Allah! Forgive all my sins, minor and major, the first

وَاٰخِرَهُ وَعَلَانِيَتَهُ وَسِرَّهُ

and the last, and those which I committed openly or secretly.

﴿١٤﴾ رَبِّ اَعْطِ نَفْسِيْ تَقْوٰهَا وَزَكِّهَا اَنْتَ خَيْرُ

14. O Allah! Bless me with taqwa (Your fear) and purify my soul as You are the Best

| 13. Muslim # 483 | 14. Musnad Ahmad # 25229 |

مَنْ زَكَّاهَا اَنْتَ وَلِيُّهَا وَمَوْلٰهَا

Purifier. You are the Guardian and Master of my soul.

اَللّٰهُمَّ اِنِّيْ ظَلَمْتُ نَفْسِيْ ظُلْمًا كَثِيْرًا وَّلَا ۱۵

15. O Allah! I have seriously wronged myself and none

يَغْفِرُ الذُّنُوْبَ اِلَّا اَنْتَ فَاغْفِرْلِيْ مَغْفِرَةً مِّنْ

besides You can forgive sins, so forgive me

عِنْدِكَ وَارْحَمْنِيْ اِنَّكَ اَنْتَ الْغَفُوْرُ الرَّحِيْمُ

and have mercy on me. Verily You are Most Forgiving and Most
Merciful.

اَللّٰهُمَّ حَاسِبْنِيْ حِسَابًا يَّسِيْرًا ۱۶

16. O Allah! Put me through an easy reckoning.

15. Bukhaari # 834	16. Mustadrak # 190

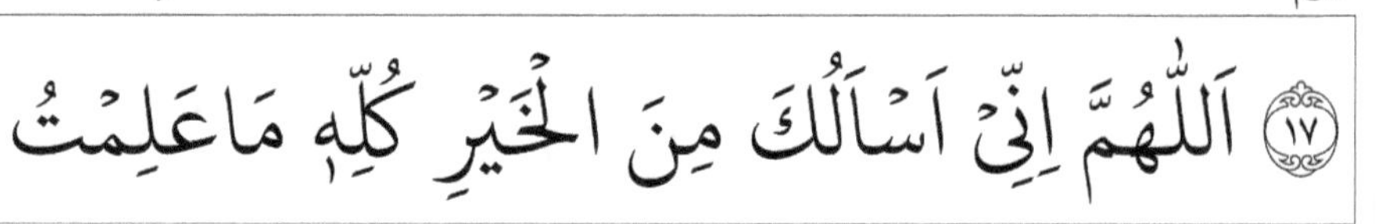

17. O Allah! I beg You for all kinds of good, that which I know

and that which I do not know. And I seek Your protection from all evil

that which I know and that which I do not know. O Allah! I beg of You

all the good which was asked for by Your pious servants

and I seek Your protection from all kinds of evil which they had sought Your protection from.

17. Musannaf ibn Abi Shaybah # 3025

الصَّالِحُوْنَ. رَبَّنَآ اٰتِنَا فِى الدُّنْيَا حَسَنَةً وَّفِى

O Allah! Grant us the good of this world,

الْاٰخِرَةِ حَسَنَةً وَّقِنَا عَذَابَ النَّارِ

the good of the hereafter and save us from the punishment of Jahannum.

رَبَّنَآ اِنَّنَآ اٰمَنَّا فَاغْفِرْ لَنَا ذُنُوْبَنَا وَكَفِّرْ عَنَّا

O Allah! We have believed, so forgive our sins and pardon our transgressions

سَيِّاٰتِنَا وَتَوَفَّنَا مَعَ الْاَبْرَارِ. رَبَّنَا وَاٰتِنَا مَا

and let us die with the righteous. O Allah! Grant us whatever You have

وَعَدتَّنَا عَلٰى رُسُلِكَ وَلَا تُخْزِنَا يَوْمَ الْقِيٰمَةِ

promised to us through Your Messengers and do not disgrace us on the Day of Qiyaamah.

اِنَّكَ لَا تُخْلِفُ الْمِيْعَادَ

Verily You never break Your promise.

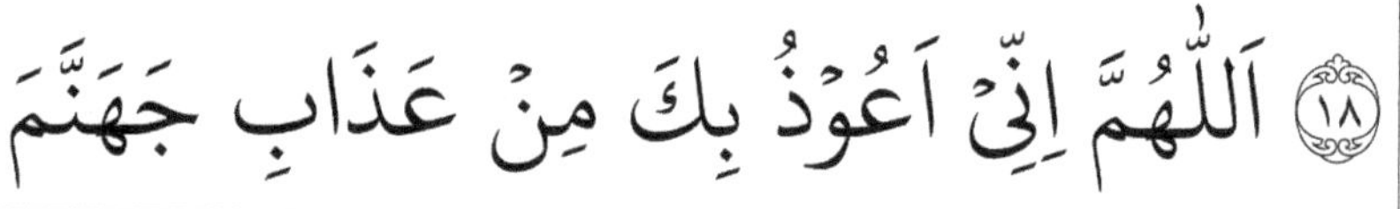

(١٨) اَللّٰهُمَّ اِنِّيْ اَعُوْذُ بِكَ مِنْ عَذَابِ جَهَنَّمَ

18. O Allah! I seek Your protection from the punishment of Jahannum,

وَاَعُوْذُ بِكَ مِنْ عَذَابِ الْقَبْرِ وَاَعُوْذُ بِكَ مِنْ

the punishment of the grave, from the

فِتْنَةِ الْمَسِيْحِ الدَّجَّالِ وَاَعُوْذُ بِكَ مِنْ فِتْنَةِ

mischief of Dajjaal, from the trials

الْمَحْيَا وَالْمَمَاتِ وَاَعُوْذُ بِكَ مِنَ الْمَأْثَمِ

of life and death, from sins

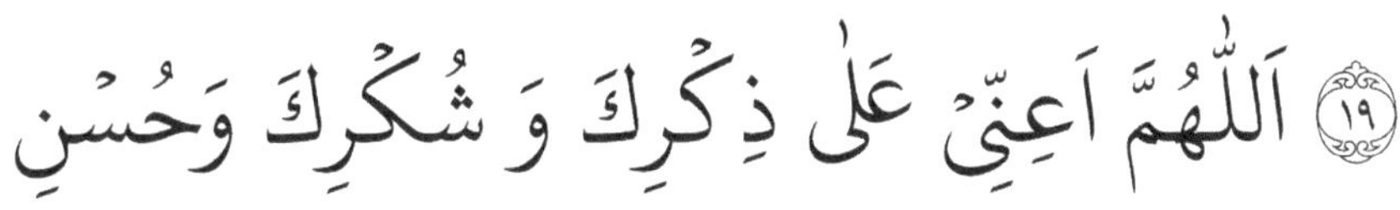

and from debts.

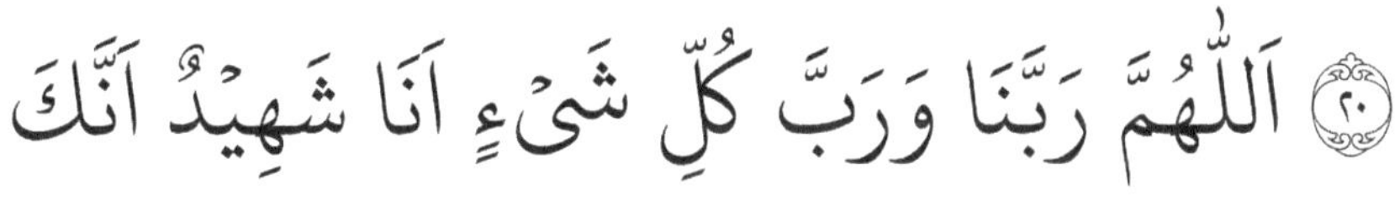

19. O Allah! Help me in remembering You, being grateful to You and

عِبَادَتِكَ

worshipping You well.

اَللّٰهُمَّ رَبَّنَا وَرَبَّ كُلِّ شَىْءٍ اَنَا شَهِيْدٌ اَنَّكَ

20. O Allah! Our Rabb and the Rabb of all things, I bear witness that You

اَنْتَ الرَّبُّ وَحْدَكَ لَا شَرِيْكَ لَكَ

are the Sole Nourisher, You are One and have no partner.

19. Abu Dawood # 1522   20. Abu Dawood # 1508

اَللّٰهُمَّ رَبَّنَا وَرَبَّ كُلِّ شَىْءٍ اَنَا شَهِيْدٌ اَنَّ

O Allah! Our Rabb and the Rabb of all things, I bear witness that

مُحَمَّدًا صَلَّى اللّٰهُ عَلَيْهِ وَسَلَّمَ عَبْدُكَ

Hadhrat Muhammad ﷺ is Your servant

وَرَسُوْلُكَ. اَللّٰهُمَّ رَبَّنَا وَرَبَّ كُلِّ شَىْءٍ اَنَا

and Messenger. O Allah! Our Rabb and the Rabb of all things, I

شَهِيْدٌ اَنَّ الْعِبَادَ كُلَّهُمْ اِخْوَةٌ. اَللّٰهُمَّ رَبَّنَا

bear witness that all Your slaves are brothers. O Allah! Our Rabb

وَرَبَّ كُلِّ شَىْءٍ اِجْعَلْنِيْ مُخْلِصًا لَّكَ وَاَهْلِيْ فِيْ

and the Rabb of all things, Make me and my family sincere in our devotion to You

كُلِّ سَاعَةٍ فِى الدُّنْيَا وَالْأٰخِرَةِ يَاذَا الْجَلَالِ

for every moment in this world and in the hereafter. O The Majestic,

وَالْاِكْرَامِ اِسْمَعْ وَاسْتَجِبْ اَللهُ اَكْبَرُ الْاَكْبَرُ

The Benevolent, hear my dua and please accept it. Allah is the Greatest, Allah is the Greatest of all.

اَللهُ نُوْرُ السَّمٰوَاتِ وَالْاَرْضِ اَللهُ اَكْبَرُ الْاَكْبَرُ

Allah is the light of the heavens and the earth. Allah is the Greatest, Allah is the Greatest of all.

حَسْبِىَ اللهُ وَنِعْمَ الْوَكِيْلُ اَللهُ اَكْبَرُ الْاَ كْبَرُ

Allah is enough for me and what an excellent Supporter He is. Allah is the Greatest, Allah is the Greatest of all.

﴿٢١﴾ اَللّٰهُمَّ اَصْلِحْ لِى دِيْنِىَ الَّذِىْ هُوَ عِصْمَةُ

21. O Allah! Correct my Deeni affairs which is in fact a protection

21. Muslim # 2720

اَمۡرِىۡ وَاَصۡلِحۡ لِىۡ دُنۡيَاىَ الَّتِىۡ فِيۡهَا مَعَاشِىۡ

for all my affairs, rectify my worldly life which is a source of my survival,

وَاَصۡلِحۡ لِىۡ اٰخِرَتِىَ الَّتِىۡ فِيۡهَا مَعَادِىۡ وَاَحۡيِنِىۡ

rectify for me the life of the hereafter to which I have to return. Keep me alive

مَا كَانَتِ الۡحَيَاةُ خَيۡرًا لِّىۡ وَتَوَفَّنِىۡ اِذَا كَانَتِ

as long as life is good for me and take me away from this world when

الۡوَفَاةُ خَيۡرًا لِّىۡ وَاجۡعَلِ الۡحَيَاةَ زِيَادَةً لِّىۡ فِىۡ كُلِّ

death is in my best interest. Make my life a means of doing more

خَيۡرٍ وَاجۡعَلِ الۡمَوۡتَ رَاحَةً لِّىۡ مِنۡ كُلِّ شَرٍّ

good, and make my death a tranquillity against all troubles.

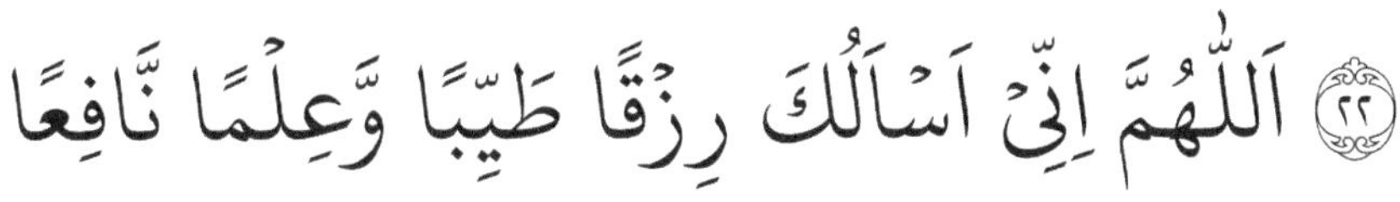

اَللّٰهُمَّ اِنِّيْ اَسْاَلُكَ رِزْقًا طَيِّبًا وَّعِلْمًا نَّافِعًا ۲۲

22. O Allah! I beg You for Halaal (pure) sustenance, beneficial knowledge

وَّعَمَلًا مُّتَقَبَّلًا

and deeds that are accepted.

اَللّٰهُمَّ اَشْبَعْتَ وَاَرْوَيْتَ فَهَنِّئْنَا وَرَزَقْتَنَا ۲۳

23. O Allah! You have satiated us (with food and drink) so make it wholesome for us and You have granted us sustenance

فَاَكْثَرْتَ وَاَطَبْتَ فَزِدْنَا

which You have made abundant and pure, so (please) increase it. for us

اَللّٰهُمَّ قَنِّعْنِيْ بِمَا رَزَقْتَنِيْ وَبَارِكْ لِيْ فِيْهِ ۲۴

24. O Allah! Make me content with whatever You have provided for me and give me *barakah* (blessings) in it

| 22. Mu'jamus Sagheer # 152 | 23. Musannaf ibn Abi Shaybah # 24513 | 24. Mustadrak # 1878 |

وَاخْلُفْ عَلٰى كُلِّ غَآئِبَةٍ لِّيْ بِخَيْرٍ

and be a Protector on my behalf over that which is not in front of me (i.e. my family and wealth).

﴿٢٥﴾ رَبِّ اغْفِرْ وَارْحَمْ اِنَّكَ اَنْتَ الْاَعَزُّ

25. O Allah! Forgive me and have mercy on me. Verily You are the most dignified

الْاَكْرَمُ

and honoured.

﴿٢٦﴾ اَللّٰهُمَّ اشْرَحْ لِيْ صَدْرِيْ وَيَسِّرْ لِيْ

26. O Allah! Expand my chest and make my work easy

اَمْرِيْ وَاَعُوْذُ بِكَ مِنْ وَّسَاوِسِ الصَّدْرِ

for me. I seek Your protection from the whispers of the heart,

25. Musannaf ibn Abi Shaybah # 15565	26. Musannaf ibn Abi Shaybah # 15135

وَشَتَاتِ الْاَمْرِ وَفِتْنَةِ الْقَبْرِ. اَللّٰهُمَّ اِنِّيْ اَعُوْذُ

from my affairs becoming complicated and having to face
difficulties in the grave. O Allah! I seek Your protection

بِكَ مِنْ شَرِّ مَا يَلِجُ فِى اللَّيْلِ وَمِنْ شَرِّ مَا يَلِجُ

from any calamity occurring at night, any calamity occurring

فِى النَّهَارِ وَمِنْ شَرِّ مَا تَهُبُّ بِهِ الرِّيَاحُ

during the day and from calamities that fly with the wind.

(۲۷) اَللّٰهُمَّ اهْدِنِيْ بِالْهُدٰى وَنَقِّنِيْ بِالتَّقْوٰى

27. O Allah! Guide me with (divine) guidance, cleanse me with
taqwa (piety)

وَاغْفِرْ لِيْ فِى الْاٰخِرَةِ وَالْاُوْلٰى

and forgive me in this life and the hereafter.

27. Musannaf ibn Abi Shaybah # 14704

اَللّٰهُمَّ اِنِّىْ اَسْاَلُكَ عِلْمًا نَّافِعًا وَّرِزْقًا

28. O Allah! I beg You for beneficial knowledge, abundant sustenance

وَّاسِعًا وَّشِفَآءً مِّنْ كُلِّ دَآءٍ

and cure from all illnesses.

اَللّٰهُمَّ اَنْتَ عَضُدِىْ وَ نَصِيْرِىْ بِكَ

29. O Allah! You are the strength of my arms and my True Helper.

اَحُوْلُ وَبِكَ اَصُوْلُ وَبِكَ اُقَاتِلُ وَلَاحَوْلَ

I charge and fight the enemy with Your help and strength and I have no ability to do good actions or avoid evil except

وَلَاقُوَّةَ اِلَّا بِكَ

with Your help.

28. Mustadrak # 1739	29. Abu Dawood # 2632

اَللّٰهُمَّ لَكَ الْحَمْدُ كُلُّهُ لَا قَابِضَ لِمَا ﴿٣٠﴾

30. O Allah! All praise is due to You. None can restrict what

بَسَطْتَ وَلَا بَاسِطَ لِمَا قَبَضْتَ وَلَاهَادِىَ لِمَنْ

You expand and none can expand what You have restricted. None can guide whom

اَضْلَلْتَ وَلَا مُضِلَّ لِمَنْ هَدَيْتَ وَلَا مُعْطِىَ لِمَا

You have caused to fall into error and none can mislead whom You have guided. None can bestow what

مَنَعْتَ وَلَا مَانِعَ لِمَا اَعْطَيْتَ وَلَا مُقَرِّبَ لِمَا

You prevent, and none can prevent what You bestow. None can bring near what

بَاعَدْتَ وَلَا مُبَاعِدَ لِمَا قَرَّبْتَ ۰ اَللّٰهُمَّ ابْسُطْ

You have distanced, and none can distance what You have brought near. O Allah! Grant us in abundance

30. Mustadrak # 4308

عَلَيْنَا مِنْ بَرَكَاتِكَ وَرَحْمَتِكَ وَفَضْلِكَ وَرِزْقِكَ

Your blessings, Your mercy, Your grace and Your sustenance.

اَللّٰهُمَّ اِنِّى اَسْاَلُكَ النَّعِيْمَ الْمُقِيْمَ الَّذِىْ لَا

O Allah! I beg of You to grant me Your everlasting favours which

يَحُوْلُ وَلَا يَزُوْلُ ۭ اَللّٰهُمَّ اِنِّى اَسْاَلُكَ الْاَمَنَ

never ends nor is taken away. O Allah! I beg of You to grant me safety

يَوْمَ الْخَوْفِ ۭ اَللّٰهُمَّ اِنِّى عَائِذٌ بِكَ مِنْ شَرِّ مَا

on the fearful Day (of Judgment). O Allah! I ask You for protection against the evil of what

اَعْطَيْتَنَا وَمِنْ شَرِّ مَا مَنَعْتَنَا ۭ اَللّٰهُمَّ حَبِّبْ

You have given us and the evil of what You have not given us. O Allah! enable us to love

اِلَيْنَا الْاِيْمَانَ وَزَيَّنْهُ فِيْ قُلُوْبِنَا وَكَرِّهْ اِلَيْنَا

Imaan and beautify our hearts with it and make us hate

الْكُفْرَ وَالْفُسُوْقَ وَالْعِصْيَانَ وَاجْعَلْنَا مِنَ

kufr (disbelief), immorality and sin and include us among

الرَّاشِدِيْنَ۔ اَللّٰهُمَّ تَوَفَّنَا مُسْلِمِيْنَ وَاَلْحِقْنَا

the pious. O Allah! Cause us to die as Muslims and join us

بِالصَّالِحِيْنَ غَيْرَ خَزَايَا وَّلَا مَفْتُوْنِيْنَ

with the pious, not amongst those who were put to shame nor from those who were tested.

اَللّٰهُمَّ قَاتِلِ الْكَفَرَةَ الَّذِيْنَ يُكَذِّبُوْنَ رُسُلَكَ

O Allah! Fight the disbelievers, those who deny Your Messengers and

وَ يَصُدُّوْنَ عَنْ سَبِيْلِكَ وَاجْعَلْ عَلَيْهِمْ

prevent people from treading Your path. Inflict on them

رِجْزَكَ وَعَذَابَكَ اِلٰهَ الْحَقِّ اٰمِيْنَ

Your severity and punishment, O The True Deity! *Aameen.*

(۳۱) اَللّٰهُمَّ مُنْزِلَ الْكِتَابِ وَمُجْرِىَ السَّحَابِ

31. O Allah! The Being Who revealed the Book, The One who moves the clouds

وَهَازِمَ الْاَحْزَابِ اِهْزِمْهُمْ وَانْصُرْنَا عَلَيْهِمْ

and The One who causes defeat to the enemy troops, do defeat the disbelievers and enable us to overcome them.

(۳۲) اَللّٰهُمَّ اِنَّا نَجْعَلُكَ فِيْ نُحُوْرِهِمْ وَنَعُوْذُ

32. O Allah! We place You in front of us when fighting them and seek Your protection

31. Bukhaari # 2966	32. Abu Dawood # 1537

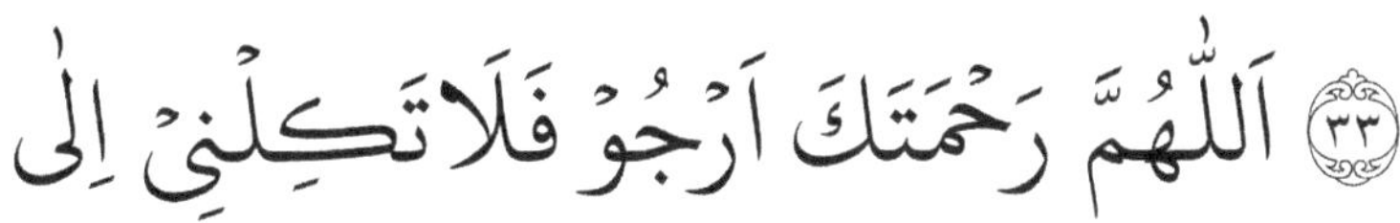

بِكَ مِنْ شُرُوْرِهِمْ

against their evil plots.

اَللّٰهُمَّ رَحْمَتَكَ اَرْجُوْ فَلَا تَكِلْنِيْ اِلٰى ۝

33. O Allah! I am hopeful of Your mercy, so do not leave me to myself

نَفْسِيْ طَرْفَةَ عَيْنٍ وَاَصْلِحْ لِيْ شَأْنِيْ كُلَّهٗ

for the blink of an eye and ease all my affairs. There is no deity besides

لَاۤ اِلٰهَ اِلَّا اَنْتَ

You.

يَا حَيُّ يَا قَيُّوْمُ بِرَحْمَتِكَ اَسْتَغِيْثُ ۝

34. O The Everlasting and The Sustainer, persistently do I beg Your mercy.

33. Abu Dawood # 5090	34. Tirmizi # 3524

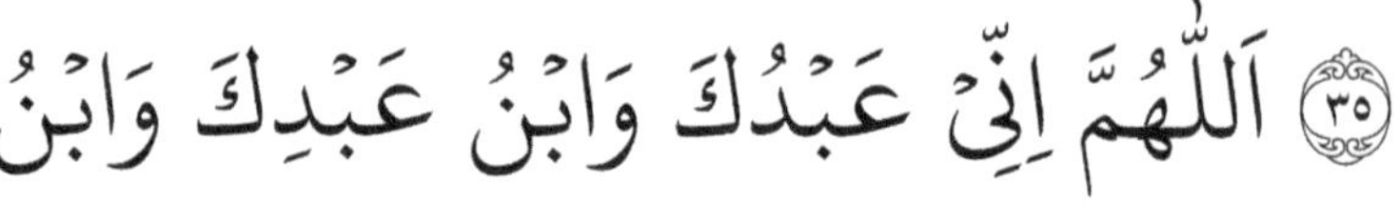

اَللّٰهُمَّ اِنِّیْ عَبْدُكَ وَابْنُ عَبْدِكَ وَابْنُ

35. O Allah! I am Your slave, the son of Your slave the son of

اَمَتِكَ نَاصِيَتِیْ بِيَدِكَ مَاضٍ فِیَّ حُكْمُكَ عَدْلٌ

Your slave woman, my forelock is in Your control, Your decree will definitely prevail over me which is full of justice.

فِیَّ قَضَآؤُكَ اَسْاَلُكَ بِكُلِّ اسْمٍ هُوَ لَكَ سَمَّيْتَ

I beg of You by whatever names You have given

بِهٖ نَفْسَكَ اَوْ اَنْزَلْتَهٗ فِیْ كِتَابِكَ اَوْ عَلَّمْتَهٗ

to Yourself, or You have revealed in Your Book, or which You have taught

اَحَدًا مِّنْ خَلْقِكَ اَوِ اسْتَاْثَرْتَ بِهٖ فِیْ عِلْمِ

to any one of Your creation, or which You have preserved within Your knowledge,

35. Ibnu Hibbaan # 968

اَلْغَيْبِ عِنْدَكَ اَنْ تَجْعَلَ الْقُرْاٰنَ الْعَظِيْمَ رَبِيْعَ

that You make the Holy Qur-aan

قَلْبِيْ وَنُوْرَ بَصَرِيْ وَجَلَاۤءَ حُزْنِيْ وَذَهَابَ

a source of delight to my heart, the light of my eyes and the healer of my sorrow

هَمِّيْ

and my worry and a source of removing my worries.

اَللّٰهُمَّ لَاسَهْلَ اِلَّا مَا جَعَلْتَهٗ سَهْلًا وَاَنْتَ ۳٦

36. O Allah! There is no ease except in that which You have made easy. And You convert

تَجْعَلُ الْحَزَنَ سَهْلًا اِذَا شِئْتَ

difficulties into ease if you so desire.

36. Ibnu Hibbaan # 970

٣٧ ﴾ لَآ اِلٰهَ اِلَّا اللهُ الْحَلِيْمُ الْكَرِيْمُ سُبْحَانَ

37. There is no deity besides Allah, The Most Tolerant and generous, who is free from any fault and

اللهِ رَبِّ الْعَرْشِ الْعَظِيْمِ

The Rabb of the Great Throne (Arsh).

اَلْحَمْدُ لِلّٰهِ رَبِّ الْعٰلَمِيْنَ اَسْاَلُكَ مُوْجِبَاتِ

Praise be to Allah, the Cherisher of the worlds. I ask You for all those things that will make Your Mercy

رَحْمَتِكَ وَعَزَآئِمَ مَغْفِرَتِكَ وَالْعِصْمَةَ مِنْ كُلِّ

necessary on me, and all those things that will secure for me Your forgiveness. (I ask for) safety from

ذَنْبٍ وَّالْغَنِيْمَةَ مِنْ كُلِّ بِرٍّ وَّالسَّلَامَةَ مِنْ كُلِّ

sin, and desire a full share of virtuous deeds and complete safety from

37. Tirmizi # 479

اِثْمٍ لَا تَدَعْ لِيْ ذَنْبًا اِلَّا غَفَرْتَهُ وَلَا هَمًّا اِلَّا

vice. (O Allah) let not a single sin of mine be left without it being forgiven, nor let any worry or pain be left without it

فَرَّجْتَهُ وَلَا كَرْبًا اِلَّا نَفَّسْتَهُ وَلَا ضُرًّا اِلَّا

being relieved, nor let any grief be left without it being dispelled, nor let any difficulty be left without it

كَشَفْتَهُ وَلَا حَاجَةً هِىَ لَكَ رِضًا اِلَّا قَضَيْتَهَا

being removed and nor any need of mine be left which You will be pleased except that it will be fulfilled.

يَآ اَرْحَمَ الرَّاحِمِيْنَ

O The Most Merciful of those who show mercy.

اَللّٰهُمَّ ارْحَمْنِيْ بِتَرْكِ الْمَعَاصِيْ اَبَدًا مَّا

1. O Allah! Have Mercy on me by allowing me to leave out sins for the rest of

اَبْقَيْتَنِيْ ۬ وَارْحَمْنِيْ اَنْ اَتَكَلَّفَ مَا لَا يَعْنِيْنِيْ ۬

my life and have mercy on me by preventing me from falling into matters that do not concern me.

وَارْزُقْنِيْ حُسْنَ النَّظَرِ فِيْ مَا يُرْضِيْكَ عَنِّيْ

And bless me with the ability of recognising those things that will make You happy with me.

اَللّٰهُمَّ بَدِيْعَ السَّمٰوَاتِ وَالْاَرْضِ ذَاالْجَلَالِ

O Allah! The Originator of the heavens and the earth, Majestic and

---

1. Tirmizi # 357

وَالْاِكْرَامِ وَالْعِزَّةِ الَّتِيْ لَا تُرَامُ اَسْاَلُكَ يَا اَللّٰهُ

Kind, Possessor of dignity which cannot be imagined by anyone else, I beg of You, O Allah!

يَا رَحْمٰنُ بِجَلَالِكَ وَنُوْرِ وَجْهِكَ اَنْ تُلْزِمَ قَلْبِيْ

O The Compassionate One, by the Majesty and the Noor of Your Countenance, that You grant my heart

حِفْظَ كِتَابِكَ كَمَا عَلَّمْتَنِيْ وَارْزُقْنِيْ اَنْ اَتْلُوَهٗ

the capacity to memorise Your Book just as You had blessed me with its knowledge and allow me to recite it

عَلَى النَّحْوِ الَّذِيْ يُرْضِيْكَ عَنِّيْ. اَللّٰهُمَّ بَدِيْعَ

in a manner that is pleasing to You. O Allah! The Originator of

السَّمٰوَاتِ وَالْاَرْضِ ذَاالْجَلَالِ وَالْاِكْرَامِ

the heavens and the earth, Majestic and Kind,

وَالْعِزَّةِ الَّتِيْ لَاتُرَامُ اَسْاَلُكَ يَا اَللهُ يَا رَحْمٰنُ

Possessor of dignity which cannot be imagined by anyone else, I beg of You, O Allah! O The Compassionate One,

بِجَلَالِكَ وَنُوْرِ وَجْهِكَ اَنْ تُنَوِّرَ بِكِتَابِكَ

by the Majesty and the noor of Your countenance, that You illuminate my eyes with the noor of Your Book (The Qur-aan),

بَصَرِيْ وَاَنْ تُطْلِقَ بِهِ لِسَانِيْ وَاَنْ تُفَرِّجَ بِهِ

allow its recitation to flow from my tongue, and remove the

عَنْ قَلْبِيْ وَاَنْ تَشْرَحَ بِهِ صَدْرِيْ وَاَنْ

grief of my heart through it, expand my chest

تَسْتَعْمِلَ بِهِ بَدَنِيْ فَاِنَّهٗ لَايُعِيْنُنِيْ عَلَى

and make my body act in accordance to it, for verily it is only You that can help me

اَلْحَقِّ غَيْرُكَ وَلَا يُؤْتِيهِ اِلَّاۤ اَنْتَ وَلَا حَوْلَ

realise the truth, and no one else can bless me with this besides you. There is no power to do good or ability to refrain from evil

وَلَا قُوَّةَ اِلَّا بِاللهِ الْعَلِيِّ الْعَظِيْمِ.

except with the help of Allah! The Most High, The Great.

(٢) اَللّٰهُمَّ اِنِّيْ اَتُوْبُ اِلَيْكَ مِنَ الْمَعَاصِيْ

2. O Allah! I make taubah (repent) before You from all sins and

لَاۤ اَرْجِـعُ اِلَيْهَا اَبَدًا

I promise never to return to them ever.

(٣) اَللّٰهُمَّ مَغْفِرَتُكَ اَوْسَعُ مِنْ ذُنُوْبِيْ

3. O Allah! Your forgiveness is much more vast than my sins, and

2. Mustadrak # 1899 | 3. Mustadrak # 1994

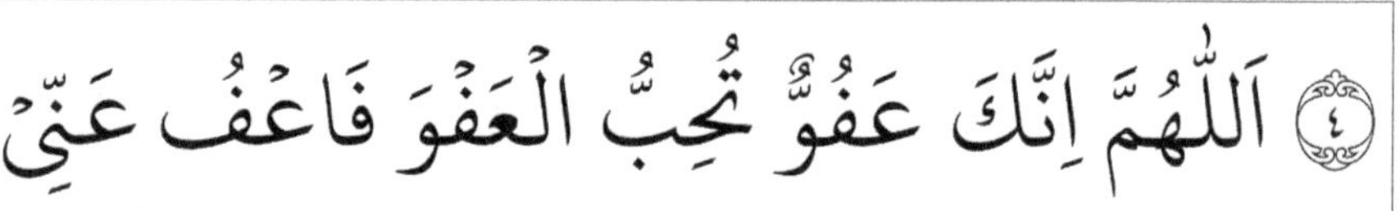

I am much more hopeful of Your Mercy than my (good) deeds.

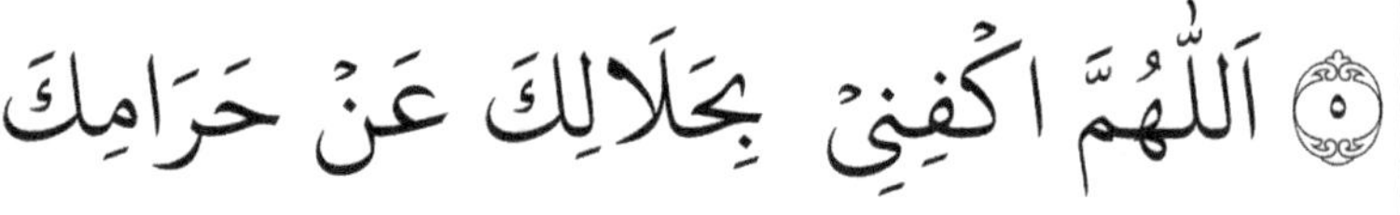

4. O Allah! You are the most Forgiving and You love to forgive so please forgive me.

5. O Allah! Provide me with halaal rizq (sustenance) that is sufficient to fulfil my needs rather than haraam (forbidden)

وَاَغْنِنِيْ بِفَضْلِكَ عَمَّنْ سِوَاكَ

wealth. And with Your grace make me independent from (asking anything from anyone) besides Yourself.

اَللّٰهُمَّ فَارِجَ الْهَمِّ كَاشِفَ الْغَمِّ مُجِيْبَ

6. O Allah! The Remover of worry and grief, The One who answers

| 4. Tirmizi # 3513 | 5. Tirmizi # 3563 | 6. Mustadrak # 1898 |

دَعْوَةِ الْمُضْطَرِّيْنَ رَحْمٰنَ الدُّنْيَا وَالْاٰخِرَةِ

the duas of helpless people, the Giver of mercy and grace in this world and the Hereafter.

وَرَحِيْمَهُمَا اَنْتَ تَرْحَمُنِيْ فَارْحَمْنِيْ بِرَحْمَةٍ

You alone can have mercy on me so favour me in a way

تُغْنِيْنِيْ بِهَا عَنْ رَّحْمَةٍ مَّنْ سِوَاكَ.

that I may no longer be in need of the sympathy of others.

۞ اَللّٰهُمَّ رَبَّ السَّمٰوَاتِ وَالْأَرْضِ عَالِمَ الْغَيْبِ

7. O Allah! The Cherisher of the heavens and the earth, The Knower of the unseen

وَالشَّهَادَةِ اِنِّيْ اَعْهَدُ اِلَيْكَ فِيْ هٰذِهِ الْحَيَاةِ

and the visible, I firmly declare in this world before You

7. Musnad Ahmad # 3906

اَلدُّنْيَا اَنِّيْ اَشْهَدُ اَنْ لَّاۤ اِلٰهَ اِلَّا اَنْتَ وَحْدَكَ لَا

that I bear witness that there is no deity besides You. You are One and there is no partner for You and

شَرِيْكَ لَكَ وَاَنَّ مُحَمَّدًا صَلَّى اللهُ عَلَيْهِ وَسَلَّمَ

that Hadhrat Muhammad ﷺ is

عَبْدُكَ وَرَسُوْلُكَ فَلَا تَكِلْنِيْ اِلٰى نَفْسِيْ فَاِنَّكَ

Your servant and Messenger. Hence do not entrust me to myself for verily if You

اِنْ تَكِلْنِيْ اِلٰى نَفْسِيْ تُقَرِّبْنِيْ مِنَ الشَّرِّ

entrust me to myself, I will be drawn closer to evil

وَتُبَاعِدْنِيْ مِنَ الْخَيْرِ وَاِنِّيْ لَاۤ اَثِقُ اِلَّا

and thrown far away from goodness. I place my full trust in

بِرَحْمَتِكَ فَاجْعَلْ لِّى عِنْدَكَ عَهْدًا تُوَفِّيْنِيْهِ

Your Mercy, hence grant me a promise, to be fulfilled on the

يَوْمَ الْقِيَامَةِ اِنَّكَ لَا تُخْلِفُ الْمِيْعَادَ.

Day of Qiyaamah, (that You will be merciful towards me). Verily You do not break Your promise.

⑧ اَسْتَغْفِرُ اللهَ الَّذِىْ لَآ اِلٰهَ اِلَّا هُوَ الْحَىُّ

8. I beg forgiveness from Allah! The Being besides whom there is no deity. The Everlasting,

الْقَيُّوْمُ وَاَتُوْبُ اِلَيْهِ

The Sustainer. I turn to Him for repentance.

⑨ رَبِّ اغْفِرْلِىْ وَتُبْ عَلَىَّ اِنَّكَ اَنْتَ التَّوَّابُ

9. O Allah! Forgive my sins and accept my repentance. Verily, You are Most Forgiving,

| 8. Abu Dawood # 1517 | 9. Abu Dawood # 1516 |

الرَّحِيْمُ

Most Merciful.

﴿١٠﴾ اَللّٰهُمَّ اِنِّيْ اَعُوْذُ بِكَ مِنَ الْعَجْزِ وَالْكَسَلِ

10. O Allah! I seek Your protection from lethargy, laziness,

وَالْجُبْنِ وَالْهَرَمِ وَالْمَغْرَمِ وَالْمَأْثَمِ.

cowardice, evil old age, having to pay undue penalties and sins.

اَللّٰهُمَّ اِنِّيْ اَعُوْذُ بِكَ مِنْ عَذَابِ النَّارِ وَفِتْنَةِ

O Allah! I seek Your protection from the punishment of the fire, the torture of the fire, the trials and punishment

النَّارِ وَفِتْنَةِ الْقَبْرِ وَعَذَابِ الْقَبْرِ وَشَرِّ فِتْنَةِ

in the grave and from being tested by an evil kind of test

10. Al-Hisnul Azam Pg. 315

الْغِنٰى وَشَرِّ فِتْنَةِ الْفَقْرِ.

in wealth and an evil kind of test in poverty.

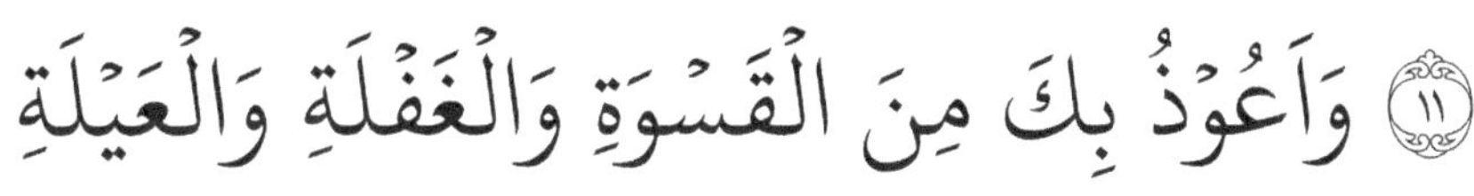

وَاَعُوْذُ بِكَ مِنَ الْقَسْوَةِ وَالْغَفْلَةِ وَالْعَيْلَةِ

11. I seek Your protection O Allah from hard heartedness,
carelessness, extreme poverty,

وَالذِّلَّةِ وَالْمَسْكَنَةِ وَاَعُوْذُ بِكَ مِنَ الْفَقْرِ

disgrace and destitution. I seek Your protection from poverty,

وَالْكُفْرِ وَالْفُسُوْقِ وَالشِّقَاقِ وَالسُّمْعَةِ

(kufr) disbelief, transgression, stubbornness, and showing off.

وَالرِّيَآءِ. وَاَعُوْذُ بِكَ مِنَ الصَّمَمِ وَالْبَكَمِ

I seek Your protection from deafness, dumbness,

11. Mustadrak # 1944

وَالْبَرَصِ وَالْجُنُوْنِ وَالْجُذَامِ وَسَيِّءِ

leprosy, insanity,

الْاَسْقَامِ

and other evil diseases.

اَللّٰهُمَّ اِنِّیْ اَعُوْذُ بِعِزَّتِكَ لَاۤ اِلٰهَ اِلَّا اَنْتَ اَنْ

12. O Allah! I seek refuge in You with Your Greatness beside whom there is no other deity

تُضِلَّنِیْ اَنْتَ الْحَیُّ الَّذِیْ لَایَمُوْتُ وَالْجِنُّ

from being led astray by You. You are alive The Being that does not die. Jinn

وَالْاِنْسُ يَمُوْتُوْنَ.

and men are prone to die.

12. Muslim # 2717

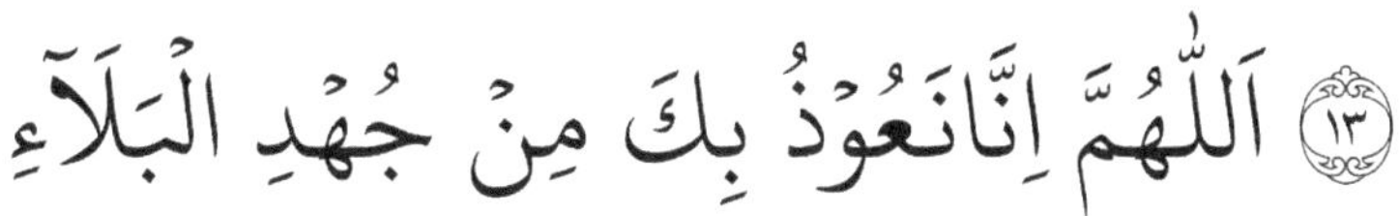

﴿١٣﴾ اَللّٰهُمَّ اِنَّا نَعُوْذُ بِكَ مِنْ جُهْدِ الْبَلَآءِ

13. O Allah! I seek Your protection from severe trials,

وَدَرْكِ الشَّقَآءِ وَسُوْءِ الْقَضَآءِ وَشَمَاتَةِ

unfortunate disasters, evil decrees and the ridicule

الْاَعْدَآءِ

of the enemies.

﴿١٤﴾ اَللّٰهُمَّ اِنِّيْ اَعُوْذُ بِكَ مِنْ شَرِّ مَا عَلِمْتُ

14. O Allah! I seek Your protection from the evil of what I know and

وَمِنْ شَرِّ مَا لَمْ اَعْلَمْ.

the evil of what I do not know.

| 13. Bukhaari # 6347 | 14. Ihyaa Pg. 291 |

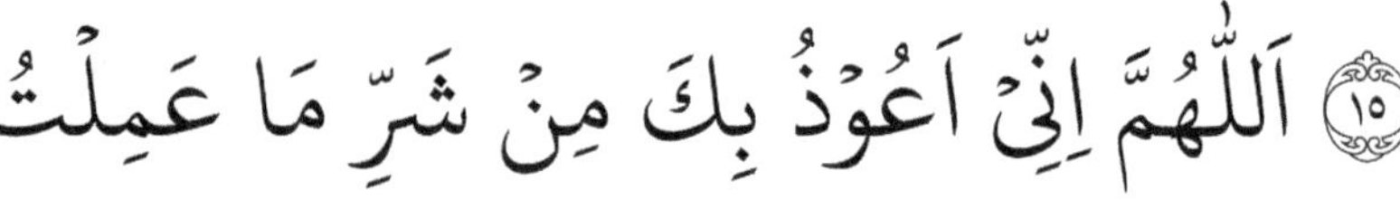

اَللّٰهُمَّ اِنِّيْ اَعُوْذُ بِكَ مِنْ شَرِّ مَا عَمِلْتُ

15. O Allah! I seek Your protection from the evil of what I have done

وَمِنْ شَرِّ مَا لَمْ اَعْمَلْ

as well as what I have not done.

اَللّٰهُمَّ اِنِّيْ اَعُوْذُ بِكَ مِنْ زَوَالِ نِعْمَتِكَ

16. O Allah! I seek Your protection from being deprived of Your favours,

وَتَحَوُّلِ عَافِيَتِكَ وَفُجَآءَةِ نِقْمَتِكَ وَجَمِيْعِ

and that your aafiyat (complete protection) turns away from me and from sudden calamities striking me and from all those things

سَخَطِكَ.

that will bring Your wrath.

15. Muslim # 2739	16. Muslim # 2739

﴿١٧﴾ اَللّٰهُمَّ اِنِّیْ اَعُوْذُ بِكَ مِنْ شَرِّ سَمْعِیْ وَمِنْ

17. O Allah! I seek Your protection from the evil of my ears,

شَرِّ بَصَرِیْ وَمِنْ شَرِّ لِسَانِیْ وَمِنْ شَرِّ قَلْبِیْ

the evil of my eyes, my tongue, my heart

وَمِنْ شَرِّ مَنِیِّیْ

and my semen.

﴿١٨﴾ اَللّٰهُمَّ اِنِّیْ اَعُوْذُ بِكَ مِنَ الْهَدْمِ وَاَعُوْذُ

18. O Allah! I seek Your protection from being buried under the
debris of a building and I seek Your protection

بِكَ مِنَ التَّرَدِّیْ وَاَعُوْذُ بِكَ مِنَ الْغَرَقِ

from falling down from the roof of a building, from being drowned
in water and

17. Tirmizi # 3492	18. Abu Dawood # 1552

وَالْحَرَقِ وَالْهَرَمِ وَاَعُوْذُ بِكَ مِنْ اَنْ

from being burnt, and from the despicable old age and I seek Your protection

يَّتَخَبَّطَنِيَ الشَّيْطَانُ عِنْدَ الْمَوْتِ وَاَعُوْذُ بِكَ

to be saved from the whispers of shaytaan at the time of death, and I seek Your protection

اَنْ اَمُوْتَ فِيْ سَبِيْلِكَ مُدْبِرًا وَاَعُوْذُ بِكَ اَنْ

from being killed in jihaad with my back towards the enemy (i.e., while I am fleeing from the battlefield). And I seek Your protection

اَمُوْتَ لَدِيْغًا.

from death caused by the biting of a venomous animal.

اَللّٰهُمَّ اِنِّيْ اَعُوْذُ بِكَ مِنْ مُّنْكَرَاتِ ۝١٩

19. O Allah! I seek Your protection from bad manners,

19. Kanzul Ummaal # 3671

الْاَخْلَاقِ وَالْاَعْمَالِ وَالْاَهْوَآءِ وَالْاَدْوَآءِ

evil actions, evil desires and dreadful diseases.

اَللّٰهُمَّ اِنِّىْ اَسْاَلُكَ مِنْ خَيْرِ مَا سَاَلَكَ مِنْهُ

20. O Allah! I beg of You (to bless me) with all the good things which

نَبِيُّكَ مُحَمَّدٌ صَلَّى اللهُ عَلَيْهِ وَسَلَّمَ وَاَعُوْذُ بِكَ

Nabi Muhammad ﷺ asked of You and I seek Your protection

مِنْ شَرِّ مَا اسْتَعَاذَ مِنْهُ نَبِيُّكَ مُحَمَّدٌ صَلَّى اللهُ

from all the evil things which Nabi Muhammad ﷺ sought protection from

عَلَيْهِ وَسَلَّمَ اَنْتَ الْمُسْتَعَانُ وَعَلَيْكَ الْبَلَاغُ

You are the only Being from whom help is sought . Upon You is the fulfilment of our needs and

20. Tirmizi # 3521

وَلَاحَوْلَ وَلَاقُوَّةَ اِلَّا بِاللهِ الْعَلِيِّ الْعَظِيْمِ

there is no power to do good deeds nor any strength to avoid evil except with the help of Allah who is Most High and The Greatest.

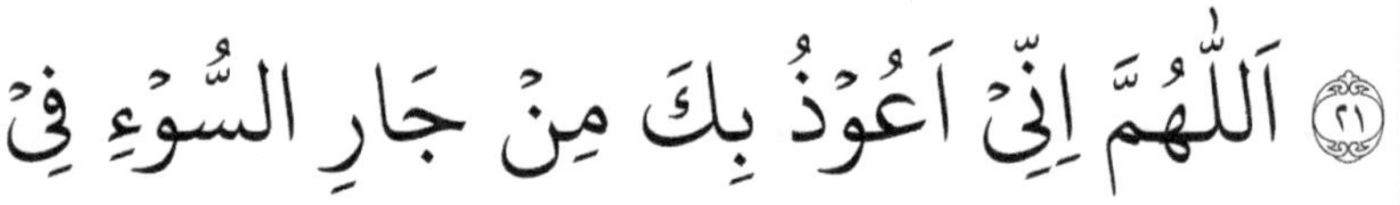

اَللّٰهُمَّ اِنِّيْ اَعُوْذُ بِكَ مِنْ جَارِ السُّوْءِ فِيْ

21. O Allah! I seek Your protection from a bad neighbour in my

دَارِ الْمُقَامَةِ فَاِنَّ جَارَ الْبَادِيَةِ يَتَحَوَّلُ وَمِنَ

locality as neighbours on a journey eventually go their own way.

الْجُوْعِ فَاِنَّهُ بِئْسَ الضَّجِيْعُ وَمِنَ الْخِيَانَةِ

(I seek protection) from hunger as it is an evil companion and from dishonesty

فَاِنَّهَا بِئْسَتِ الْبِطَانَةُ

as it is an evil quality.

21. Mustadrak # 1951	22. Mustadrak # 1957

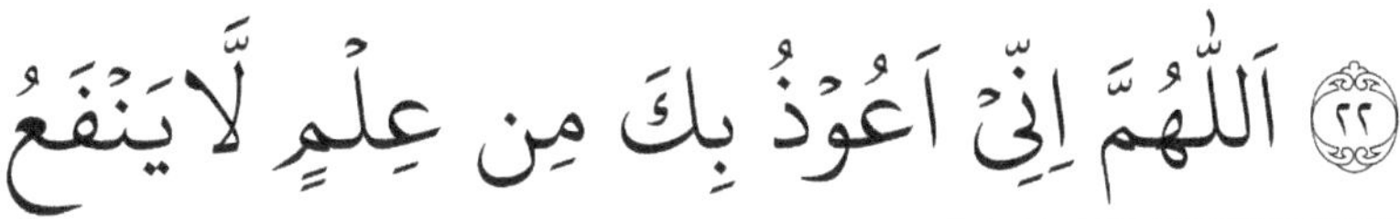

22. O Allah! I seek Your protection from knowledge that has no benefit,

from a heart which does not fear You, from a dua which is not answered by You,

from insatiable desires and from all the four said evils.

23. O Allah! We seek Your protection from turning back on our heels (turning away from Imaan)

or that our Imaan should ever be put to test.

<table>
<tr><td>23. Bukhaari # 6593</td><td>24. Mu'jamul Kabeer # 810</td></tr>
</table>

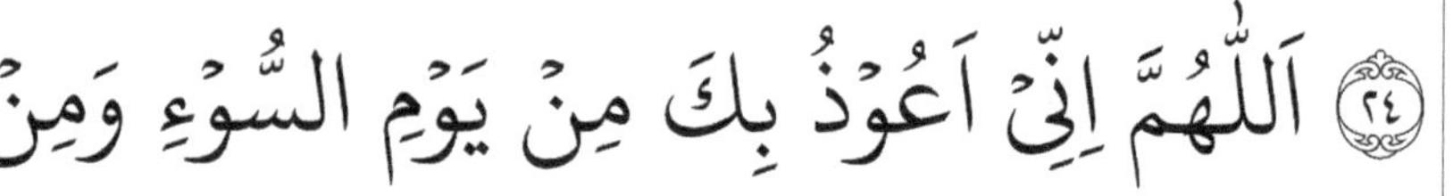

﴿٢٤﴾ اَللّٰهُمَّ اِنِّىْ اَعُوْذُ بِكَ مِنْ يَوْمِ السُّوْءِ وَمِنْ

24. O Allah! I seek Your protection from an evil day,

لَيْلَةِ السُّوْءِ وَمِنْ سَاعَةِ السُّوْءِ وَمِنْ صَاحِبِ

an evil night, an evil hour, an evil companion

السُّوْءِ وَمِنْ جَارِ السُّوْءِ فِىْ دَارِ الْمُقَامَةِ

and a bad neighbour in my locality.

﴿٢٥﴾ اَللّٰهُمَّ اِنِّىْ اَعُوْذُ بِكَ مِنَ الشِّقَاقِ وَالنِّفَاقِ

25. O Allah! I seek Your protection from causing disunity, from hypocrisy

وَسُوْءِ الْاَخْلَاقِ

and from bad manners.

25. Abu Dawood 1546	26. Muslim # 2719

26. O Allah! Forgive my sins whether committed deliberately or unintentionally, jokingly or mistakenly

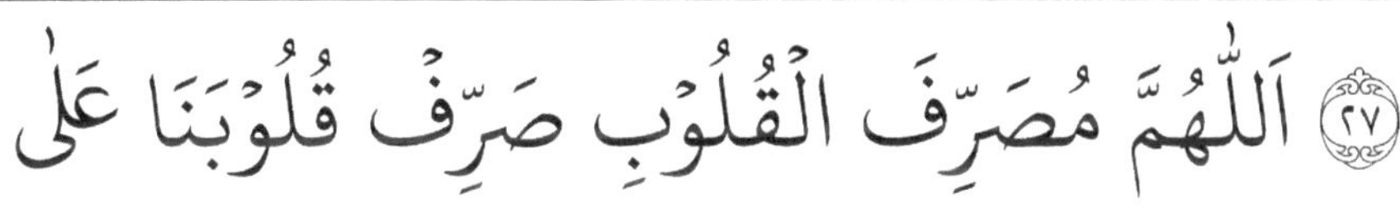

or intentionally. And I am responsible for all these sins.

27. O Allah! The controller of hearts, turn my heart towards

Your obedience.

28. O Allah! I beg of You for correct guidance, piety, chastity

27. Muslim # 2654	28. Muslim # 2721

وَالْغِنٰى

and freedom from being needy towards others.

﴿٢٩﴾ رَبِّ اَعِنِّیْ وَلَا تُعِنْ عَلَیَّ وَانْصُرْنِیْ وَلَا

29. O Allah! Help me and do not help anyone against me. Assist me and do not

تَنْصُرْ عَلَیَّ وَامْکُرْ لِیْ وَلَاتَمْکُرْ عَلَیَّ وَاهْدِنِی

assist (my enemy) to get the better of me. Plan in support of me and do not plan against me, guide me and

الْهُدٰی وَیَسِّرِ الْهُدٰی لِیْ وَانْصُرْنِیْ عَلٰی مَنْ

make it easy for me to pursue the path of guidance and help me in the event of

بَغٰی عَلَیَّ. رَبِّ اجْعَلْنِیْ لَكَ ذَكَّارًا لَّكَ شَكَّارًا

an enemy rising up against me. O Allah! Make me remember You intensely and make me extremely grateful to You.

29. Tirmizi # 3551

لَّكَ رَهَّابًا لَّكَ مِطْوَاعًا لَّكَ مُخْبِتًا اِلَيْكَ اَوَّاهًا

Make me fear and obey You thoroughly and make me one who pleads with You greatly and turns to You

مُنِيْبًا. رَبِّ تَقَبَّلْ تَوْبَتِيْ وَاغْسِلْ حَوْبَتِيْ

with constant tears and devotion. O Allah! Accept my repentance, wash away my sins,

وَاَجِبْ دَعْوَتِيْ وَثَبِّتْ حُجَّتِيْ وَسَدِّدْ لِسَانِيْ

accept my duas, strengthen my case, straighten my tongue,

وَاهْدِ قَلْبِيْ وَاسْلُلْ سَخِيْمَةَ صَدْرِيْ

guide my heart and remove malice from it.

۳۰ اَللّٰهُمَّ اغْفِرْ لَنَا وَارْحَمْنَا وَارْضَ عَنَّا

30. O Allah! Forgive us, have mercy on us, be pleased with us,

30. Ibnu Majah # 3836

وَتَقَبَّلْ مِنَّا وَاَدْخِلْنَا الْجَنَّةَ وَنَجِّنَا مِنَ النَّارِ

accept our actions, admit us in to Jannah, save us from the fire of Jahannam

وَاَصْلِحْ لَنَا شَاْنَنَا كُلَّهٗ

and put right for us all our affairs.

(٣١) اَللّٰهُمَّ اِنِّيْ اَسْاَلُكَ الثَّبَاتَ فِي الْاَمْرِ

31. O Allah! I beg of You steadfastness in all my affairs,

وَاَسْاَلُكَ عَزِيْمَةَ الرُّشْدِ وَاَسْاَلُكَ شُكْرَ

determination to follow the path of virtue, gratitude for Your gifts

نِعْمَتِكَ وَحُسْنَ عِبَادَتِكَ وَاَسْاَلُكَ لِسَانًا

and the ability to worship You well. I beg of You for a tongue that is

31. Tirmizi # 3407

صَادِقًا وَّقَلْبًا سَلِيْمًا وَّخُلُقًا مُّسْتَقِيْمًا

truthful, a heart that is sound and an upright conduct.

وَاَعُوْذُ بِكَ مِنْ شَرِّ مَا تَعْلَمُ وَاَسْاَلُكَ مِنْ

I seek Your protection from the evil of those things which You know and I beg of You for the good of

خَيْرِ مَا تَعْلَمُ وَاَسْتَغْفِرُكَ مِمَّا تَعْلَمُ اِنَّكَ

what You know. I beg Your forgiveness for my sins which are known to You. Verily

اَنْتَ عَلَّامُ الْغُيُوْبِ

You are fully aware of all hidden things.

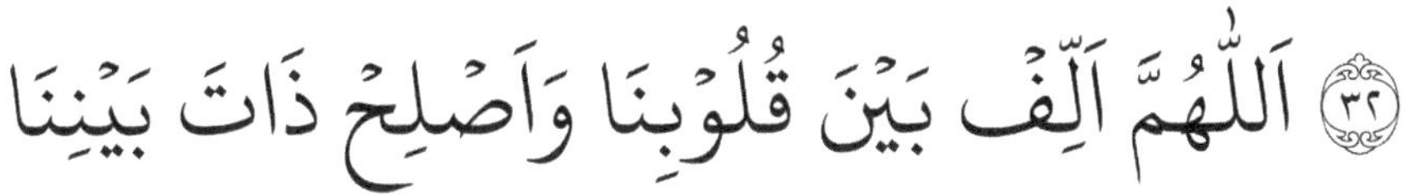

٣٢ اَللّٰهُمَّ اَلِّفْ بَيْنَ قُلُوْبِنَا وَاَصْلِحْ ذَاتَ بَيْنِنَا

32. O Allah! Unite our hearts and put right for us our mutual affairs.

32. Abu Dawood # 969

وَاهْدِنَا سُبُلَ السَّلَامِ وَنَجِّنَا مِنَ الظُّلُمَاتِ

guide us to the path of peace, release us from

اِلَى النُّورِ وَجَنِّبْنَا الْفَوَاحِشَ مَا ظَهَرَ

darkness to light, save us from obscene practices whether open

مِنْهَا وَمَا بَطَنَ وَبَارِكْ لَنَا فِي اَسْمَاعِنَا

or hidden. Bless us in our ears,

وَاَبْصَارِنَا وَقُلُوْبِنَا وَاَزْوَاجِنَا وَذُرِّيَّاتِنَا وَتُبْ

our eyes, our hearts, our wives and our children and accept our
repentance.

عَلَيْنَا اِنَّكَ اَنْتَ التَّوَّابُ الرَّحِيْمُ.

Verily You are Most Forgiving Most Merciful.

وَاجْعَلْنَا شَاكِرِيْنَ لِنِعْمَتِكَ مُثْنِيْنَ بِهَا

Make us thankful to You for Your favours that we may praise You for it,

قَابِلِيْهَا وَاَتِمَّهَا عَلَيْنَا

make us worthy of Your favours and please complete Your bounty upon us.

﴿٣٣﴾ اَللّٰهُمَّ اقْسِمْ لَنَا مِنْ خَشْيَتِكَ مَا تَحُوْلُ

33. O Allah! Grant us Your fear in such a way that it becomes a barrier

بِهٖ بَيْنَنَا وَبَيْنَ مَعَاصِيْكَ وَمِنْ طَاعَتِكَ مَا

between us and committing sins. Make us obedient to You in such a way

تُبَلِّغُنَا بِهٖ جَنَّتَكَ وَمِنَ الْيَقِيْنِ مَا تُهَوِّنُ بِهٖ

that it will take us to Jannah. Bless us with such conviction that enables us to face

33. Tirmizi # 3502

عَلَيْنَا مَصَآئِبَ الدُّنْيَا وَمَتِّعْنَا بِاَسْمَاعِنَا

worldly calamities with ease. Let us enjoy the benefits of our ears,

وَاَبْصَارِنَا وقُوَّتِنَا مَا اَحْيَيْتَنَا واجْعَلْهُ الْوَارِثَ

our eyes and bodily strength as long as You keep us alive and continue their goodness after our death.

مِنَّا وَاجْعَلْ ثَأْرَنَا عَلٰى مَنْ ظَلَمَنَا وَانْصُرْنَا

Take revenge on those who have been cruel to us and help us

عَلٰى مَنْ عَادَانَا وَلَا تَجْعَلْ مُصِيْبَتَنَا فِيْ دِيْنِنَا

against those who oppress us and let not any calamity spoil our Imaan.

وَلَا تَجْعَلِ الدُّنْيَا اَكْبَرَ هَمِّنَا وَلَا مَبْلَغَ عِلْمِنَا

Let not this worldly life become our main objective nor the limit of our knowledge.

وَلَا تُسَلِّطْ عَلَيْنَا مَنْ لَّا يَرْحَمُنَا

And do not put us under the control of such people who will have no pity on us.

٣٤) اَللّٰهُمَّ زِدْنَا وَلَا تَنْقُصْنَا وَاَكْرِمْنَا وَلَا

34. O Allah! Increase (Your grace) for us and do not decrease it. Grant us honour

تُهِنَّا وَاَعْطِنَا وَلَا تَحْرِمْنَا وَاٰثِرْنَا وَلَا تُؤْثِرْ

and do not disgrace us, Give us and do not deprive us, grant us preference and let not others be preferred over us.

عَلَيْنَا وَاَرْضِنَا عَنْكَ وَارْضَ عَنَّا

Allow us to be pleased with You and You be pleased with us.

٣٥) اَللّٰهُمَّ اَلْهِمْنِيْ رُشْدِيْ وَاَعِذْنِيْ مِنْ شَرِّ

35. O Allah! Inspire my heart with thoughts that will be good for my guidance and save me from the evil

34. Tirmizi # 3173   35. Tirmizi # 3473

نَفْسِيْ

of my base desires.

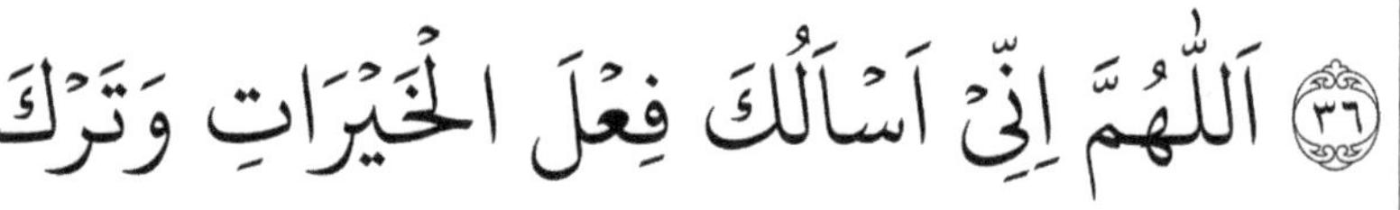

٣٦ اَللّٰهُمَّ اِنِّيْ اَسْاَلُكَ فِعْلَ الْخَيْرَاتِ وَتَرْكَ

36. O Allah! I beg of You the ability to perform good deeds and to abstain

الْمُنْكَرَاتِ وَحُبَّ الْمَسَاكِيْنِ وَاَنْ تَغْفِرَلِيْ

from evil deeds. (I beg of You the ability) to love the poor. Forgive me

وَتَرْحَمَنِيْ وَاِذَا اَرَدْتَّ بِقَوْمٍ فِتْنَةً فَتَوَفَّنِيْ غَيْرَ

and have mercy on me. (O Allah) when You intend to test a nation then take me away from this world

مَفْتُوْنٍ. اَللّٰهُمَّ اِنِّيْ اَسْاَلُكَ حُبَّكَ وَحُبَّ مَنْ

without being tested. O Allah! I beg of You to grant me Your love and the love of those

36. Tirmizi # 3235

يُحِبُّكَ وَالْعَمَلَ الَّذِىْ يُبَلِّغُنِىْ حُبَّكَ

who love You, as well as those deeds that will make me acquire Your love.

(٣٧) اَللّٰهُمَّ اجْعَلْ حُبَّكَ اَحَبَّ اِلَىَّ مِنْ نَفْسِىْ

37. O Allah! Make Your love more beloved to me than myself,

وَاَهْلِىْ وَمِنَ الْمَآءِ الْبَارِدِ

my family and cool water.

(٣٨) اَللّٰهُمَّ ارْزُقْنِىْ حُبَّكَ وَحُبَّ مَنْ يَّنْفَعُنِىْ

38. O Allah! Grant me Your love as well as the love of those people whose love will be beneficial

حُبُّهٗ عِنْدَكَ اَللّٰهُمَّ فَكَمَا رَزَقْتَنِىْ مِمَّا اُحِبُّ

to me by You. O Allah! As You have blessed me with gifts that I love,

فَاجْعَلْهُ قُوَّةً لِّيْ فِيْمَا تُحِبُّ اَللّٰهُمَّ وَمَا زَوَيْتَ

so allow me to use it in avenues that You love. O Allah! Whatever You have kept away from me which I love (but are to my

عَنِّيْ مِمَّا أُحِبُّ فَاجْعَلْهُ فَرَاغًا لِّيْ فِيْمَا تُحِبُّ

detriment), make them a source of freedom for me so that I may be able to fulfil all that which You love.

(٣٩) يَا مُقَلِّبَ الْقُلُوْبِ ثَبِّتْ قَلْبِيْ عَلٰى دِيْنِكَ

39. O Controller of hearts, let my heart hold fast onto Your religion.

(٤٠) اَللّٰهُمَّ اِنِّيْ اَسْاَلُكَ اِيْمَانًا لَّا يَرْتَدُّ وَنَعِيْمًا

40. O Allah! I beg of You to bless me with Imaan which does not waver, bounties

لَّا يَنْفَدُ وَمُرَافَقَةَ نَبِيِّنَا مُحَمَّدٍ صَلَّى اللهُ

which never terminate and the company of our beloved Nabi Muhammad ﷺ

---

39. Tirmizi # 2140 | 40. Mustadrak # 1928

عَلَيْهِ وَسَلَّمَ فِي اَعْلٰى دَرَجَةِ الْجَنَّةِ جَنَّةِ

in the highest stages of Jannah,

الْخُلْدِ

the Everlasting Jannah.

(٤١) اَللّٰهُمَّ انْفَعْنِيْ بِمَا عَلَّمْتَنِيْ وَعَلِّمْنِيْ مَا

41. O Allah! Allow me to take benefit from my knowledge, teach
me what

يَنْفَعُنِيْ وَزِدْنِيْ عِلْمًا. اَلْحَمْدُ لِلّٰهِ عَلٰى كُلِّ

will be useful to me and increase me in knowledge. All praise is
due to Allah Ta'ala under all

حَالٍ وَاَعُوْذُ بِاللّٰهِ مِنْ حَالِ اَهْلِ النَّارِ

conditions and I seek Allah's protection from the condition of the
inmates of Hell.

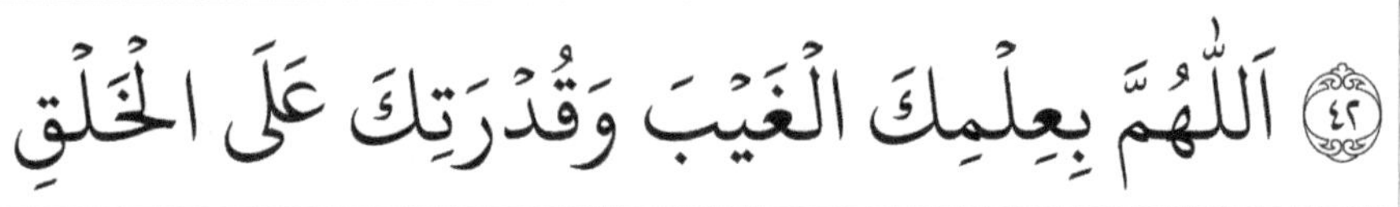

42. O Allah! By Your knowledge of the unseen and the power
which You have over Your creation,

keep me alive for as long as it is in my best interest to be alive and
grant me death

when it is best for me. Grant me the ability to fear You both

in secret and in public and to speak with truth and sincerity in
moments of joy

and anger. I also ask for moderation in spending, both in poverty
and in prosperity.

وَاَسْاَلُكَ نَعِيمًا لَّا يَنْفَدُ وَقُرَّةَ عَيْنٍ لَّا تَنْقَطِعُ

And I ask for Your favours which never end. I ask You to cool my eyes with such favours that will never end.

وَاَسْاَلُكَ الرِّضَا بِالْقَضَآءِ وَبَرْدَ الْعَيْشِ بَعْدَ

I ask You to make me submit happily to Your decrees, a comfortable life after

الْمَوْتِ وَلَذَّةَ النَّظَرِ اِلٰى وَجْهِكَ وَالشَّوْقَ اِلٰى

death, the delight of seeing Your blessed countenance and the deep desire

لِقَآئِكَ وَاَعُوْذُ بِكَ مِنْ ضَرَّآءَ مُضِرَّةٍ وَّفِتْنَةٍ

to meet You. I seek Your protection from disastrous calamities and *fitnahs* (tests and trials) which cause me

مُّضِلَّةٍ. اَللّٰهُمَّ زَيِّنَّا بِزِيْنَةِ الْاِيْمَانِ وَاجْعَلْنَا

to go astray. O Allah! Beautify me with the beauty of Imaan, guide us

هُدَاةً مُّهْتَدِيْنَ

and make us guides for others as well (to the right path).

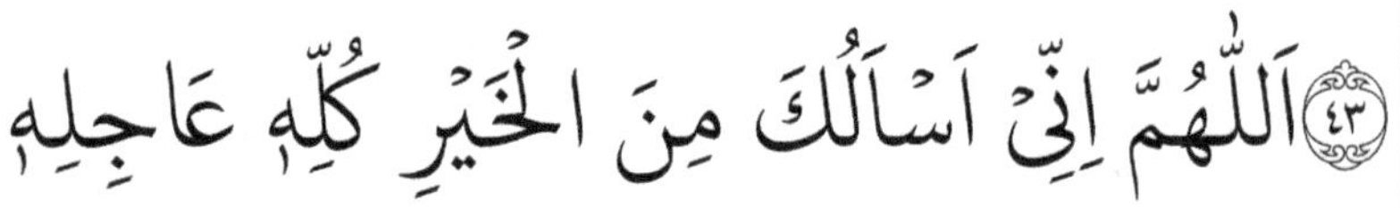

اَللّٰهُمَّ اِنِّيْ اَسْأَلُكَ مِنَ الْخَيْرِ كُلِّهِ عَاجِلِهِ

43. O Allah! I beg of You for all good whether it comes sooner or

وَاٰجِلِهِ مَا عَلِمْتُ مِنْهُ وَمَا لَمْ اَعْلَمْ وَاَعُوْذُ

later and whether I know of it or not.

بِكَ مِنَ الشَّرِّ كُلِّهِ عَاجِلِهِ وَاٰجِلِهِ مَا عَلِمْتُ

I seek Your protection from all evil whether it comes sooner or
later

مِنْهُ وَمَالَمْ اَعْلَمْ. اَللّٰهُمَّ اِنِّيْ اَسْأَلُكَ الْجَنَّةَ وَمَا

and whether I know of it or not. O Allah! I beg of You to grant me
Jannah and all such

43. Ibnu Majah # 3846

قَرَّبَ اِلَيْهَا مِنْ قَوْلٍ اَوْعَمَلٍ وَاَعُوْذُ بِكَ مِنَ

words and deeds which will lead me to it.

النَّارِ وَمَا قَرَّبَ اِلَيْهَا مِنْ قَوْلٍ اَوْعَمَلٍ

And I seek Your protection from the Fire of Hell and all such words and deeds which will lead me to it.

وَاَسْاَلُكَ اَنْ تَجْعَلَ كُلَّ قَضَاءٍ لِّيْ خَيْرًا

I beg of You that Your decree be favourable to me

وَاَسْاَلُكَ مَا قَضَيْتَ لِيْ مِنْ اَمْرٍ اَنْ تَجْعَلَ

and I beg You that whatever decision You have taken concerning me,

عَاقِبَتَهٗ رُشْدًا

let the ultimate end be favourable.

44. Mustadrak # 6508

44. O Allah! Grant us the best possible results in all things of our life

and save us from disgrace in this world and punishment in the hereafter.

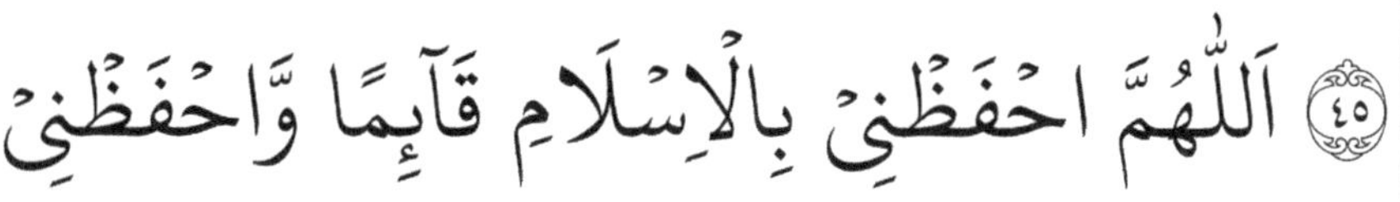

45. O Allah! Protect me with Islam whilst standing, protect me whilst

sitting and protect me whilst

sleeping and do not give my enemy or a jealous person the chance to ridicule me.

45. Mustadrak # 1924

اَللّٰهُمَّ اِنِّیْ اَسْاَلُكَ مِنْ كُلِّ خَيْرٍ خَزَائِنُهٗ

O Allah! I beg of You all good things the treasures of which are in
Your Hands

بِيَدِكَ وَاَعُوْذُ بِكَ مِنْ كُلِّ شَرٍّ خَزَائِنُهٗ بِيَدِكَ

and I seek Your protection from all evil things the treasures of
which are in Your Hands

وَاَعُوْذُ بِكَ مِنْ شَرِّ مَا اَنْتَ اٰخِذٌ بِنَاصِيَتِه

and I seek Your protection from the evil of all things which You
have control of by its forelocks.

﴿٤٦﴾ اَللّٰهُمَّ اِنِّیْ اَسْاَلُكَ عِيْشَةً نَّقِيَّةً وَّمِيْتَةً

46. O Allah! I beg of You a pure and honourable life, an easy death

سَوِيَّةً وَّمَرَدًّا غَيْرَ مَخْزِيٍّ وَّلَا فَاضِحٍ

and a place of ultimate return (hereafter) which is free from any
misery and disgrace.

46. Mustadrak # 1986

47. O Allah! I am weak, grant me strength in this weakness of mine in seeking Your pleasure.

Lead me towards good by my forelock and make Islam

the source of greatest happiness for me. O Allah! Verily I am weak, grant me strength.

I am disgraced, so please grant me respect and I am poor, so please grant me sustenance.

47. Mustadrak # 1931

TUESDAY

اَللّٰهُمَّ اِنِّىْ اَسْأَلُكَ خَيْرَ الْمَسْأَلَةِ وَخَيْرَ

الدُّعَآءِ وَخَيْرَ النَّجَاحِ وَخَيْرَ الْعَمَلِ وَخَيْرَ

الثَّوَابِ وَخَيْرَ الْحَيَاةِ وَخَيْرَ الْمَمَاتِ وَثَبِّتْنِىْ

وَثَقِّلْ مَوَازِيْنِىْ وَحَقِّقْ اِيْمَانِىْ وَارْفَعْ

1. O Allah! I ask of You the best of whatever can be asked, the best

dua, true success, good deeds, the best

reward, the best life and an excellent death. Grant me firmness (in Deen),

cause my good actions to outweigh my evil ones, strengthen my Imaan,

Mustadrak # 1911

دَرَجَتِيْ وَتَقَبَّلْ صَلَاتِيْ وَاغْفِرْ خَطِيْئَتِيْ

exalt me, accept my salaah and forgive my sins.

وَاَسْأَلُكَ الدَّرَجَاتِ الْعُلٰى مِنَ الْجَنَّةِ اٰمِيْنَ

I beg You for a lofty position in Jannah. Aameen.

اَللّٰهُمَّ اِنِّيْ اَسْأَلُكَ فَوَاتِحَ الْخَيْرِ وَخَوَاتِمَهٗ

O Allah! I beg of You to bless me with goodness at the beginning, and at the end

وَجَوَامِعَهٗ وَكَوَامِلَهٗ وَاَوَّلَهٗ وَاٰخِرَهٗ وَظَاهِرَهٗ

grant me the perfection of all virtuous deeds, the sum and substance of virtue and, the first and last and outer

وَبَاطِنَهٗ وَالدَّرَجَاتِ الْعُلٰى مِنَ الْجَنَّةِ اٰمِيْنَ

and inner ingredients of virtue and I beg of You for a lofty position in Jannah. "Aameen".

اَللّٰهُمَّ نَجِّنِيْ مِنَ النَّارِ وَارْزُقْنِيْ مَغْفِرَةً

O Allah! Save me from the fire of Hell and grant me Your forgiveness

بِالَّيْلِ وَالنَّهَارِ وَالْمَنْزِلَ الصَّالِحَ مِنَ الْجَنَّةِ

during the night and the day and bless me with a good home in Jannah.

أُمِيْنَ۔ اَللّٰهُمَّ اِنِّيْ اَسْاَلُكَ خَلَاصًا مِّنَ النَّارِ

"Aameen". O Allah! I beg of You for freedom from the fire of Hell

سَالِمًا وَاَنْ تُدْخِلَنِيَ الْجَنَّةَ أُمِنًا۔ اَللّٰهُمَّ اِنِّيْ

safely and (I beg You) to grant me a safe entry into Jannah. O Allah! I

اَسْاَلُكَ خَيْرَ مَآ اٰتِيْ وَخَيْرَ مَآ اَفْعَلُ وَخَيْرَ مَآ

beg of You good conduct as well as virtuous actions, goodness in

اَعْمَلُ وَخَيْرَ مَا بَطَنَ وَخَيْرَ مَا ظَهَرَ

all that which is hidden and what is apparent (in my deeds)

وَالدَّرَجَاتِ الْعُلٰى مِنَ الْجَنَّةِ اٰمِيْنَ۰ اَللّٰهُمَّ اِنِّیْ

and (I beg You) for a lofty position in Jannah. "Aameen". O Allah! I

اَسْئَلُكَ اَنْ تَرْفَعَ ذِكْرِیْ وَتَضَعَ وِزْرِیْ وَتُصْلِحَ

beg of You to raise my reputation, free me from the burden of sins, correct

اَمْرِیْ وَتُطَهِّرَ قَلْبِیْ وَتُحَصِّنَ فَرْجِیْ وَتُنَوِّرَ لِیْ

my affairs, purify my heart, protect the chastity of my private parts, illuminate

فِیْ قَبْرِیْ وَتَغْفِرَلِیْ ذَنْبِیْ وَاَسْئَلُكَ

my grave, forgive my sins and I beg You for

اَلدَّرَجَاتِ الْعُلٰى مِنَ الْجَنَّةِ اٰمِيْنَ. اَللّٰهُمَّ اِنِّى

a lofty position in Jannah. "Aameen". O Allah! I

اَسْاَلُكَ اَنْ تُبَارِكَ لِىْ فِىْ سَمْعِىْ وَفِىْ بَصَرِىْ

beg of You to bless me in my hearing, my seeing,

وَفِىْ رُوْحِىْ وَفِىْ خَلْقِىْ وَفِىْ خُلُقِىْ وَفِىْ اَهْلِىْ

my soul, my physical body, my character, my family,

وَفِىْ مَالِىْ وَفِىْ مَحْيَاىَ وَفِىْ مَمَاتِىْ وَفِىْ عَمَلِىْ

my wealth, in my life and death and in my actions.

اَللّٰهُمَّ وَتَقَبَّلْ حَسَنَاتِىْ وَاَسْاَلُكَ الدَّرَجَاتِ

O Allah! Accept my good deeds, and I beg You for a lofty

الْعُلٰى مِنَ الْجَنَّةِ اٰمِيْنَ

position in Jannah. "Aameen"

٢ اَللّٰهُمَّ اجْعَلْ اَوْسَعَ رِزْقِكَ عَلَىَّ عِنْدَ كِبَرِ

2. O Allah! Make my rizq (sustenance) the most abundant during my old

سِنِّيْ وَانْقِطَاعِ عُمْرِيْ

age and at the last portion of my life.

٣ يَامَنْ لَّاتَرَاهُ الْعُيُوْنُ وَلَا تُخَالِطُهُ

3. O The One whom eyes cannot see, minds cannot fully

الظُّنُوْنُ وَلَايَصِفُهُ الْوَاصِفُوْنَ وَلَا تُغَيِّرُهُ

comprehend, admirers cannot praise sufficiently, One who situations do not affect him,

2. Mustadrak # 1987	3. Mu'jamul Awsat # 9448

الْحَوَادِثُ وَلَا يَخْشَى الدَّوَائِرَ يَعْلَمُ

One who does not fear the changing times , Who fully knows

مَثَاقِيْلَ الْجِبَالِ وَمَكَايِيْلَ الْبِحَارِ وَعَدَدَ

the weight of mountains, the measure of the seas, the number of

قَطْرِ الْأَمْطَارِ وَعَدَدَ وَرَقِ الْأَشْجَارِ وَعَدَدَ مَا

droplets of rain, the number of leaves on the trees, the number of things

أَظْلَمَ عَلَيْهِ اللَّيْلُ وَأَشْرَقَ عَلَيْهِ النَّهَارُ وَلَا

over which the night throws its darkness and the day sheds its light,

تُوَارِىٰ مِنْهُ سَمَآءٌ سَمَآءً وَلَاۤ أَرْضٌ أَرْضًا وَلَا

The One from Whom one heaven cannot hide the other heaven nor can one layer of earth hide the other nor are

بَحْرُ مَّا فِیْ قَعْرِهٖ وَلَاجَبَلُ مَّا فِیْ وَعْرِهٖ اِجْعَلْ

the contents at the bottom of the oceans hidden from Him nor is the inner substance of the mountains hidden from Him. (O Allah)

خَيْرَ عُمْرِیْ اٰخِرَهٗ وَخَيْرَ عَمَلِیْ خَوَاتِمَهٗ

make the last part of my life the best part, my last action the best one

وَخَيْرَ اَيَّامِیْ يَوْمَ اَلْقَاكَ فِيْهِ

and the best day in my life the day I meet with You. (O Allah)

يَا وَلِیَّ الْاِسْلَامِ وَاَهْلِهٖ ثَبِّتْنِیْ بِهٖ حَتّٰی

4. O The Master of Islam and The Master of the followers of Islam, keep me firm on Islam until

اَلْقَاكَ

I meet You.

4. Mu'jamul Awsat # 661   5. Musnad Ahmad # 15327

5. O Allah! I beg of You for prosperity for myself and for my family members.

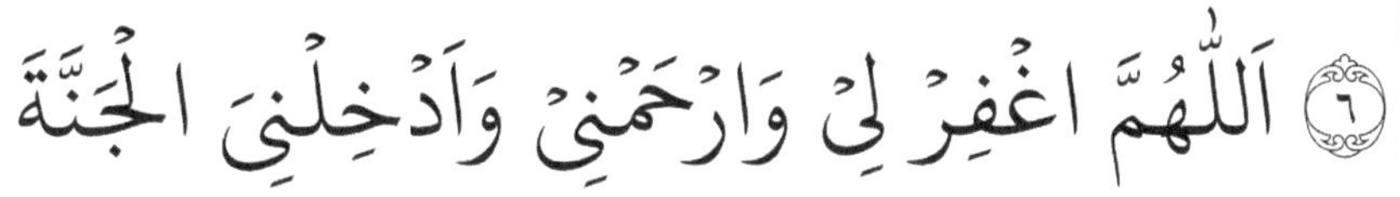

6. O Allah! Forgive me, have mercy on me and admit me into Jannah.

اَللّٰهُمَّ اجْعَلْنِيْ صَبُوْرًا وَّاجْعَلْنِيْ شَكُوْرًا ⑦

7. O Allah! Make me patient and make me be grateful to You.

وَاجْعَلْنِيْ فِيْ عَيْنِيْ صَغِيْرًا وَفِيْ اَعْيُنِ النَّاسِ

make me look small in my eyes but great in the

كَبِيْرًا

eyes of others.

| 6. Mu'jamul Kabeer # 667 | 7. Majma'uz Zawaaid # 181 | 8. Musnad Ahmad # 2616 |

اَللّٰهُمَّ اِنِّیْ اَسْاَلُكَ عِلْمًا نَّافِعًا وَّعَمَلًا ⟨٨⟩

8. O Allah! I beg of You to bless me with beneficial knowledge, deeds that are accepted,

مُّتَقَبَّلًا وَّرِزْقًا حَلَالًا طَيِّبًا

and pure, well-earned sustenance.

اَللّٰهُمَّ اِنِّیْ اَسْتَغْفِرُكَ لِذَنْبِیْ وَاَسْتَهْدِيْكَ ⟨٩⟩

9. O Allah! I seek Your forgiveness for my sins and I beg You to guide me

لِمَرَاشِدِ اَمْرِیْ وَاَسْتَجِيْرُكَ مِنْ شَرِّ نَفْسِیْ

to the ways of achieving success in my efforts. I seek refuge in You from the evil of my carnal desires

وَاَتُوْبُ اِلَيْكَ فَتُبْ عَلَیَّ اِنَّكَ اَنْتَ رَبِّیْ

and I repent before You. Please accept my repentance as You are indeed my Rabb.

9. Musannaf ibn Abi Shaybah # 29268

اَللّٰهُمَّ فَاجْعَلْ رَغْبَتِيْ اِلَيْكَ وَاجْعَلْ غِنَايَ فِيْ

O Allah! Incline my heart towards You, grant me contentment

صَدْرِيْ وَبَارِكْ لِيْ فِيْمَا رَزَقْتَنِيْ وَتَقَبَّلْ مِنِّيْ

of the heart and grant me barakah in my sustenance given by You to me. Accept my good deeds

اِنَّكَ اَنْتَ رَبِّيْ

as You are indeed my Rabb.

﴿١٠﴾ يَامَنْ اَظْهَرَ الْجَمِيْلَ وَسَتَرَ عَلَىَّ الْقَبِيْحَ

10. O The One who has publicised my good actions but concealed my sins.

يَامَنْ لَّا يُؤَاخِذْ بِالْجَرِيْرَةِ وَلَا يَهْتِكُ السِّتْرَ

O The One who does not penalise me for every fault nor does he remove the curtain, (exposing my faults).

10. Mustadrak # 1998

يَا عَظِيمَ الْعَفْوِ يَا حَسَنَ التَّجَاوُزِ يَا وَاسِعَ

O, The Giver of limitless forgiveness, The Most Tolerant, The One with everlasting

الْمَغْفِرَةِ يَا بَاسِطَ الْيَدَيْنِ بِالرَّحْمَةِ

forgiveness, The One with both hands stretched out to dispense mercy.

يَا صَاحِبَ كُلِّ نَجْوَى يَا مُنْتَهَى كُلِّ شَكْوَى

O You who is aware of even a whisper, Who is the last resort for every complaint,

يَا كَرِيْمَ الصَّفْحِ يَا عَظِيْمَ الْمَنِّ يَا مُبْدِئَ

Who is extremely generous in forgiving sins, Extremely Compassionate, Who initiates

النِّعَمِ قَبْلَ اسْتِحْقَاقِهَا يَا رَبَّنَا وَيَا سَيِّدَنَا

His Grace even before it is merited. O our Rabb, our Master,

وَيَا مَوْلَانَا وَيَا غَايَةَ رَغْبَتِنَا اَسْأَلُكَ يَا اَللّٰهُ

our protector The Sole purpose of the yearning of our hearts, we beg You, O Allah!

اَنْ لَّا تَشْوِىَ خَلْقِىْ بِالنَّارِ

Do not roast our bodies in the Fire.

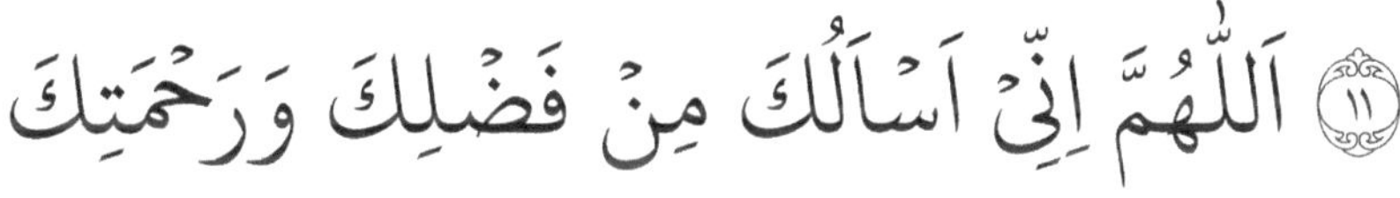

اَللّٰهُمَّ اِنِّىْ اَسْأَلُكَ مِنْ فَضْلِكَ وَرَحْمَتِكَ

11. O Allah! I beg of You Your Grace and Your Mercy

فَاِنَّهٗ لَا يَمْلِكُهَا اِلَّا اَنْتَ

as none possesses it besides You.

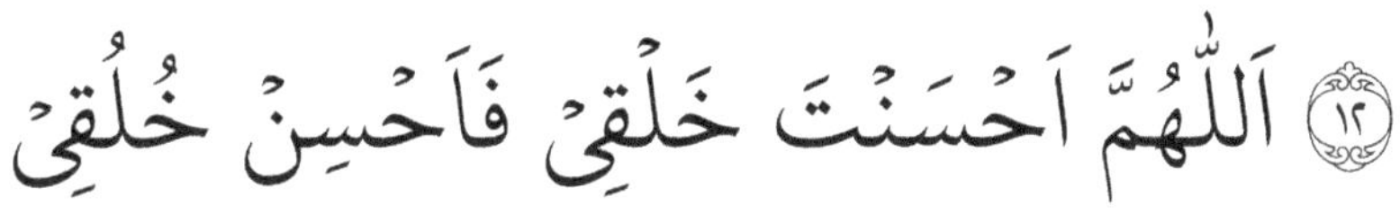

اَللّٰهُمَّ اَحْسَنْتَ خَلْقِىْ فَاَحْسِنْ خُلُقِىْ

12. O Allah! You have given me a good physical form. So bless me with good manners as well.

11. Mu'jamul Kabeer # 10379 | 12. Musnad Ahmad # 3813 | 13. Musnad Ahmad # 26145

۱۳ رَبِّ اغْفِرْ وَارْحَمْ وَاهْدِنِى السَّبِيْلَ

13. O My Rabb, forgive me, have mercy on me, guide me to the

الْاَقْوَمَ

straight path

۱٤ اَللّٰهُمَّ رَبَّ النَّبِيِّ مُحَمَّدٍ صَلَّى اللهُ عَلَيْهِ

14. O Allah! The Rabb of Nabi Muhammad ﷺ,

وَسَلَّمَ اغْفِرْ لِى ذَنْبِى وَاَذْهِبْ عَنِّى غَيْظَ قَلْبِى

forgive my sins, quench the fire (of anger) in my heart,

وَاَجِرْنِى مِنْ مُضِلَّاتِ الْفِتَنِ مَا اَحْيَيْتَنَا.

save me from tests that will lead me astray as long as You keep me alive.

| 14. Musnad Ahmad # 26036 | 15. Kanzul Ummaal # 3861 |

$$\text{(١٥)}\ \text{اَللّٰهُمَّ ارْزُقْنِيْ طَيِّبًا وَّاسْتَعْمِلْنِيْ طَيِّبًا.}$$

15. O Allah! Grant me pure sustenance and engage me in good actions.

$$\text{(١٦)}\ \text{اَللّٰهُمَّ اِنِّيْ اَسْأَلُكَ مِنْ فُجَاءَةِ الْخَيْرِ وَاَعُوْذُ}$$

16. O Allah! I beg You to please bless me with good though it is without any preceding means and

$$\text{بِكَ مِنْ فُجَاءَةِ الشَّرِّ}$$

I seek Your protection from sudden calamities.

$$\text{(١٧)}\ \text{اَللّٰهُمَّ اَنْتَ السَّلَامُ وَمِنْكَ السَّلَامُ}$$

17. O Allah! Your name is As-Salaam (The Giver of Peace) and peace comes only from You

$$\text{وَاِلَيْكَ يَعُوْدُ السَّلَامُ اَسْأَلُكَ يَاذَا الْجَلَالِ}$$

and to You does it return. I beg of You, O Majestic

16. Musnad Abi Ya'laa # 3371   17. Majma'uz Zawaaid #

وَالْاِكْرَامِ اَنْ تَسْتَجِيْبَ لَنَا دَعْوَتَنَا وَاَنْ

and Benevolent One that You accept all our duas,

تُعْطِيَنَا رَغْبَتَنَا وَاَنْ تُغْنِيَنَا عَمَّنْ اَغْنَيْتَهٗ عَنَّا

You fulfil our desires and You make us independent from

مِنْ خَلْقِكَ

Your creatures who have no need towards us.

﴿١٨﴾ رَبِّ قِنِيْ عَذَابَكَ يَوْمَ تَبْعَثُ عِبَادَكَ

18. O Allah! Save me from Your punishment on the Day You will resurrect Your servants.

﴿١٩﴾ اَللّٰهُمَّ خِرْ لِيْ وَاخْتَرْ لِيْ

19. O Allah! You choose for me what is best for me and then grant it to me.

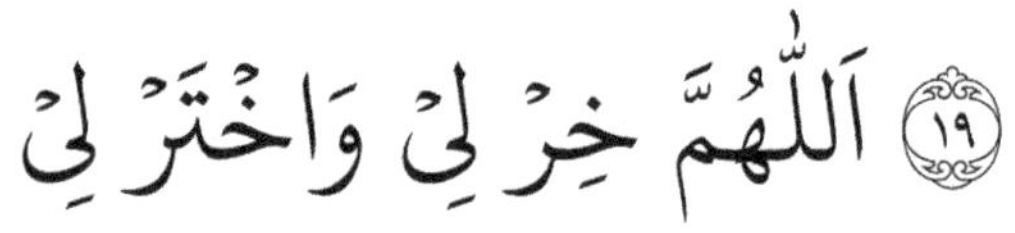

18. Mu'jamul Awsat # 3206	19. Tirmizi # 3516	20. Kanzul Ummaal # 3692

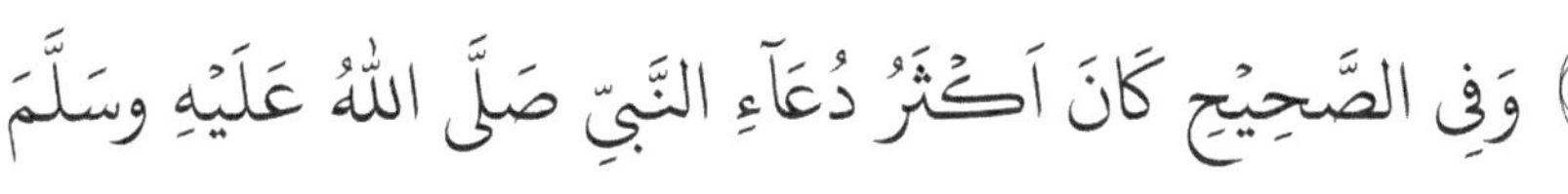

﴿٢٠﴾ وَفِى الصَّحِيْحِ كَانَ اَكْثَرُ دُعَآءِ النَّبِيّ صَلَّى اللهُ عَلَيْهِ وَسَلَّمَ

20. (It is reported in authentic Ahaadith that Rasulullah ﷺ used to recite the following dua very often):

اَللّٰهُمَّ رَبَّنَا اٰتِنَا فِى الدُّنْيَا حَسَنَةً وَّفِى الْاٰخِرَةِ

"O Allah! Give us the good of this world and in the Aakhirah (hereafter) also

حَسَنَةً وَّقِنَا عَذَابَ النَّارِ

grant us goodness and save us from the punishment of the fire."

﴿٢١﴾ بِسْمِ اللهِ عَلٰى نَفْسِىْ وَمَالِىْ وَدِيْنِىْ. اَللّٰهُمَّ

May the blessings of the name of Allah descend on me, my wealth and my Deen. O Allah!

اَرْضِنِىْ بِقَضَآئِكَ وَبَارِكْ لِىْ فِيْمَا قُدِّرَلِىْ حَتّٰى

Make me pleased with Your decree and grant me *barakah* (blessings) in whatever You have decreed for me so that

21. Amalul Yawmi Wal Laylah # 113

لَا أُحِبُّ تَعْجِيلَ مَا اَخَّرْتَ وَلَا تَأْخِيرَ مَا

I do not desire to hasten that which You have delayed or delay what

عَجَّلْتَ

You have hastened.

(٢٢) اَللّٰهُمَّ لَاعَيْشَ اِلَّا عَيْشُ الْاٰخِرَةِ

22. O Allah! There is no life but the life of the hereafter.

(٢٣) اَللّٰهُمَّ اَحْيِنِيْ مِسْكِيْنًا وَّاَمِتْنِيْ مِسْكِيْنًا

23. O Allah! Allow me to live as a humble person, cause me to die as a humble person

وَّاحْشُرْنِيْ فِيْ زُمْرَةِ الْمَسَاكِيْنِ

and raise me (on the Day of Judgement) in the company of the humble.

| 22. Bukhaari # 2961 | 23. Ibn Maajah # 4126 | 24. Ibn Maajah # 3820 |

اَللّٰهُمَّ اجْعَلْنِيْ مِنَ الَّذِيْنَ اِذَا اَحْسَنُوْا

24. O Allah! Make me from those who when they do good deeds

اِسْتَبْشَرُوْا وَاِذَا اَسَآءُوْا اِسْتَغْفَرُوْا

they rejoice and when they do wrong they ask for forgiveness.

اَللّٰهُمَّ اِنِّيْ اَسْاَلُكَ رَحْمَةً مِّنْ عِنْدِكَ تَهْدِىْ

25. O Allah! I beg of You Your special mercy by which You would guide

بِهَا قَلْبِيْ وَتَجْمَعُ بِهَاۤ اَمْرِىْ وَتَلُمُّ بِهَا

my heart, consolidate my affairs, straighten out for me

شَعَثِيْ وَتُصْلِحُ بِهَا دِيْنِيْ، وَتَقْضِيْ بِهَا دِيْنِيْ،

my muddled dealings, improve my religious life, settle my debts,

25. Tirmizi # 3419

وَتَحْفَظُ بِهَا غَآئِبِيْ، وَتَرْفَعُ بِهَا شَاهِدِیْ،

protect my interests in my absence, promote my outer matters,

وَتُبَيِّضُ بِهَا وَجْهِیْ، وَتُزَكِّیْ بِهَا عَمَلِیْ،

illuminate my face, purify my actions (from pride),

وَتُلْهِمُنِیْ بِهَا رُشْدِیْ، وَتَرُدُّ بِهَا الْفِتَنِ،

inspire my heart with righteousness, divert my passions (to desirable things)

وَتَعْصِمُنِیْ بِهَا مِنْ كُلِّ سُوْءٍ. اَللّٰهُمَّ اَعْطِنِیْ

and save me from all evil. O Allah! Bless me with

اِيْمَانًا لَّا يَرْتَدُّ، وَيَقِيْنًا لَّيْسَ بَعْدَهُ كُفْرٌ

Imaan that will never terminate, such *yaqeen* (firm conviction) after which there is no possibility of disbelief

وَرَحْمَةً اَنَالُ بِهَا شَرَفَ كَرَامَتِكَ فِي الدُّنْيَا

and (bless me with) *rahmat* (mercy) through which I can attain Your special favours in this world

وَالْاٰخِرَةِ، اَللّٰهُمَّ اِنِّيْ اَسْأَلُكَ الْفَوْزَ فِي الْقَضَآءِ

and the hereafter. O Allah! I beg of You to bless me with success in the decisions You have passed in my favour,

وَنُزُلَ الشُّهَدَآءِ، وَعَيْشَ السُّعَدَآءِ،

the hospitality afforded to the martyrs, happiness bestowed upon the fortunate,

وَمُرَافَقَةَ الْاَنْبِيَآءِ، وَالنَّصْرَ عَلَى الْاَعْدَآءِ،

the company of the Ambiyaa (messengers) and victory over the enemies.

اِنَّكَ سَمِيْعُ الدُّعَآءِ. اَللّٰهُمَّ اِنِّيْ اُنْزِلُ بِكَ

Verily, You hear all duas. O Allah! I place before You

حَاجَتِيْ، وَاِنْ قَصُرَ رَأْيِيْ وَضَعُفَ عَمَلِيْ

my needs despite my limited understanding, and my weak actions.

اِفْتَقَرْتُ اِلٰى رَحْمَتِكَ فَاَسْاَلُكَ يَا قَاضِيَ الْاُمُوْرِ

I am desperately in need of Your mercy. O The One who accomplishes all matters

وَيَا شَافِيَ الصُّدُوْرِ كَمَا تُجِيْرُ بَيْنَ الْبُحُوْرِ اَنْ

and O The One who fulfils the desires of the hearts and cures its illnesses,

تُجِيْرَنِيْ مِنْ عَذَابِ السَّعِيْرِ وَمِنْ دَعْوَةِ الثُّبُوْرِ

keep me far away from the punishment of Hell just as You have kept the oceans far away from each other. Save me from the

وَمِنْ فِتْنَةِ الْقُبُوْرِ. اَللّٰهُمَّ مَا قَصُرَ عَنْهُ رَأْيِيْ

agonies of Hell and from the trials of the grave. O Allah! If there is any good thing which my mind was unable to grasp,

وَضَعُفَ عَنْهُ عَمَلِي وَلَمْ تَبْلُغْهُ مُنِيَتِي

my actions unable to fulfil, or any other good which I neither desired

وَمَسْأَلَتِي مِنْ خَيْرٍ وَّعَدْتَّهُ اَحَدًا مِّنْ خَلْقِكَ

nor asked for, or any other good which You have promised to any of Your creation

اَوْ خَيْرٍ اَنْتَ مُعْطِيهِ اَحَدًا مِّنْ عِبَادِكَ فَاِنِّيْ

or any good which You intend to bless anyone of Your creation, then I also

اَرْغَبُ اِلَيْكَ فِيهِ وَاَسْاَلُكَ بِرَحْمَتِكَ رَبَّ

long for all that good and beg You for the same by Your mercy, O Cherisher of

الْعَالَمِيْنَ. اَللّٰهُمَّ ذَا الْحَبْلِ الشَّدِيدِ وَالْاَمْرِ

the worlds. O Allah! The Maker of strong covenants, The Source of all

الرَّشِيدِ اَسْاَلُكَ الْاَمَنَ يَوْمَ الْوَعِيدِ، وَالْجَنَّة

virtuous deeds, I beg of You to grant me safety on the Day of Judgement and to grant me entry into Jannah

يَوْمَ الْخُلُوْدِ مَعَ الْمُقَرَّبِيْنَ الشُّهُوْدِ، اَلرُّكَّع

on the day that is everlasting with Your close servants who enjoy your proximity and your countenance and are perpetually in ruku

السُّجُوْدُ، اَلْمُوْفِيْنَ بِالْعُهُوْدِ اِنَّكَ رَحِيْمٌ وَّدُوْدٌ

and sajdah before You and who fulfil their promises. Verily, You are Merciful and loving

اِنَّكَ تَفْعَلُ مَا تُرِيْدُ. اَللّٰهُمَّ اجْعَلْنَا هَادِيْنَ

and You do what You wish. O Allah! Make us from those who are rightly guided and from those who

مُهْتَدِيْنَ غَيْرَ ضَآلِّيْنَ وَلَا مُضِلِّيْنَ، سِلْمًا

guides others. Not from those who are misguided and those who misguides others. (Make us) from those who make peace

لِاَوْلِيَآئِكَ وَحَرْبًا لِاَعْدَآئِكَ، نُحِبُّ بِحُبِّكَ

with Your friends and are constantly at war with Your enemies,
who loves those that love You solely on account of

مَنْ اَحَبَّكَ، وَنُعَادِىْ بِعَدَاوَتِكَ مَنْ خَالَفَكَ

their love for You and show hatred towards Your enemies
amongst Your creation because of their enmity towards You.

مِنْ خَلْقِكَ. اَللّٰهُمَّ هٰذَا الدُّعَآءُ وَعَلَيْكَ

O Allah! Making dua is our duty and accepting our duas

الْاِجَابَةُ، وَهٰذَا الْجُهْدُ وَعَلَيْكَ التُّكْلَانُ

is Your promise. We make the effort but our total reliance is on
You.

اَللّٰهُمَّ اجْعَلْ لِّىْ نُوْرًا فِىْ قَلْبِىْ، وَنُوْرًا فِىْ قَبْرِىْ،

O Allah! Pour Your noor (light) into my heart and into my grave.

وَنُوْرًا مِّنْ بَيْنِ يَدَيَّ، وَنُوْرًا مِّنْ خَلْفِيْ، وَنُوْرًا

shower Your noor in front of me and behind me,

عَنْ يَّمِيْنِيْ، وَنُوْرًا عَنْ شِمَالِيْ وَنُوْرًا مِنْ فَوْقِيْ

on my right and my left, above me

وَنُوْرًا مِّنْ تَحْتِيْ، وَنُوْرًا فِيْ سَمْعِيْ، وَنُوْرًا فِيْ

and beneath me. Pour Your Noor into my ears

بَصَرِيْ، وَنُوْرًا فِيْ شَعْرِيْ، وَنُوْرًا فِيْ بَشَرِيْ،

and my eyes, into my hair and into my skin,

وَنُوْرًا فِيْ لَحْمِيْ، وَنُوْرًا فِيْ دَمِيْ، وَنُوْرًا فِيْ مُخِّيْ

my flesh, my blood, the marrow of my bones

وَنُوْرًا فِيْ عِظَامِيْ، اَللّٰهُمَّ اَعْظِمْ لِيْ نُوْرًا

and in all the bones of my body. O Allah! Expand Your light for me.

وَاَعْطِنِيْ نُوْرًا، وَاجْعَلْ لِّيْ نُوْرًا، وَزِدْنِيْ نُوْرًا،

bestow it upon me and make me an embodiment of light (from head to toe). Increase Your light for me,

وَزِدْنِيْ نُوْرًا، وَزِدْنِيْ نُوْرًا. سُبْحَانَ الَّذِيْ تَعَطَّفَ

increase Your light for me, increase Your light for me. Perfect is Allah whose covering is

بِالْعِزِّ، وَقَالَ بِهٖ، سُبْحَانَ الَّذِيْ لَبِسَ الْمَجْدَ

dignity and whose word is dignified, Whose garb is sanctity and

وَتَكَرَّمَ بِهٖ، سُبْحَانَ الَّذِيْ لَا يَنْبَغِيْ

He favours others with it as well. Unblemished is He who

التَّسْبِيحِ اِلَّا لَهٗ سُبْحَانَ مَنْ اَحْصٰى كُلَّ شَىْءٍ

alone may be called such. Whose knowledge encompasses everything,

بِعِلْمِهٖ، سُبْحَانَ ذِى الْفَضْلِ وَالطَّوْلِ، سُبْحَانَ

Glory be to Him Who possesses great kindness,

ذِى الْمَنِّ وَالنِّعَمِ، سُبْحَانَ ذِى الْمَجْدِ

Glory be to Him Who is extremely generous and kind (to His creation). Glory be to Him Who is perfectly adorable,

وَالْكَرَمِ سُبْحَانَ ذِى الْجَلَالِ وَالْاِكْرَامِ.

Glory be to Him Who is extremely Great and Kind.

۲۶ اَللّٰهُمَّ لَاتَكِلْنِيْ اِلٰى نَفْسِيْ طَرْفَةَ عَيْنٍ

26. O Allah! Do not entrust me to my self for the blinking of an eye

وَّلَاتَنْزِعْ مِنِّيْ صَالِحَ مَا اَعْطَيْتَنِيْ.

and do not snatch away any good which You have already bestowed upon me.

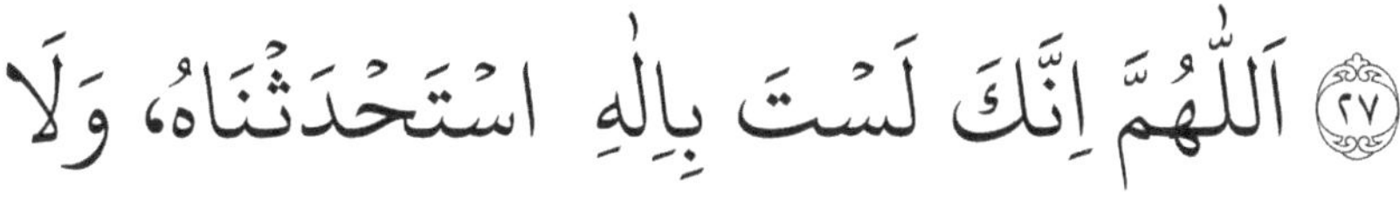 اَللّٰهُمَّ اِنَّكَ لَسْتَ بِاِلٰهٍ اسْتَحْدَثْنَاهُ، وَلَا

27. O Allah! You are not a deity who was made by us, nor

بِرَبٍّ يَّبِيْدُ ذِكْرُهُ ابْتَدَعْنَاهُ، وَلَاعَلَيْكَ

a Rabb who we made, nor a Rabb whose remembrance will ever end, nor do you have

شُرَكَآءُ يَقْضُوْنَ مَعَكَ، وَلَا كَانَ لَنَا قَبْلَكَ مِنْ

any partners who make decisions with You. Nor was there any deity before yourself that

اِلٰهٍ نَّلْجَأُ اِلَيْهِ وَنَذَرُكَ، وَلَا اَعَانَكَ عَلٰى خَلْقِنَا

could make us leave you and seek refuge in him. Nor has any one aided You in creating us

27. Mustadrak # 5708

اَحَدٌ فَنُشْرِكَهُ فِيكَ، تَبَارَكْتَ وَتَعَالَيْتَ،

that we may take him also as a Supreme being. You are indeed full of blessings and most exalted.

فَنَسْاَلُكَ لَآ اِلٰهَ اِلَّا اَنْتَ اِغْفِرْلِى

So we ask from You, as there is no other deity besides You, (O Allah) to please forgive us.

(۲۸) اَللّٰهُمَّ اِنَّكَ تَسْمَعُ كَلَامِى، وَتَرٰى مَكَانِى،

28. O Allah! You hear my speech and You can see my position (where I am),

وَتَعْلَمُ سِرِّى وَعَلَانِيَتِى، لَا يَخْفٰى عَلَيْكَ شَىْءٌ

You know what I conceal and what I reveal. Nothing in me can be hidden from You.

مِّنْ اَمْرِى، وَاَنَا الْبَآئِسُ الْفَقِيرُ الْمُسْتَغِيثُ

I am suffering and I am in desperate need of your help. I beg of You (O Allah)

28. Mu'jamus Sagheer # 696

الْمُسْتَجِيرُ الْوَجِلُ الْمُشْفِقُ الْمُقِرُّ الْمُعْتَرِفُ

and seek refuge in You whilst trembling with Your fear and confessing fully of

بِذَنْبِي اَسْاَلُكَ مَسْاَلَةَ الْمِسْكِينِ، وَاَبْتَهِلُ

my sins. I beg of You like how a beggar begs, and I plead

اِلَيْكَ ابْتِهَالَ الْمُذْنِبِ الذَّلِيلِ، وَاَدْعُوكَ دُعَاءَ

to You most humbly in the manner a disgraceful criminal does. I call onto You

الْخَآئِفِ الضَّرِيرِ، وَدُعَآءَ مَنْ خَضَعَتْ لَكَ

like the one who is struck with fear and misery, like the one whose neck is bowed

رَقَبَتُهُ وَفَاضَتْ لَكَ عَبْرَتُهُ وَذَلَّ لَكَ جِسْمُهُ

before You, whose tears are flowing, whose body is lowered before You

وَرَغِمَ لَكَ اَنْفُهُ اَللّٰهُمَّ لَا تَجْعَلْنِيْ بِدُعَآئِكَ

and whose nose is soiled in dust. O Allah! Do not make me among those who have been deprived, in this dua of mine.

شَقِيًّا، وَكُنْ لِّيْ رَءُوْفًا رَّحِيْمًا

Please be Kind and Merciful to me,

يَا خَيْرَ الْمَسْئُوْلِيْنَ وَيَا خَيْرَ الْمُعْطِيْنَ.

O the best of those who are petitioned and O the best of those who grant.

﴿٢٩﴾ اَللّٰهُمَّ اِلَيْكَ اَشْكُوْ ضَعْفَ قُوَّتِيْ وَقِلَّةَ حِيْلَتِيْ

29. O Allah! I complain only to You the lack of my strength and I do not have the resources

وَهَوَانِيْ عَلَى النَّاسِ يَآ اَرْحَمَ الرَّاحِمِيْنَ، اِلٰى مَنْ

and that I do not hold any significance in the eyes of people. O The Most Merciful of all those who show mercy, to whom are

29. Kanzul Ummaal # 3613

وَكِلُنِيْ، اِلٰى عَدُوٍّ يَّتَجَهَّمُنِيْ اَمْ اِلٰى قَرِيْبٍ

You going to entrust me ? To an enemy who would look at me harshly or to a friend

مَلَّكْتَهٗ اَمْرِىْ، اِنْ لَّمْ تَكُنْ سَاخِطًا عَلَىَّ فَلَآ

whom You have given the control of my affairs. If You are not angry with me, then (O Allah)

اُبَالِىْ غَيْرَ اَنَّ عَافِيَتَكَ اَوْسَعُ لِىْ، اَعُوْذُ بِنُوْرِ

I do not care for anything except that I should enjoy Your protection. I seek protection in the Noor of

وَجْهِكَ الْكَرِيْمِ الَّذِىْ اَضَآءَتْ لَهُ السَّمٰوَاتُ

Your Noble Countenance which brightens up the skies and which

وَاَشْرَقَتْ لَهُ الظُّلُمٰتُ وَصَلُحَ عَلَيْهِ اَمْرُ الدُّنْيَا

removes all kinds of darkness and controls the affairs of this world

وَالْاٰخِرَةِ اَنْ تُحِلَّ عَلَيَّ غَضَبَكَ وَ تُنْزِلَ عَلَيَّ

and the hereafter. May it never be that you become angry with me or Your wrath descends upon me

سَخَطَكَ وَلَكَ الْعُتْبٰى حَتّٰى تَرْضٰى، وَلَاحَوْلَ

I must continue to please You until You are happy with me. There is no strength (to refrain from evil)

وَلَاقُوَّةَ اِلَّا بِكَ

nor any power (to do any good) except with Your help.

﴿۳۰﴾ اَللّٰهُمَّ وَاقِيَةً كَوَاقِيَةِ الْوَلِيدِ.

30. O Allah! Grant me protection like the protection given to a new born baby.

﴿۳۱﴾ اَللّٰهُمَّ اِنَّا نَسْاَلُكَ قُلُوبًا اَوَّاهَةً مُّخْبِتَةً

31. O Allah! Grant us hearts which sigh in admiration for You, which are full of humility towards You

30. Kanzul Ummaal # 3678	31. Mustadrak # 1957

مُنِيْبَةً فِىْ سَبِيْلِكَ

and strongly inclined to follow Your path.

اَللّٰهُمَّ اِنِّىْ اَسْاَلُكَ اِيْمَانًا يُّبَاشِرُ قَلْبِىْ،

32. O Allah! I beg of You to bless me with such Imaan which penetrates my heart

وَّيَقِيْنًا صَادِقًا حَتّٰى اَعْلَمَ اَنَّهٗ لَايُصِيْبُنِىْ اِلَّا

and a true conviction so that I realise that whatever happens to me was

مَا كَتَبْتَ لِىْ وَرِضًا مِّنَ الْمَعِيْشَةِ بِمَا قَسَمْتَ

already decreed by You and I ask You for contentment in the income which You have granted to

لِىْ

me.

32. Kanzul Ummaal # 3657   33. Tirmizi # 3520

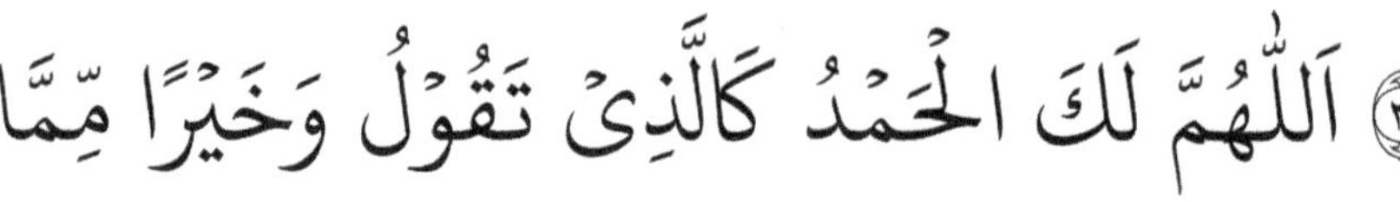

﴿٣٣﴾ اَللّٰهُمَّ لَكَ الْحَمْدُ كَالَّذِىْ تَقُوْلُ وَخَيْرًا مِّمَّا

33. O Allah! Your praises are like how You have expressed it and much more than what

نَقُوْلُ. اَللّٰهُمَّ لَكَ صَلَاتِىْ وَنُسُكِىْ وَمَحْيَاىَ

we can ever express. O Allah! For You is my salaah, my ibaadat (worship), my life

وَمَمَاتِىْ وَاِلَيْكَ مَاٰبِىْ وَلَكَ رَبِّ تُرَاثِىْ

and my death and unto You lies my ultimate return and all my assets belong to You.

اَللّٰهُمَّ اِنِّىْ اَعُوْذُ بِكَ مِنْ عَذَابِ الْقَبْرِ وَوَسْوَسَةِ

O Allah! I seek Your protection from the punishment of the grave, the whispers of

الصَّدْرِ وَشَتَاتِ الْاَمْرِ. اَللّٰهُمَّ اِنِّىْ اَسْأَلُكَ مِنْ

the heart and the complication of my affairs. O Allah! I beg of You

خَيْرِ مَا تَجِيْءُ بِهِ الرِّيَاحُ، وَاَعُوْذُ بِكَ مِنْ شَرِّ

all the good which is brought by the winds and I seek Your protection from all the evil

مَا تَجِيْءُ بِهِ الرِّيَاحُ.

which it carries.

﴿٣٤﴾ اَللّٰهُمَّ اجْعَلْنِيْ اُعَظِّمُ شُكْرَكَ وَاُكْثِرُ

34. O Allah! Make me one who is extremely grateful to You, remembers You

ذِكْرَكَ وَاَتَّبِعُ نَصِيْحَتَكَ وَاَحْفَظُ وَصِيَّتَكَ

frequently, obeys Your advices and remembers Your commandments.

﴿٣٥﴾ اَللّٰهُمَّ اِنَّ قُلُوْبَنَا وَنَوَاصِيْنَا وَجَوَارِحَنَا

35. O Allah! Our hearts, foreheads and limbs

34. Musnad Ahmad # 8040   35. Kanzul Ummaal # 3644

بِيَدِكَ لَمْ تُمَلِّكْنَا مِنْهَا شَيْئًا فَاِذَا فَعَلْتَ ذٰلِكَ

are all in Your control. You did not make us the owners of any one of these things. Since You have decreed it in this way,

بِنَا فَكُنْ اَنْتَ وَلِيَّنَا وَاهْدِنَاۤ اِلٰى سَوَآءِ

then be our guardian and guide us to the straight

السَّبِيْلِ

path.

㊱ اَللّٰهُمَّ اجْعَلْ حُبَّكَ اَحَبَّ الْاَشْيَآءِ اِلَيَّ،

36. O Allah! Make Your love the most beloved of things to me

وَاجْعَلْ خَشْيَتَكَ اَخْوَفَ الْاَشْيَآءِ عِنْدِىْ،

and make Your fear the most fearful of things to me.

36. Kanzul Ummaal # 3648

وَاقْطَعْ عَنِّيْ حَاجَاتِ الدُّنْيَا بِالشَّوْقِ اِلٰى

remove all worldly needs from my heart by infusing it with a burning passion for

لِقَآئِكَ، وَاِذَا اَقْرَرْتَ اَعْيُنَ اَهْلِ الدُّنْيَا مِنْ

meeting with You. And when You cool the eyes of the worldly class with

دُنْيَاهُمْ فَاَقْرِرْ عَيْنِيْ مِنْ عِبَادَتِكَ.

their worldly pursuits then cool my eyes with acts of ibaadah (devotion) towards You.

(٣٧) اَللّٰهُمَّ اِنِّيْ اَعُوْذُ بِكَ مِنْ شَرِّ الْاَعْمَيَيْنِ

37. O Allah! I seek Your protection from the evil of the two blind things,

السَّيْلِ وَالْبَعِيْرِ الصَّؤُوْلِ.

the mountain floods and the onslaught of the camel. (Both these calamites come blindly and destroy everything.)

37. Kanzul Ummaal # 3649	38. Kanzul Ummaal # 3650

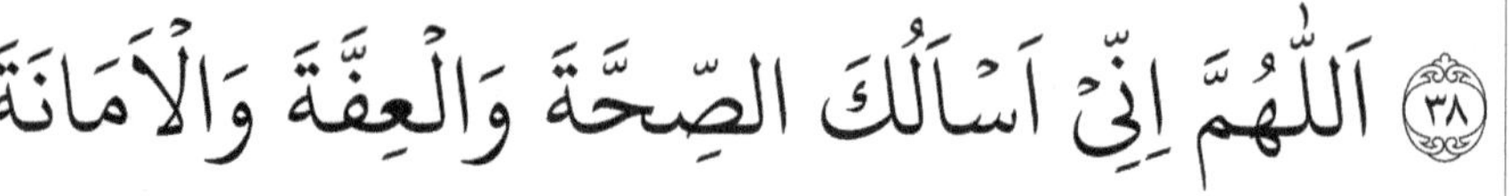

38. O Allah! I beg of You good health, chastity, trustworthiness,

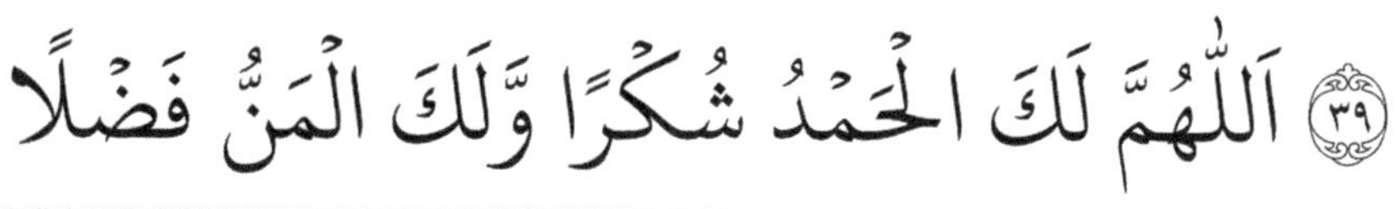

good manners and to be happy with Your decree.

39. O Allah! All praise is due to You with gratefulness and all kindness is due to You with grace.

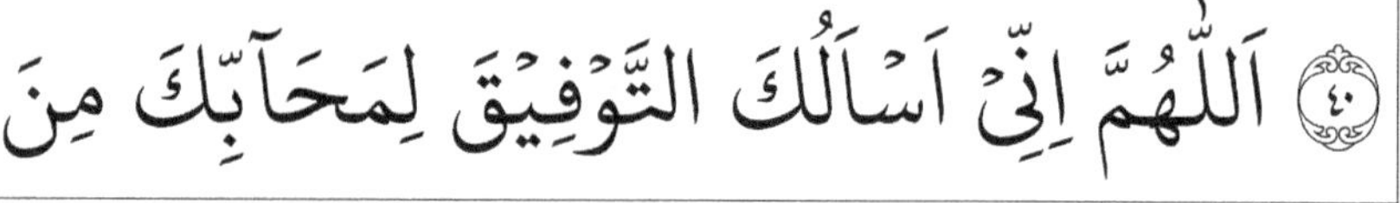

40. O Allah! I beg of You the ability to perform deeds which are pleasing to You,

true reliance on You and I ask of You to bless me with good thoughts

39. Mu'jamul Kabeer # 316   40. Kanzul Ummaal # 3654

بِكَ

concerning You.

اَللّٰهُمَّ افْتَحْ مَسَامِعَ قَلْبِيْ لِذِكْرِكَ وَارْزُقْنِيْ

41. O Allah! Open up the pores of my heart for Your remembrance, grant me the ability to be

طَاعَتَكَ وَطَاعَةَ رَسُوْلِكَ وَعَمَلاً بِكِتَابِكَ

obedient to You and Your Rasul ﷺ and grant me the ability to practice on the Qur-aan.

اَللّٰهُمَّ اجْعَلْنِيْ اَخْشَاكَ كَاَنِّيْ اَرَاكَ اَبَدًا

42. O Allah! Make me such that I fear You forever, as if I can see you before me,

حَتّٰى اَلْقَاكَ، وَاَسْعِدْنِيْ بِتَقْوَاكَ، وَلَا تُشْقِنِيْ

until the day I meet You. Make me amongst the fortunate on account of my fear for you and do not make me amongst the

41. Mu'jamul Awsat # 1286	42. Mu'jamul Awsat # 5982

بِمَعْصِيَتِكَ، وَخِرْلِى فِى قَضَآئِكَ، وَبَارِكْ لِى فِى

wretched because of my disobedience to You. Grant me good in what ever You have decreed for me and grant me *barkat*

قَدْرِكَ حَتَّى لَا أُحِبَّ تَعْجِيلَ مَا أَخَّرْتَ وَلَا

(blessings) in it, to this extent that I would not like to hasten what You have delayed for me

تَأْخِيرَ مَا عَجَّلْتَ، وَاجْعَلْ غِنَايِى فِى نَفْسِى

and delay that which You have chosen to hasten for me, and create contentment within me.

۴۳ اَللّٰهُمَّ الْطُفْ بِى فِى تَيْسِيرِ كُلِّ عَسِيرٍ،

43. O Allah! Be kind to me by making every difficulty easy for me

فَاِنَّ تَيْسِيرَ كُلِّ عَسِيرٍ عَلَيْكَ يَسِيرٌ وَاَسْاَلُكَ

as it is absolutely easy for You to do so. And I ask You

43. Mu'jamul Awsat # 1250

الْيُسْرَ وَالْمُعَافَاةَ فِى الدُّنْيَا وَالْاٰخِرَةِ

for ease and forgiveness in this world and the hereafter.

٤٤ اَللّٰهُمَّ اعْفُ عَنِّىْ فَاِنَّكَ عَفُوٌّ كَرِيْمٌ.

44. O Allah! Forgive me as You are Most Forgiving and Most Kind.

44. Mu'jamul Awsat # 7746

اَللّٰهُمَّ طَهِّرْ قَلْبِىْ مِنَ النِّفَاقِ، وَعَمَلِىْ مِنَ

1. O Allah! Cleanse my heart from hypocrisy, my actions from

الرِّيَآءِ، وَلِسَانِىْ مِنَ الْكِذْبِ، وَعَيْنِىْ مِنَ

show, my tongue from lies, my eyes from

الْخِيَانَةِ، فَاِنَّكَ تَعْلَمُ خَآئِنَةَ الْاَعْيُنِ وَمَا

deception. Verily You know well the deception of the eyes and whatever

تُخْفِى الصُّدُوْرُ

the hearts conceal.

1. Kanzul Ummaal # 3660

اَللّٰهُمَّ ارْزُقْنِيْ عَيْنَيْنِ هَطَّالَتَيْنِ تَسْقِيَانِ ۝

2. O Allah! Grant me such eyes which tear profusely and thereby water

الْقَلْبَ بِذُرُوْفِ الدَّمْعِ مِنْ خَشْيَتِكَ قَبْلَ اَنْ

the heart with flowing tears out of Your fear, before

تَكُوْنَ الدُّمُوْعُ دَمًا وَّالْاَضْرَاسُ جَمْرًا

the arrival of the time when tears turn into blood and jaws turn into embers.

اَللّٰهُمَّ عَافِنِيْ فِيْ قُدْرَتِكَ، وَاَدْخِلْنِيْ فِيْ ۝

3. O Allah! Protect me by Your power and admit me into

رَحْمَتِكَ، وَاقْضِ اَجَلِيْ فِيْ طَاعَتِكَ، وَاخْتِمْ لِيْ

Your mercy, make me devote my life to worshipping You, and allow my life to end

2. Kanzul Ummaal # 3661	3. Kanzul Ummaal # 3662

بِخَيْرِ عَمَلِيْ، وَاجْعَلْ ثَوَابَهُ الْجَنَّةَ

with the best of deeds and make Jannah the reward of it all.

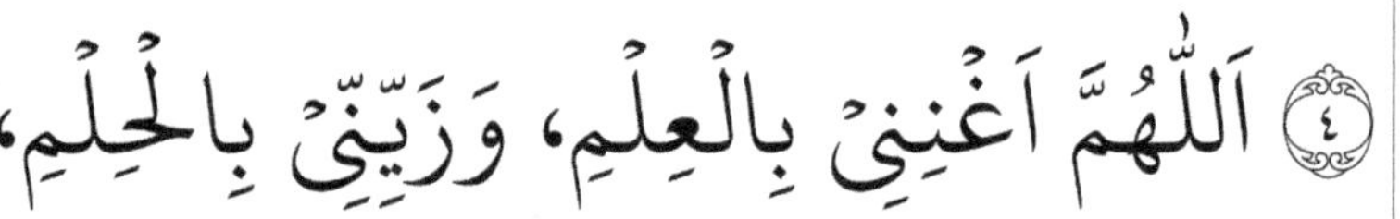

اَللّٰهُمَّ اَغْنِنِيْ بِالْعِلْمِ، وَزَيِّنِّيْ بِالْحِلْمِ،

4. O Allah! Enrich me with knowledge, beautify me with tolerance,

وَاَكْرِمْنِيْ بِالتَّقْوٰى، وَجَمِّلْنِيْ بِالْعَافِيَةِ.

and honour me with piety and beautify me with good health.

اَللّٰهُمَّ اِنِّيْ اَعُوْذُ بِكَ مِنْ خَلِيْلٍ مَّاكِرٍ

5. O Allah! I seek Your protection from a cunning friend who is constantly

عَيْنَاهُ تَرَيَانِيْ وَقَلْبُهُ يَرْعَانِيْ، اِنْ رَّاٰى حَسَنَةً

monitoring me with his eyes and observing me with his heart. When he sees any good in me he conceals it

4. Kanzul Ummaal # 3663	5. Kanzul Ummaal # 3666

دَفَنَهَا، وَاِنْ رَّاٰى سَيِّئَةً اَذَاعَهَا.

and when he sees any wrong in me he publicises it.

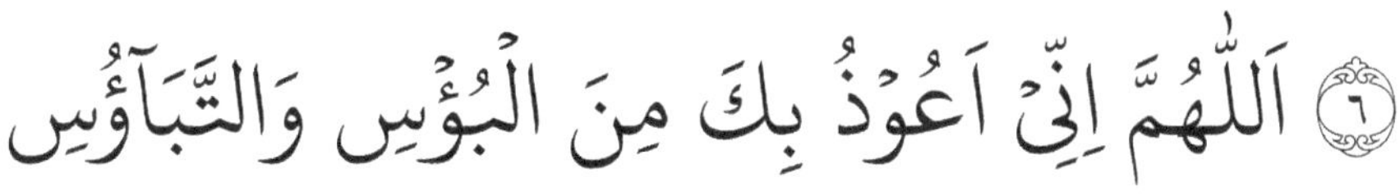

اَللّٰهُمَّ اِنِّىْ اَعُوْذُ بِكَ مِنَ الْبُؤُسِ وَالتَّبَاؤُسِ

6. O Allah! I seek Your protection from poverty and from becoming a pauper.

اَللّٰهُمَّ لَا يُدْرِكُنِىْ زَمَانٌ وَّلَا يُدْرِكُوْا زَمَانًا

7. O Allah! Save me and others from such a time where people will

لَّا يُتَّبَعُ فِيْهِ الْعَلِيْمُ وَلَا يُسْتَحْيٰى فِيْهِ مِنَ

refuse to follow the learned Ulama and have no regard for

الْحَلِيْمِ قُلُوْبُهُمْ قُلُوْبُ الْاَعَاجِمِ وَاَلْسِنَتُهُمْ

tolerant/gentle people. Their hearts will be like those of non-Arabs and their tongues

---

6. Mu'jamus Sahaabah # 1559 | 7. Kanzul Ummaal # 3686

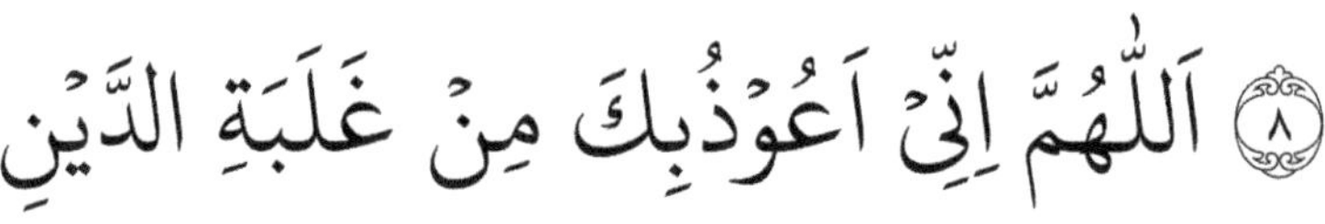

will be like that of Arabs.

اَللّٰهُمَّ اِنِّىْ اَعُوْذُبِكَ مِنْ غَلَبَةِ الدَّيْنِ

8. O Allah! I seek Your protection from being overpowered by debt,

وَغَلَبَةِ الْعَدُوِّ، وَمِنْ بَوَارِ الْاَيِّمِ وَمِنْ فِتْنَةِ

being overpowered by an enemy, from a widow who is unable to find a suitable partner and from the fitnah (trial)

اَلْمَسِيْحِ الدَّجَّالِ

of Dajjaal.

اَللّٰهُمَّ اِنِّىْ اَعُوْذُ بِكَ مِنْ فِتْنَةِ النِّسَآءِ،

9. O Allah! I seek Your protection from the temptation of women

8. Mu'jamul Awsat # 2142	9. Kanzul Ummaal # 36

وَاَعُوْذُبِكَ مِنْ عَذَابِ الْقَبْرِ

and the punishment in the grave.

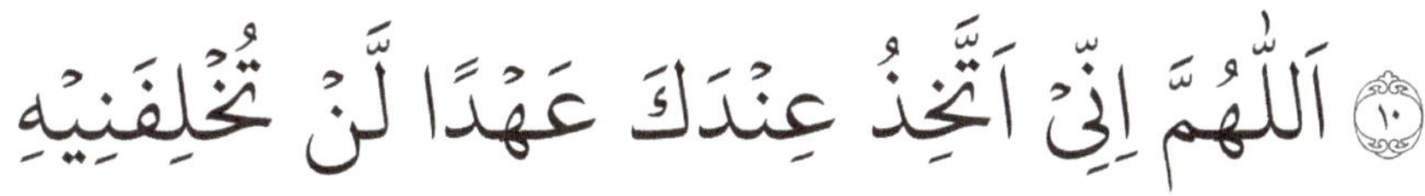

اَللّٰهُمَّ اِنِّى اَتَّخِذُ عِنْدَكَ عَهْدًا لَّنْ تُخْلِفَنِيْهِ ۝

10. O Allah! I have taken a promise with You which You would never violate.

فَاِنَّمَآ اَنَا بَشَرٌ فَاَيُّمَا مُؤْمِنٍ اٰذَيْتُهٗ اَوْ شَتَمْتُهٗ اَوْ

Indeed I am a human being (liable to err) and if I have hurt or scolded a Muslim or

جَلَدْتُّهٗ اَوْ لَعَنْتُهٗ فَاجْعَلْهَا لَهٗ صَلٰوةً وَّزَكَاةً

hit him or cursed him then I beg You to please make this (hurt) a means of peace, purification

وَّقُرْبَةً تُقَرِّبُهٗ بِهَآ اِلَيْكَ

and nearness for him, which in turn will allow him to gain Your closeness.

10. Musnad Ahmad # 8053

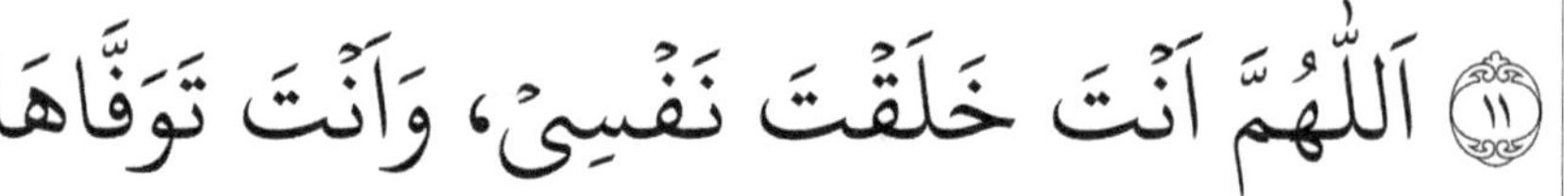

اَللّٰهُمَّ اَنْتَ خَلَقْتَ نَفْسِيْ، وَاَنْتَ تَوَفَّاهَا

11. O Allah! You have created me and You will also cause me to die.

لَكَ مَمَاتُهَا وَمَحْيَاهَا اِنْ اَحْيَيْتَهَا فَاحْفَظْهَا

Hence, life and death are both in Your control. If You are going to keep me alive then protect me

بِمَا تَحْفَظُ بِهٖ عِبَادَكَ الصَّالِحِيْنَ، وَاِنْ اَمَتَّهَا

in the way You have protected Your virtuous servants and if I am to die

فَاغْفِرْ لَهَا وَارْحَمْهَا،

then please forgive me and have mercy on me.

اَللّٰهُمَّ اِنِّيْ اَسْاَلُكَ الْعَافِيَةَ

O Allah! I beg You for ease.

11. Muslim # 2712

12. O Allah! Guard my private parts and make my work easy for me.

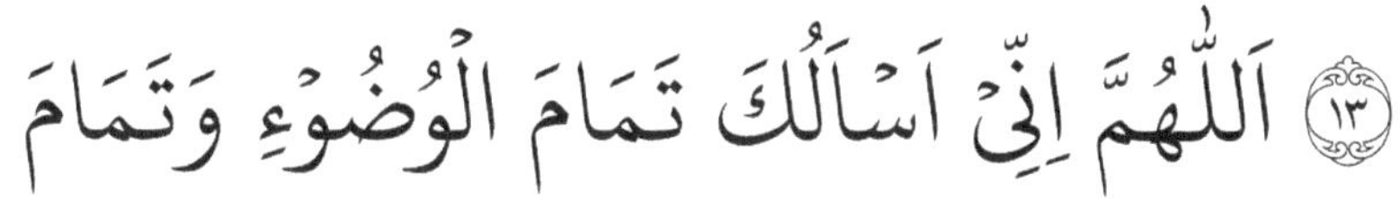

13. O Allah! I beg of You to grant me perfection in wudhu and perfection in

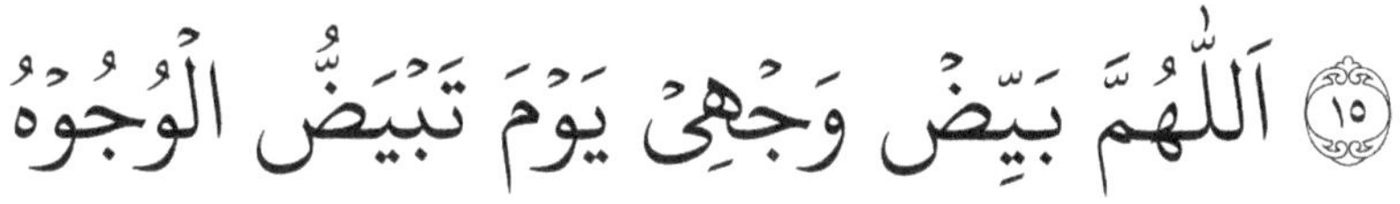

salaah and your complete pleasure (towards me) and (grant me) Your complete forgiveness.

14. O Allah! Give me my book of deeds in my right hand.

15. O Allah! Grant me a shining face on the day when the faces of the pious will shine.

12. T. Muhtaaj # 89	13. M. Haaris # 469	14. Azkaar # 65	15. Azkaar # 65

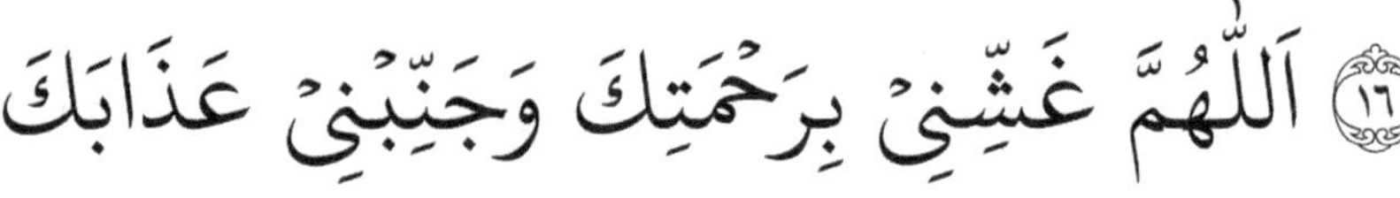

16. O Allah! Cover me with Your mercy and save me from Your punishment.

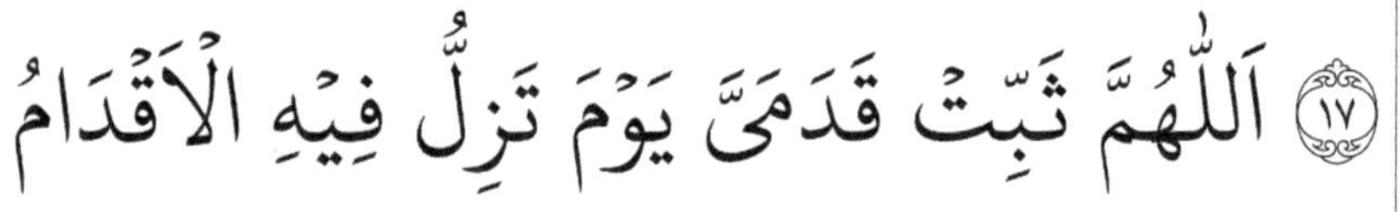

17. O Allah! Keep my feet firm on that Day when the feet will begin to slip.

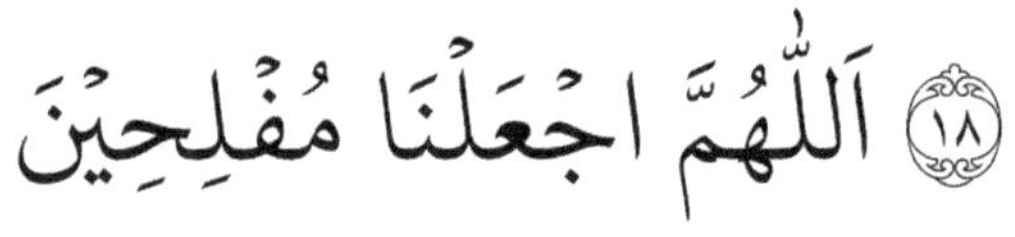

18. O Allah! Make us from the successful ones.

19. O Allah! Open up the locks of our hearts with Your remembrance, complete

عَلَيْنَا نِعْمَتَكَ، وَاَسْبِغْ عَلَيْنَا مِنْ فَضْلِكَ،

Your favour upon us, pour Your grace and bounty over us

16. Kanzul U #26985	17. Kanzul U #26987	18. Amalul Y.W.L #92	19. Kanzul U #20990

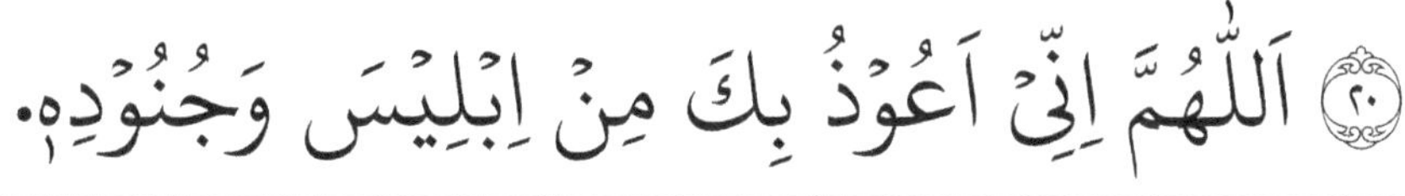

and make us Your pious servants.

اَللّٰهُمَّ اِنِّیْ اَعُوْذُ بِكَ مِنْ اِبْلِیْسَ وَجُنُوْدِهٖ۔

20. O Allah! I seek Your protection from the devil and his troops.

اَللّٰهُمَّ اٰتِنِیْ اَفْضَلَ مَا تُؤْتِیْ عِبَادَكَ

21. O Allah! Bless me with the best of that which You have granted Your

الصَّالِحِیْنَ۔

pious servants.

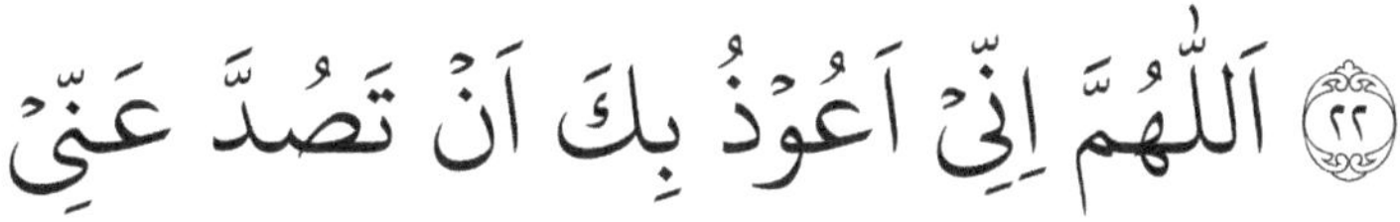

اَللّٰهُمَّ اِنِّیْ اَعُوْذُ بِكَ اَنْ تَصُدَّ عَنِّیْ

22. O Allah! I seek Your protection that You should turn Your

وَجْهَكَ يَوْمَ الْقِيٰمَةِ

face away from me on the Day of Judgement.

اَللّٰهُمَّ اَحْيِنِيْ مُسْلِمًا وَّاَمِتْنِيْ مُسْلِمًا

O Allah! Keep me alive as a Muslim and cause me to die as a Muslim.

اَللّٰهُمَّ عَذِّبِ الْكَفَرَةَ، وَاَلْقِ فِيْ قُلُوْبِهِمُ ﴿٢٣﴾

23. O Allah! Punish the unbelievers, fill their hearts with

الرُّعْبَ، وَخَالِفْ بَيْنَ كَلِمَتِهِمْ، وَاَنْزِلْ عَلَيْهِمْ

terror, cause a conflict in their planning and bring upon them

رِجْزَكَ وَعَذَابَكَ

Your anger and punishment.

اَللّٰهُمَّ عَذِّبِ الْكَفَرَةَ اَهْلَ الْكِتَابِ ﴿٢٤﴾

24. O Allah! Punish the disbelievers and the people of the book,

وَالْمُشْرِكِيْنَ الَّذِيْنَ يَجْحَدُوْنَ اٰيَاتِكَ

and the polytheists, those who reject Your verses,

وَيُكَذِّبُوْنَ رُسُلَكَ وَيَصُدُّوْنَ عَنْ سَبِيْلِكَ

deny Your Messengers, prevent the people from following Your path,

وَيَتَعَدَّوْنَ حُدُوْدَكَ وَيَدْعُوْنَ مَعَكَ اِلٰـهًا اٰخَرَ

transgress the limits prescribed by You and call upon other deities besides You

لَا اِلٰهَ اِلَّا اَنْتَ تَبَارَكْتَ وَتَعَالَيْتَ عَمَّا يَقُوْلُ

There is indeed no Supreme Being besides You, You are full of blessings and far, far above what

24. Raudhatul Muhaddiseen # 292

الظَّالِمُوْنَ عُلُوًّا كَبِيْرًا

the oppressive people utter.

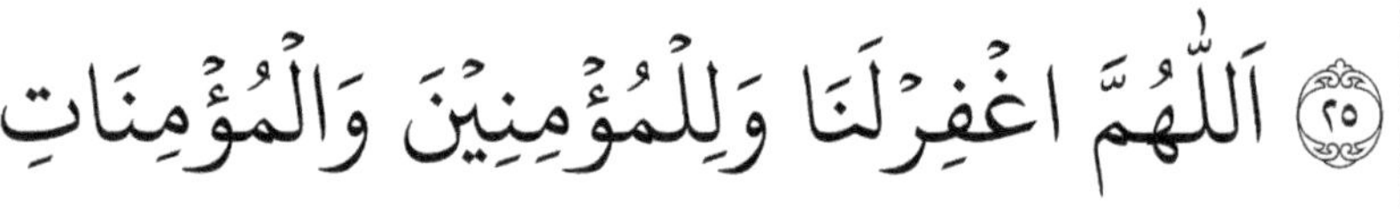

٢٥ اَللّٰهُمَّ اغْفِرْ لَنَا وَلِلْمُؤْمِنِيْنَ وَالْمُؤْمِنَاتِ

25. O Allah! Forgive us and all the believing men and women,

وَالْمُسْلِمِيْنَ وَالْمُسْلِمَاتِ، وَاَصْلِحْهُمْ وَاَصْلِحْ

all the Muslim men and women. Reform them and set right their

ذَاتَ بَيْنِهِمْ، وَاَلِّفْ بَيْنَ قُلُوْبِهِمْ، وَاجْعَلْ فِيْ

affairs, unite their hearts and, fill it

قُلُوْبِهِمُ الْاِيْمَانَ وَالْحِكْمَةَ. وَثَبِّتْهُمْ عَلٰى مِلَّةِ

with Imaan and wisdom, keep them firm on the religion of

25. Musannaf Abdur Razzaaq # 4968

رَسُوْلِكَ. وَاَوْزِعْهُمْ اَنْ يَّشْكُرُوْا نِعْمَتَكَ الَّتِيْ

Your Messenger ﷺ, grant them the ability of being grateful to You for the favours which

اَنْعَمْتَ عَلَيْهِمْ. وَاَنْ يُّوْفُوْا بِعَهْدِكَ الَّذِىْ

You have bestowed upon them and to fulfil the promise which

عَاهَدْتَّهُمْ عَلَيْهِ. وَانْصُرْهُمْ عَلٰى عَدُوِّكَ

You have taken from them and grant them victory over their enemy

وَعَدُوِّهِمْ اِلٰهَ الْحَقِّ.

and Your enemy. O the Supreme Being of Truth.

سُبْحَانَكَ لَاۤ اِلٰهَ غَيْرُكَ اِغْفِرْلِىْ ذَنْبِىْ. ﴿٢٦﴾

26. You are absolutely pure and sublime, there is no deity besides You, forgive my sins

وَاَصْلِحْ لِيْ عَمَلِيْ ۗ اِنَّكَ تَغْفِرُالذُّنُوْبَ لِـمَـنْ

and correct my actions. Verily You forgive the sins of whomsoever

تَشَآءُ وَاَنْتَ الْغَفُوْرُ الرَّحِيْمُ يَا غَفَّارُ اِغْفِرْلِيْ

You please and You are indeed Most Forgiving and Most Merciful. O the One who is most forgiving, forgive me.

يَاتَوَّابُ تُبْ عَلَيَّ ۗ يَا رَحْمٰنُ ارْحَمْنِيْ ۗ يَا عَفُوُّ

O the One who accepts repentance, accept my repentance. O the One who is full of mercy, have mercy on me. O the One who

اعْفُ عَنِّيْ ۗ يَارَءُوْفُ ارْؤُفْ بِيْ ۗ يَارَبِّ اَوْزِعْنِيْ

pardons sins, pardon me. O the One who is most kind, be kind to me. O Allah! Grant me the ability

اَنْ اَشْكُرَ نِعْمَتَكَ الَّتِيْ اَنْعَمْتَ عَلَيَّ وَطَوِّقْـنِيْ

to be grateful to You for Your favours, which You have bestowed upon me and grant me the ability to worship You

26. Jam'ul Fawaaid # 1536

حُسْنَ عِبَادَتِكَ. يَارَبِّ اَسْاَلُكَ مِنَ الْخَيْرِ

in the best manner. O Allah! I beg of You all kinds of good.

كُلِّهٖ. يَارَبِّ افْتَحْ لِىْ بِخَيْرٍ وَّاخْتِمْ لِىْ بِخَيْرٍ.

O Allah! Let me begin with good and make me breathe my last in a state of goodness,

وَّاٰتِنِىْ تَشَوُّقًا اِلٰى لِقَآئِكَ مِنْ غَيْرِ ضَرَّاءَ

grant me a strong passion for meeting with You in a condition where there is no

مُضِرَّةٍ وَّلَافِتْنَةٍ مُّضِلَّةٍ وَقِنِى السَّيِّاٰتِ وَمَنْ تَقِ

suffering or a test. (i.e. it should be a meeting of a blessed servant with his Supreme Creator) and save me from all types of evil.

السَّيِّاٰتِ يَوْمَئِذٍ فَقَدْ رَحِمْتَهٗ وَذٰلِكَ هُوَالْفَوْزُ

Surely The one whom You save from evils on that Day is truly blessed by You and it is indeed a

الْعَظِيمُ

great success.

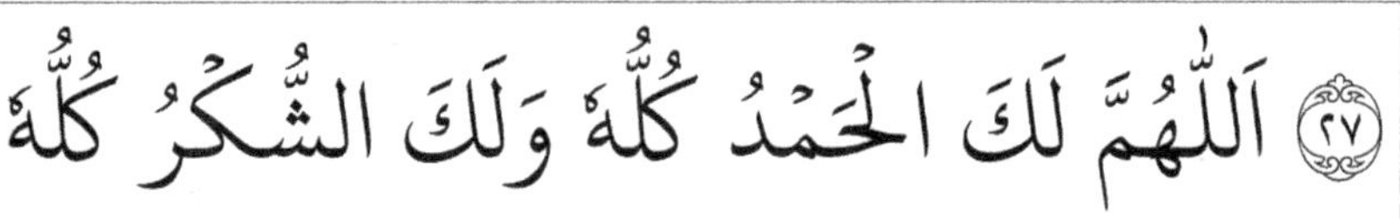

اَللّٰهُمَّ لَكَ الْحَمْدُ كُلُّهُ وَلَكَ الشُّكْرُ كُلُّهُ ۝

27. O Allah! All praise and gratitude is for You,

وَلَكَ الْمُلْكُ كُلُّهُ وَلَكَ الْخَلْقُ كُلُّهُ بِيَدِكَ

the entire kingdom and creation belong to You. All good is in Your

الْخَيْرُ كُلُّهُ وَاِلَيْكَ يَرْجِعُ الْاَمْرُ كُلُّهُ

hands and all matters ultimately return to You.

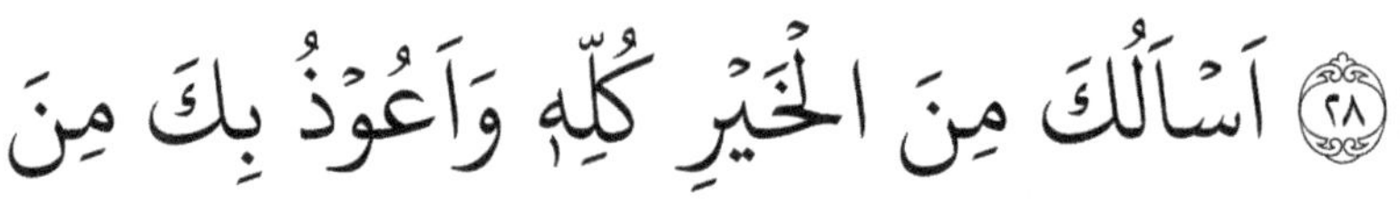

اَسْاَلُكَ مِنَ الْخَيْرِ كُلِّهِ وَاَعُوْذُ بِكَ مِنَ ۝

28. I beg of You for all kinds of goodness and I also beg to be saved
from

27. Musnad Ahmad # 396

الشَّرِّ كُلِّهٖ

all kinds of evil.

٢٩ بِسْمِ اللّٰهِ الَّذِیْ لَاۤ اِلٰهَ غَيْرُهٗ.

29. In the name of Allah besides whom there is no Supreme Being.

اَللّٰهُمَّ اَذْهِبْ عَنِّی الْهَمَّ وَالْحُزْنَ.

O Allah! Relieve me of all worry and grief.

٣٠ اَللّٰهُمَّ بِحَمْدِكَ انْصَرَفْتُ وَبِذَنْبِیْ

30. O Allah! I turn towards You while praising You and confessing my sins.

اعْتَرَفْتُ. وَاَعُوْذُبِكَ مِنْ شَرِّ مَا اقْتَرَفْتُ.

I seek Your protection from the sins I've committed,

| 28. Kanzul Ummaal # 22546 | 29. Jaami'us Saghir #6741 | 30. Akhbaar. A # 446 |

وَاَعُوْذُ بِكَ مِنْ جُهْدِ الْبَلَاۤءِ. وَمِنْ عَذَابِ

protection from severe tests and from the punishment

الْاٰخِرَةِ.

of the hereafter.

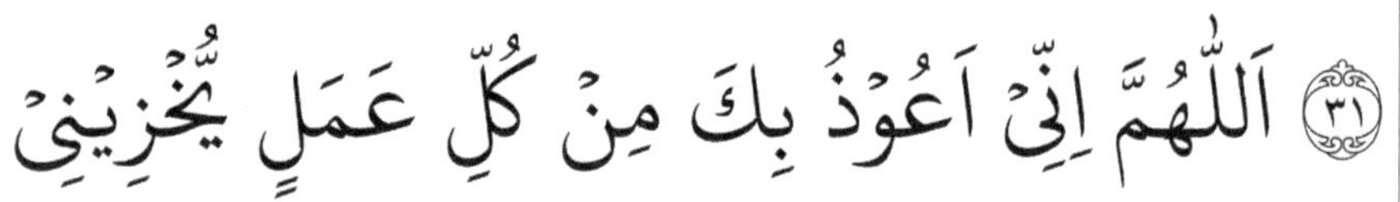

(٣١) اَللّٰهُمَّ اِنِّيْ اَعُوْذُ بِكَ مِنْ كُلِّ عَمَلٍ يُّخْزِيْنِيْ

31. O Allah! I seek Your protection from all such actions that will bring disgrace upon me,

وَاَعُوْذُ بِكَ مِنْ كُلِّ صَاحِبٍ يُّؤْذِيْنِيْ

from friends who may cause harm to me,

وَاَعُوْذُبِكَ مِنْ كُلِّ اَمَلٍ يُّلْهِيْنِيْ وَاَعُوْذُ بِكَ

from having high hopes in things that may make me unmindful (of my duties). I seek Your protection

31. Majma'uz Zawaaid # 110

مِنْ كُلِّ فَقْرٍ يُّنْسِيْنِيْ وَاَعُوْذُ بِكَ مِنْ كُلِّ غِنَّى

from all kinds of poverty which may make me forgetful of you and from all kinds of wealth which may make me

يُطْغِيْنِيْ.

disobedient to you.

(۳۲) اَللّٰهُمَّ اِلٰهِيْ وَاِلٰهَ اِبْرَاهِيْمَ وَاِسْحٰقَ

32. O Allah! My Rabb and the Rabb of Ibraaheem عَلَيْهِٱلسَّلَامُ, Ishaaq عَلَيْهِٱلسَّلَامُ,

وَيَعْقُوْبَ وَاِلٰهَ جِبْرِيْلَ وَمِيْكَائِيْلَ وَاِسْرَافِيْلَ

Ya'qoob عَلَيْهِٱلسَّلَامُ, the Rabb of Jibraaeel عَلَيْهِٱلسَّلَامُ, Mikaaeel عَلَيْهِٱلسَّلَامُ and Israafeel عَلَيْهِٱلسَّلَامُ.

اَسْاَلُكَ اَنْ تَسْتَجِيْبَ دَعْوَتِيْ فَاَنَا مُضْطَرٌّ.

I beg You to accept my dua for I am very restless

32. Kanzul Ummaal # 3476

وَتَعْصِمَنِيْ فِيْ دِيْنِيْ فَاِنِّيْ مُبْتَلًى. وَتَنَالَنِيْ

and guard my Imaan as I am going through trying circumstances. Receive me into

بِرَحْمَتِكَ فَاِنِّيْ مُذْنِبٌ. وَتَنْفِىَ عَنِّى الْفَقْرَ فَاِنِّيْ

Your arms of Mercy as I am extremely sinful and relieve me from poverty as I am

مُتَمَسْكِنٌ

extremely poor.

اَللّٰهُمَّ اِنِّيْ اَسْاَلُكَ بِحَقِّ السَّآئِلِيْنَ عَلَيْكَ. ۝

33. O Allah! I beg You by the rights which beggars have over You

فَاِنَّ لِلسَّآئِلِ عَلَيْكَ حَقًّا. اَيَّمَا عَبْدٍ اَوْ اَمَةٍ

and verily beggars do have rights over You. If You have accepted the duas of any one of Your slaves amongst

33. Kanzul Ummaal # 4977

مِّنْ اَهْلِ الْبَرِّ وَالْبَحْرِ تَقَبَّلْتَ دَعْوَتَهُمْ

the inhabitants of the land and the sea,

وَاسْتَجَبْتَ دُعَآءَهُمْ۔ اَنْ تُشْرِكَنَا فِیْ صَالِح

then join us in the blessed

مَایَدْعُوْنَكَ فِیْهِ۔ وَاَنْ تُشْرِكَهُمْ فِیْ صَالِحٍ مَا

duas they have made to You and let them also be joined with us in the good

نَدْعُوْكَ فِیْهِ وَاَنْ تُعَافِیَنَا وَاِیَّاهُمْ وَاَنْ

duas we make to You. Grant us peace and grant them peace as well

تَقَبَّلَ مِنَّا وَمِنْهُمْ وَاَنْ تَجَاوَزَ عَنَّا وَعَنْهُمْ

accept from us and from them, overlook our faults and theirs.

فَاِنَّنَآ اٰمَنَّا بِمَآ اَنْزَلْتَ وَاتَّبَعْنَا الرَّسُوْلَ

Verily we believe in what You have revealed and we have obeyed Your messenger,

فَاكْتُبْنَا مَعَ الشُّهِدِيْنَ

so count us among those who testify.

(٣٤) اَللّٰهُمَّ اَعْطِ مُحَمَّدَ الْوَسِيْلَةَ وَاجْعَلْ فِى

34. O Allah! Bless Nabi Muhammad 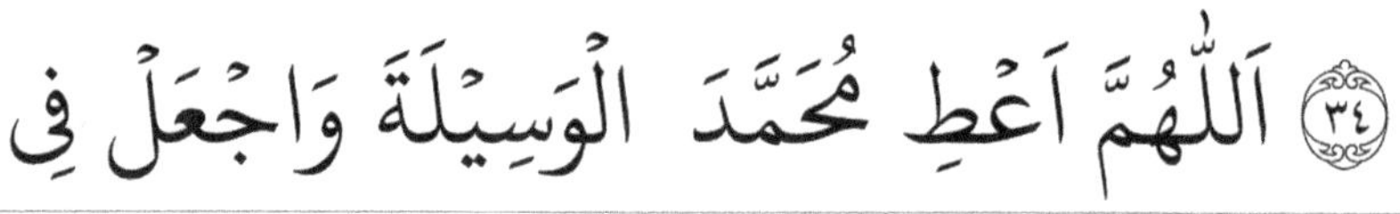 with the position of Waseelah (a special position of intercession), instil

الْمُصْطَفَيْنَ مَحَبَّتَهٗ وَفِى الْاَعْلَيْنَ دَرَجَتَهٗ وَفِىْ

his love into the hearts of the chosen ones, place him among the people of the highest rank

الْمُقَرَّبِيْنَ ذِكْرَهٗ

and allow his name to be on the lips of those who are extremely close to You.

34. Kanzul Ummaal # 3479

اَللّٰهُمَّ اهْدِنِيْ مِنْ عِنْدِكَ وَاَفِضْ عَلَيَّ مِنْ

35. O Allah! Grant me Your special guidance, pour

فَضْلِكَ وَاَسْبِغْ عَلَيَّ مِنْ رَّحْمَتِكَ وَاَنْزِلْ عَلَيَّ

Your grace upon me, shower me with Your mercy and favour me with

مِنْ بَرَكَاتِكَ

Your blessings.

اَللّٰهُمَّ اغْفِرْلِيْ وَارْحَمْنِيْ وَتُبْ عَلَيَّ اِنَّكَ

36. O Allah! Forgive me, have mercy on me, accept my taubah (repentance). Verily

اَنْتَ التَّوَّابُ الرَّحِيْمُ.

You are Most Forgiving and Most Merciful.

35. Kanzul Ummaal # 352	36. Musnad Ahmad # 5331

اَللّٰهُمَّ اِنِّى اَسْاَلُكَ تَوْفِيْقَ اَهْلِ الْهُدٰى ﴿٣٧﴾

37. O Allah! I ask of you to grant me *taufeeq* (ability) like that of the people of guidance,

وَاَعْمَالَ اَهْلِ الْيَقِيْنِ وَمُنَاصَحَةَ اَهْلِ التَّوْبَةِ

actions like that of the people of yaqeen (conviction), sincerity like those who repent for their sins,

وَعَزْمَ اَهْلِ الصَّبْرِ وَجِدَّ اَهْلِ الْخَشْيَةِ وَطَلَبَ

courage like those who make *sabr* (patience), sacrifice like those who have fear, aspirations as possessed

اَهْلِ الرَّغْبَةِ وَتَعَبُّدَ اَهْلِ الْوَرْعِ وَعِرْفَانَ اَهْلِ

by those who are endowed with Your love, *ibaadat* (worship) like that of the pious and recognition like that of the

الْعِلْمِ حَتّٰى اَلْقَاكَ. اَللّٰهُمَّ اِنِّى اَسْاَلُكَ مَخَافَةً

Ulama. And allow all of these (blessings) to remain with me till I meet with You. O Allah! I beg of You to bless me with such fear

37. Musnad Firdaus # 1841

تَحْجُزُنِيْ عَنْ مَّعَاصِيْكَ حَتّٰى اَعْمَلَ بِطَاعَتِكَ

which would prevent me from committing sins so that I may do acts of obedience for You

عَمَلًا اَسْتَحِقُّ بِهٖ رِضَاكَ وَحَتّٰى اُنَاصِحَكَ

in a way that I will receive Your pleasure, and I may

بِالتَّوْبَةِ خَوْفًا مِّنْكَ وَحَتّٰى اُخْلِصَ لَكَ

repent earnestly before You out of fear for You, that I may be encouraged to do

النَّصِيْحَةَ حَيَاءً مِّنْكَ وَحَتّٰى اَتَوَكَّلَ عَلَيْكَ فِيْ

acts of worship out of special regards for You, and I may rely purely on You in all matters and

الْاُمُوْرِ كُلِّهَا وَحُسْنَ ظَنٍّ بِكَ سُبْحَانَ خَالِقٍ

hope for the best from You, O The Unblemished Creator

النُّوْرِ

of light.

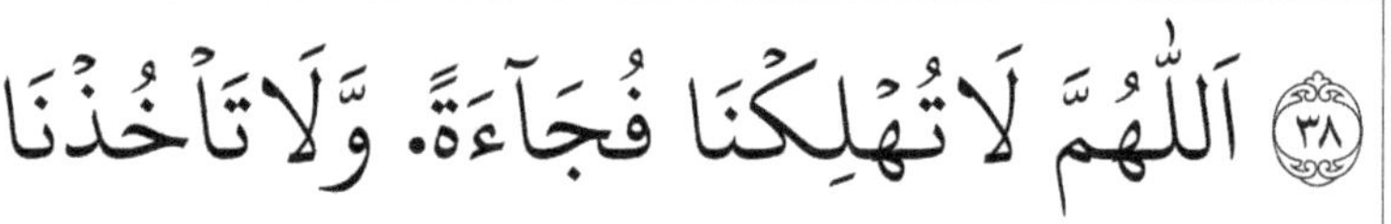

اَللّٰهُمَّ لَاتُهْلِكْنَا فُجَآءَةً. وَّلَاتَأْخُذْنَا

38. O Allah! Do not cause us to die a sudden death, nor seize us

بَغْتَةً. وَّلَاتُغْفِلْنَا عَنْ حَقٍّ وَّلَاوَصِيَّةٍ

by surprise nor make us unmindful of any duty or advice.

اَللّٰهُمَّ اٰنِسْ وَحْشَتِيْ فِيْ قَبْرِيْ

39. O Allah! Make me feel comfortable in the loneliness of the grave.

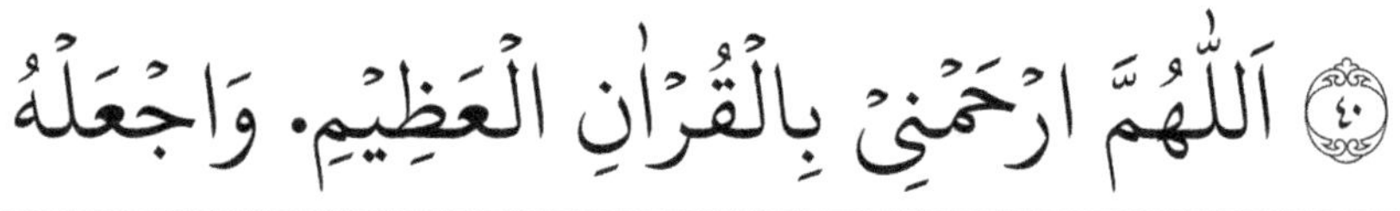

اَللّٰهُمَّ ارْحَمْنِيْ بِالْقُرْاٰنِ الْعَظِيْمِ. وَاجْعَلْهُ

40. O Allah! Have mercy on me through the blessings of the Qur-aan shareef and make it

| 38. Jam'ul Fawaaid # 108 | 39. Kanzul Ummaal # 2781 | 40. Ihyaul. U # 3551 |

لِيْ اِمَامًا وَّنُوْرًا وَّهُدًى وَّرَحْمَةً. اَللّٰهُمَّ ذَكِّرْنِيْ

a guide for me, a source of light, a source of guidance and a source of mercy as well. O Allah, make me remember

مِنْهُ مَا نَسِيْتُ. وَعَلِّمْنِيْ مِنْهُ مَا جَهِلْتُ.

what I have forgotten of the Qur-aan, and grant me an understanding of those parts which I am ignorant about.

وَارْزُقْنِيْ تِلَاوَتَهٗ اٰنَآءَ الَّيْلِ وَاٰنَآءَ النَّهَارِ.

Enable me to recite it during the hours of the night and day

وَاجْعَلْهُ لِيْ حُجَّةً يَّا رَبَّ الْعَالَمِيْنَ

and make it a proof in my favour, O Rabb of the worlds.

اَللّٰهُمَّ اَنَا عَبْدُكَ وَابْنُ عَبْدِكَ وَابْنُ ﴿٤١﴾

41. O Allah! I am Your servant and the son of Your servant, the son

41. Tanzeehush Shari'ah # 76

اَمَتِكَ نَاصِيَتِیْ بِيَدِكَ. اَتَقَلَّبُ فِیْ قَبْضَتِكَ.

of Your bondswoman. I am always within Your grasp, my movements are under Your control,

وَاُصَدِّقُ بِلِقَآئِكَ. وَاُوْمِنُ بِوَعْدِكَ. اَمَرْتَنِیْ

I testify to meeting You, I believe in Your promise. You commanded me

فَعَصَيْتُ. وَنَهَيْتَنِیْ فَاَبَيْتُ هٰذَا مَكَانُ الْعَآئِذِ

but I disobeyed You. You prohibited me (from doing certain things) but I did not restrain myself. Here is a person who is

بِكَ مِنَ النَّارِ. لَآ اِلٰهَ اِلَّآ اَنْتَ سُبْحَانَكَ ظَلَمْتُ

begging You for safety from the Fire of Hell. There is no deity besides You. You are most pure. I have wronged

نَفْسِیْ فَاغْفِرْلِیْ اِنَّهٗ لَايَغْفِرُ الذُّنُوْبَ اِلَّآ

my soul, please forgive me as none can forgive sins except

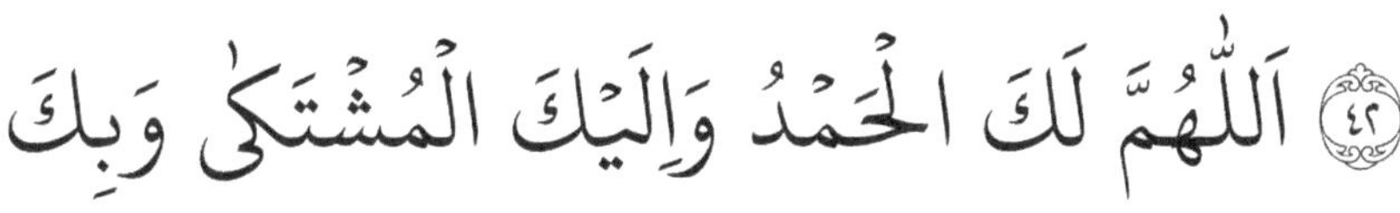

اَنْتَ

You.

اَللّٰهُمَّ لَكَ الْحَمْدُ وَاِلَيْكَ الْمُشْتَكٰى وَبِكَ ﴿٤٢﴾

42. O Allah! all praise is due to You, and before You do I present my complaints.

الْمُسْتَغَاثُ وَاَنْتَ الْمُسْتَعَانُ وَلَاحَوْلَ وَلَاقُوَّةَ

You alone do I ask for help and help is sought from You only. There is no power to do good or strength to stay away from evil

اِلَّا بِاللهِ.

except through Allah Ta'ala.

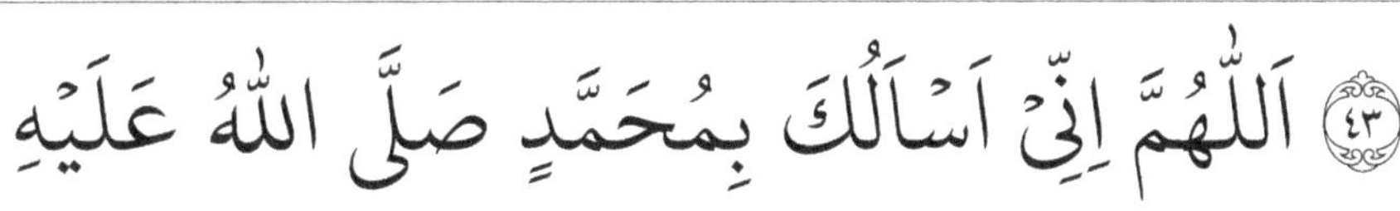

اَللّٰهُمَّ اِنِّى اَسْاَلُكَ بِمُحَمَّدٍ صَلَّى اللهُ عَلَيْهِ ﴿٤٣﴾

43. O Allah! I beg of You through Your Messenger, Muhammad صَلَّى اللّٰهُ عَلَيْهِ وَسَلَّمَ,

| 42. Mu'jamul Awsat # 17427 | 43. Al-La-'aalil Masnoo'ah |

وَسَلَّمَ نَبِيَّكَ. وَاِبْرَاهِيْمَ خَلِيْلِكَ. وَمُوْسٰى

Your friend Ibraaheem عَلَيْهِ ٱلسَّلَامُ, Musa عَلَيْهِ ٱلسَّلَامُ

نَجِيَّكَ. وَعِيْسٰى رُوْحِكَ وَكَلِمَتِكَ. وَبِكَلَامِ

who had the privilege of speaking to you privately, Isa عَلَيْهِ ٱلسَّلَامُ,
Your Rooh (spirit) and Your Word; the speech

مُوْسٰى. وَاِنْجِيْلِ عِيْسٰى. وَزَبُوْرِ دَاوِدَ. وَفُرْقَانِ

of Musa عَلَيْهِ ٱلسَّلَامُ, the Injeel of Isa عَلَيْهِ ٱلسَّلَامُ, the Zaboor of Dawood
عَلَيْهِ ٱلسَّلَامُ and the Qur-aan

مُحَمَّدٍ صَلَّى اللهُ عَلَيْهِ وَسَلَّمَ. وَبِكُلِّ وَحْيٍ

of Nabi Muhammad صَلَّى ٱللَّهُ عَلَيْهِ وَسَلَّمَ and through every revelation
which

اَوْحَيْتَهٗ اَوْقَضَاءٍ قَضَيْتَهٗ اَوْسَآئِلٍ اَعْطَيْتَهٗ

You sent (from time to time), through every decision You have
passed and by virtue of every such person whose request you have

اَوۡ فَقِيۡرٍ اَغۡنَيۡتَهٗ اَوۡ غَنِيٍّ اَفۡقَرۡتَهٗ. اَوۡ ضَآلٍّ

granted, or every poor person whom You have enriched, or every
rich person whom You have reduced to poverty, or every

هَدَيۡتَهٗ. وَاَسۡـَٔلُكَ بِاسۡمِكَ الَّذِىۡ اَنۡزَلۡتَهٗ عَلٰى

misguided person whom You have guided. I beg of You through
Your name which You revealed to

مُوۡسٰى وَاَسۡـَٔلُكَ بِاسۡمِكَ الَّذِىۡ وَضَعۡتَهٗ عَلَى

Musa ﷷ, and I beg of you, through Your name which You
placed on

الۡاَرۡضِ فَاسۡتَقَرَّتۡ. وَعَلَى السَّمٰوَاتِ

the earth, so it became steady, which You placed on the heavens

فَاسۡتَقَلَّتۡ. وَعَلَى الۡجِبَالِ فَرَسَتۡ. وَاَسۡـَٔلُكَ

and they became stationary, which You placed on the mountains
and they became firmly grounded. I beg of You through Your

بِاسْمِكَ الَّذِى اسْتَقَرَّ بِهِ عَرْشُكَ. وَاَسْاَلُكَ

name whereby Your Throne (Arsh) is stable, and through

بِاسْمِكَ الطَّاهِرِ الْمُطَهَّرِ الْمُنَزَّلِ فِى كِتَابِكَ

Your pure and clean name which is revealed in Your Book and

مِنْ لَّدُنْكَ وَبِاسْمِكَ الَّذِى وَضَعْتَهُ عَلَى النَّهَارِ

through Your name which You placed on the day

فَاسْتَنَارَ. وَعَلَى اللَّيْلِ فَاَظْلَمَ. وَبِعَظَمَتِكَ

and it brightened, and on the night so it became dark, and through
Your greatness,

وَكِبْرِيَآئِكَ وَبِنُوْرِ وَجْهِكَ اَنْ تَرْزُقَنِىَ الْقُرْاَنَ

glory and the noor (radiance) of Your countenance that You bless
me with the Qur-aan Shareef

الْعَظِيمَ وَتُخْلِطَهُ بِلَحْمِى وَدَمِى وَسَمْعِى

so that it permeates my flesh, my blood, my hearing

وَبَصَرِى وَتَسْتَعْمِلَ بِهٖ جَسَدِى بِحَوْلِكَ

and my seeing. Grant me, through Your power, the ability that I may act upon it

وَقُوَّتِكَ فَاِنَّهُ لَاحَوْلَ وَ لَاقُوَّةَ اِلَّابِكَ

as I have no ability or strength except from You.

(٤٤) بِسْمِ اللهِ ذِى الشَّاْنِ عَظِيمِ الْبُرْهَانِ

44. I begin with the name of Allah who is full of grandeur, sound arguments and

شَدِيدِ السُّلْطَانِ مَاشَآءَ اللهُ كَانَ. اَعُوْذُ بِاللهِ

overpowering might. Whatever He willed has happened. I seek the protection of Allah

44. Kanzul Ummaal # 17

مِنَ الشَّيْطَانِ الرَّجِيْمِ.

from the accursed devil.

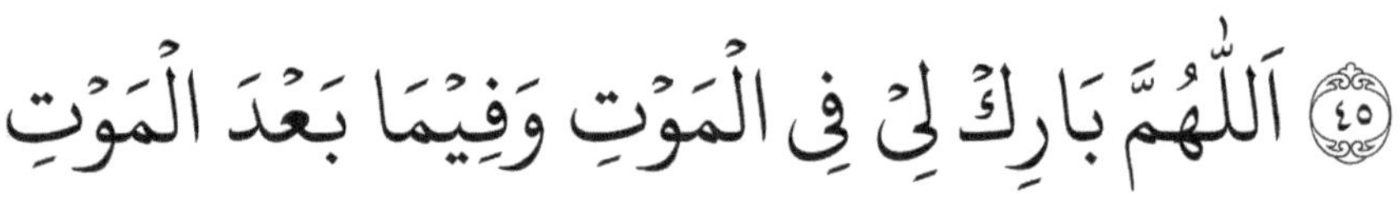

45. O Allah! Bless me at the time of my death and (bless me) in what follows after death.

Recite the above dua 25 times daily.

(٤٦) اَللّٰهُمَّ لَاتُؤَمِّنَّا مَكْرَكَ وَلَا تُنْسِنَا ذِكْرَكَ

46. O Allah! Do not make us fearless of Your secret planning, let not Your remembrance die out from our hearts,

وَلَاتَهْتِكْ عَنَّا سِتْرَكَ وَلَاتَجْعَلْنَا مِنَ

do not remove Your covering over our faults and do not make us from

---

45. Mu'jamul Awsat #7676   46. Musnadul Firdaus # 2017

الْغَافِلِيْنَ

the unmindful.

﴿٤٧﴾ اَللّٰهُمَّ اِنِّیْ اَعُوْذُ بِكَ مِنْ ضِيْقِ الدُّنْيَا

47. O Allah! I seek Your protection from narrowness (distress) in this world

وَضِيْقِ يَوْمِ الْقِيَامَةِ

and on the Day of Judgement.

﴿٤٨﴾ اَللّٰهُمَّ اِنِّیْ اَسْاَلُكَ تَعْجِيْلَ عَافِيَتِكَ وَدَفْعَ

48. O Allah! I beg of You the hastening of ease and comfort upon me, the removal

بَلَآئِكَ وَخُرُوْجًا مِّنَ الدُّنْيَاۤ اِلٰى رَحْمَتِكَ

of afflictions and leaving this world towards Your mercy.

47. Abu Dawood # 5085	48. Kanzul Ummaal # 3698

49. O The One who suffices (us) from everyone else and the One from whom none can be self-sufficient.

O The Being who is One and has no equal. O the One who does not need any support and is a support for everyone else,

all hopes have been cut off except from You. Give me salvation from

the situation in which I am and help me in the affliction that I find myself in,

through Your benevolence and by virtue of the right of Nabi Muhammad ﷺ

49. Kanzul Ummaal # 3425

عَلَيْهِ وَسَلَّمَ عَلَيْكَ اَمِيْنَ

on You. Aameen!

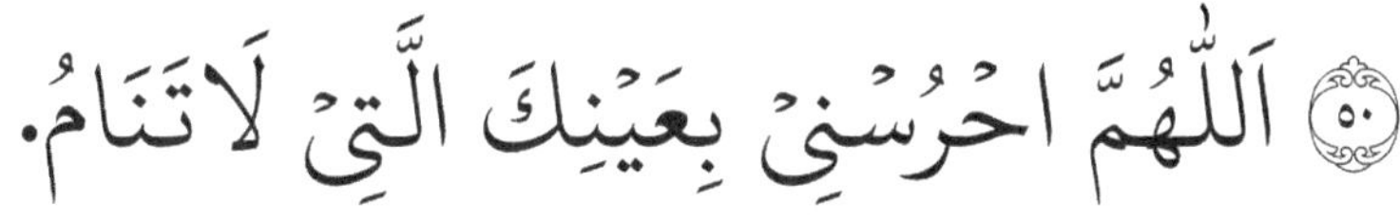

اَللّٰهُمَّ احْرُسْنِيْ بِعَيْنِكَ الَّتِيْ لَاتَنَامُ.

50. O Allah! Take care of me through Your eyes which never sleep,

وَاكْنُفْنِيْ بِرُكْنِكَ الَّذِيْ لَا يُرَامُ. وَارْحَمْنِيْ

embrace me with Your strength from which no one can be separated and have mercy on me

بِقُدْرَتِكَ عَلَيَّ فَلَآ اَهْلِكُ وَاَنْتَ رَجَآئِيْ

through Your power so that I may not be destroyed. (O Allah) You are my only hope. How many

فَكَمْ مِنْ نِّعْمَةٍ اَنْعَمْتَ بِهَا عَلَيَّ. قَلَّ لَكَ بِهَا

gifts have You showered upon me for which I was deficient in offering

50. Kanzul Ummaal # 3441

شُكْرِى وَكَمْ مِنْ بَلِيَّةٍ ابْتَلَيْتَنِى بِهَا قَلَّ لَكَ

gratitude to You. Many were the occasions on which You tested me and I was found lacking

بِهَا صَبْرِى. فَيَا مَنْ قَلَّ عِنْدَ نِعْمَتِهٖ شُكْرِى

in patience. O the One who did not deprive me of His Grace despite my ungratefulness,

فَلَمْ يَحْرِمْنِى وَيَا مَنْ قَلَّ عِنْدَ بَلِيَّتِهٖ صَبْرِى

who did not disgrace me in spite of my impatience

فَلَمْ يَخْذُلْنِى. وَيَا مَنْ رَاٰنِى عَلَى الْخَطَايَا فَلَمْ

and who witnessed my sins but did not

يَفْضَحْنِى. يَاذَا الْمَعْرُوْفِ الَّذِى لَايَنْقَضِى

expose them. O the One who is full of everlasting goodness

أَبَدًا. وَيَاذَا النَّعْمَاءِ الَّتِيْ لَا تُحْصَى أَبَدًا

that never ends and O You who distributes favours that cannot be counted,

اَسْاَلُكَ اَنْ تُصَلِّيَ عَلٰى مُحَمَّدٍ صَلَّى اللهُ عَلَيْهِ

I beg of You to shower Your blessings on Nabi Muhammad ﷺ

وَسَلَّمَ وَعَلٰى اٰلِ مُحَمَّدٍ صَلَّى اللهُ عَلَيْهِ وَسَلَّمَ

and his progeny.

وَبِكَ اَدْرَاُ فِيْ نُحُوْرِ الْاَعْدَاءِ وَالْجَبَابِرَة

O Allah! With Your help do we repel our enemies and oppressors

اَللّٰهُمَّ اَعِنِّيْ عَلٰى دِيْنِيْ بِالدُّنْيَا وَعَلٰى اٰخِرَتِيْ

O Allah! Assist me in my Deen through this world, and in my hereafter

بِالتَّقْوٰى. وَاحْفَظْنِي فِيْمَا غِبْتُ عَنْـهُ. وَلَا

through piety, look after my affairs which are hidden from me

تَكِلْنِيْ اِلٰى نَفْسِيْ فِيْمَا حَضَرْتُهٗ يَا مَنْ

and do not leave me alone to deal with those affairs which are
before me. O the One whom the sins of the creation cannot harm

لَّا تَضُرُّهُ الذُّنُوْبُ وَلَا تَنْقُصُهُ الْمَغْفِرَةُ هَبْ لِيْ مَا

and who loses nothing by forgiving, favour me with that which
does not

لَا يَنْقُصُكَ وَاغْفِرْلِيْ مَا لَا يَضُرُّكَ اِنَّكَ اَنْـتَ

cause You any loss (i.e. forgiveness) and forgive me from what
does not cause You any harm (i.e. sins). Verily You are

الْوَهَّابُ. اَسْاَلُكَ فَرَجًا قَرِيْبًا وَّصَبْرًا جَمِـيْـلًا

a Generous Giver. O Allah! I beg of You for an instant solution in
every calamity, remarkable patience,

وَّرِزْقًا وَّاسِعًا وَّالْعَافِيَةَ مِنْ جَمِيعِ الْبَلَآءِ.

abundant sustenance and safety from all trials

وَاَسْأَلُكَ تَمَامَ الْعَافِيَةِ. وَاَسْأَلُكَ دَوَامَ

and I beg of You for perfect ease and lasting

الْعَافِيَةِ. وَاَسْأَلُكَ الشُّكْرَ عَلَى الْعَافِيَةِ.

ease and the ability to be grateful for it

وَاَسْأَلُكَ الْغِنٰى عَنِ النَّاسِ وَلَاحَوْلَ وَلَاقُوَّةَ

and I beg of You for total independence from others. There is no ability or strength in us

اِلَّا بِاللهِ الْعَلِيِّ الْعَظِيْمِ

except with the help of Allah! Most High and most Great.

(٥١) يَا رَبِّ يَا رَبِّ يَا رَبِّ يَا رَبِّ

51. O my Rabb, O my Rabb, O my Rabb.

اَللّٰهُمَّ يَا كَبِيْرُ يَا سَمِيْعُ يَا بَصِيْرُ يَا مَنْ لَّا

1. O Allah! O The Greatest, O The One who hears and sees all things, O The One who has

شَرِيْكَ لَهٗ وَلَا وَزِيْرَ لَهٗ وَيَا خَالِقَ الشَّمْسِ

no partner and no advisor, O The Creator of the sun

وَالْقَمَرِ الْمُنِيْرِ وَيَا عِصْمَةَ الْبَائِسِ الْخَآئِفِ

and the brilliant moon, O The One who is the Refuge for a fearful destitute

الْمُسْتَجِيْرِ وَيَا رَازِقَ الطِّفْلِ الصَّغِيْرِ وَيَا

longing for protection. O The Nourisher of an infant, O

Tanzeehush Shari'atil Marfoo'ah # 330

جَابِرَ الْعَظْمِ الْكَسِيْرِ ۰ اَدْعُوْكَ دُعَاءَ الْبَآئِسِ

The Healer of a fractured bone, I beg You like the begging of a

الْفَقِيْرِ كَدُعَاءِ الْمُضْطَرِّ الضَّرِيْرِ ۰ اَسْاَلُكَ

poor beggar or a helpless blind man. I beg You

بِمَعَاقِدِ الْعِزِّ مِنْ عَرْشِكَ وَبِمَفَاتِيْحِ الرَّحْمَةِ

through Your Throne which is wrapped in dignity, through the keys of mercy

مِنْ كِتَابِكَ وَبِالْاَسْمَآءِ الثَّمَانِيَةِ الْمَكْتُوْبَةِ

which is contained in Your Book and through the eight names which are written

عَلَى قَرْنِ الشَّمْسِ اَنْ تَجْعَلَ الْقُرْاَنَ رَبِيْعَ

on the edge of the rising sun that You make the Qur-aan shareef a source of comfort

قَلْبِيْ وَجَلَاۤءَ حُزْنِيْ رَبَّنَاۤ اٰتِنَا فِى الدُّنْيَا

to my heart and a cure for my grief. O our Rabb, bless us in this world with.........

(كَذَا وَكَذَا)

(here mention whatever you desire).

يَا مُوْنِسَ كُلِّ وَحِيْدٍ. وَيَا صَاحِبَ كُلِّ

2. O The Comforter and Companion of every lonely person,

فَرِيْدٍ. وَيَا قَرِيْبًا غَيْرَ بَعِيْدٍ. وَيَا شَاهِدًا غَيْرَ

O The One who is near and never far, O The One who is present and never

غَاۤئِبٍ. وَيَا غَالِبًا غَيْرَ مَغْلُوْبٍ. يَا حَیُّ يَا

absent, O You who subjugates all but is never overpowered in any way, O The Everlasting

2. Kanzul Ummaal # 5103

قَيُّوْمُ. يَا ذَا الْجَلَالِ وَالْاِكْرَامِ

and Sustainer, The Majestic and Benevolent.

٣ يَا نُوْرَ السَّمٰوَاتِ وَالْاَرْضِ. يَا زَيْنَ

3. O The One who is the light of the heavens and the earth. O The One who is the beauty of the heavens

السَّمٰوَاتِ وَالْاَرْضِ. يَا جَبَّارَ السَّمٰوَاتِ

and the earth. O The Mighty Sovereign of the heavens and earth.

وَالْاَرْضِ. يَا عِمَادَ السَّمٰوَاتِ وَالْاَرْضِ. يَا

The sole supporter of the heavens and earth.

بَدِيْعَ السَّمٰوَاتِ وَالْاَرْضِ. يَا قَيَّامَ السَّمٰوَاتِ

The Originator of the heavens and earth. O The Sustainer of the heavens

3. Majma'uz Zawaaid # 10 : 179

وَالْاَرْضِ. يَاذَا الْجَلَالِ وَالْاِكْرَامِ. يَا صَرِيْخَ

and earth. The Majestic and Kind. O The One who answers

الْمُسْتَصْرِخِيْنَ. وَمُنْتَهَى الْعَآئِذِيْنَ

the pleas of people and is the last resort for those who seek protection,

وَالْمُفَرِّجَ عَنِ الْمَكْرُوْبِيْنَ وَالْمُرَوِّحَ عَنِ

O You Who relieves people in distress, soothes the sorrow

الْمَغْمُوْمِيْنَ وَمُجِيْبَ دُعَآءِ الْمُضْطَرِّيْنَ. وَيَا

of the grieving and responds favourably to the duas of those in difficulty.

كَاشِفَ الْكُرَبِ يَا اِلٰهَ الْعَالَمِيْنَ. وَيَآ اَرْحَمَ

O The One who removes all uneasiness. O The Rabb of the worlds. O The One who is Most Merciful

الرَّاحِمِيْنَ مَنْزُوْلٌ بِكَ كُلُّ حَاجَةٍ

and Compassionate, we humbly place all our needs before You.

اَللّٰهُمَّ اِنِّيْ اَعُوْذُ بِكَ مِنْ مَوْتِ الْهَمِّ ۞

4. O Allah! I seek Your protection from death in a state of worry

وَاَعُوْذُ بِكَ مِنْ مَوْتِ الْغَمِّ ۰ وَاَعُوْذُ بِكَ مِنَ

And I seek your protection from death in a state of grief, and I seek Your protection from

الْجُوْعِ فَاِنَّهُ بِئْسَ الضَّجِيْعُ وَاَعُوْذُ بِكَ مِنَ

hunger as it is an evil companion and from

الْخِيَانَةِ فَاِنَّهَا بِئْسَتِ الْبِطَانَةُ

dishonesty as it is the worst of character.

4. Kanzul Ummaal # 3775

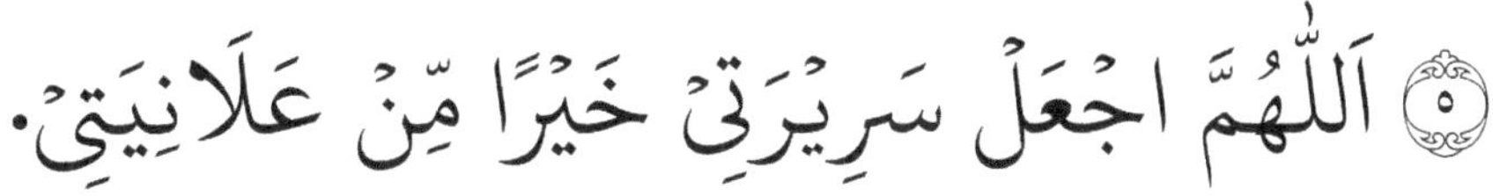

اَللّٰهُمَّ اجْعَلْ سَرِيْرَتِيْ خَيْرًا مِّنْ عَلَانِيَتِيْ.

5. O Allah! Make my inner self better than my outer self

وَاجْعَلْ عَلَانِيَتِيْ صَالِحَةً. اَللّٰهُمَّ اِنِّيْ اَسْأَلُكَ

and make my outer self pious and righteous. O Allah! I beg of You to

مِنْ صَالِحِ مَا تُؤْتِي النَّاسَ مِنَ الْمَالِ وَالْاَهْلِ

bless me with all the good that You have blessed others by way of wealth, spouse

وَالْوَلَدِ غَيْرَ ضَالٍّ وَّلَا مُضِلٍّ

and children who are not misguided and do not misguide others.

اَللّٰهُمَّ اجْعَلْنَا مِنْ عِبَادِكَ الْمُنْتَخَبِيْنَ

6. O Allah! Include us among Your selected servants whose

5. Tirmizi # 3586	6. Musnad Ahmad # 16126

اَلْغُرِّ الْمُحَجَّلِيْنَ الْوَفْدِ الْمُتَقَبَّلِيْنَ

hands and feet are shining and they belong to the group of Your accepted ones.

⑦ اَللّٰهُمَّ اِنِّىْ اَعُوْذُ بِكَ مِنْ اَنْ اُشْرِكَ بِكَ شَيْئًا

7. O Allah! I seek Your protection from joining any partners with You

وَّاَنَا اَعْلَمُ بِهٖ وَاَسْتَغْفِرُكَ لِمَا لَاۤ اَعْلَمُ بِهٖ

knowingly and I beg Your forgiveness for all that I have done unknowingly.

⑧ اَللّٰهُمَّ اِنِّىْ اَعُوْذُ بِوَجْهِكَ الْكَرِيْمِ

8. O Allah! By Your magnificent countenance and Your great name

وَبِاسْمِكَ الْعَظِيْمِ مِنَ الْكُفْرِ وَالْفَقْرِ

I seek Your protection from kufr (disbelief) and poverty.

7. Al Adabul Mufrad # 716	8. Jaami'us Sageer # 1542

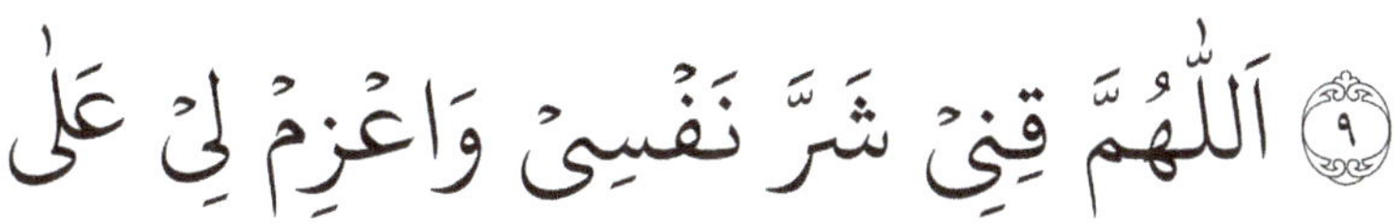

اَللّٰهُمَّ قِنِيْ شَرَّ نَفْسِيْ وَاعْزِمْ لِيْ عَلٰى

9. O Allah! Save me from the evil of my carnal desires and give me the courage to discharge

اَرْشَدِ اَمْرِيْ

my responsibilities in the best possible manner.

اَللّٰهُمَّ لَاتَكِلْنِيْ اِلٰى نَفْسِيْ طَرْفَةَ عَيْنٍ

10. O Allah! Do not leave me to myself for the blinking of an eye

وَلَا تَنْزِعْ مِنِّيْ صَالِحَ مَا اَعْطَيْتَنِيْ فَاِنَّهٗ لَانَازِعَ

and do not take away from me whatever good You have already bestowed upon me, as none can take away what

لِمَا اَعْطَيْتَ وَلَا يَعْصِمُ ذَا الْجَدِّ مِنْكَ الْجَدُّ.

You have bestowed and the wealth of the wealthy cannot safeguard them.

9. Musnad Ahmad # 1949	10. Kanzul Ummaal # 3674

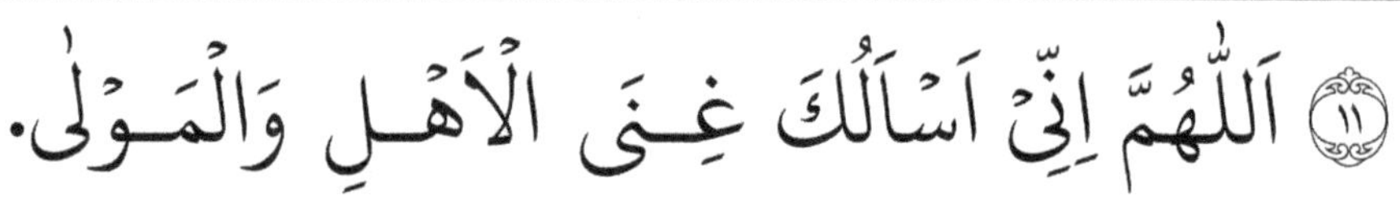

⟨١١⟩ اَللّٰهُمَّ اِنِّیْ اَسْاَلُكَ غِنَـی الْاَهْـلِ وَالْمَـوْلٰی.

11. O Allah! I beg You for the prosperity of my family members and those who bring me comfort.

وَاَعُوْذُ بِكَ اَنْ يَّدْعُوَ عَلَیَّ رَحِمٌ قَطَعْتُهَا.

and I seek Your protection from the curse of a relative whom I have cut off ties with.

⟨١٢⟩ اَللّٰهُمَّ اِنِّیْ اَسْاَلُكَ نَفْسًا بِكَ مُطْمَئِنَّةً.

12. O Allah! I beg of You for a heart which is at peace with You,

تُؤْمِنُ بِلِقَآئِكَ. وَتَـرْضٰی بِقَـضَآئِكَ. وَتَقْنَعُ

which believes in meeting You, is pleased with Your decree and is contented

بِعَطَآئِكَ

with Your gifts.

11. Mu'jamul Kabeer # 4849	12. Mu'jamul Kabeer # 749

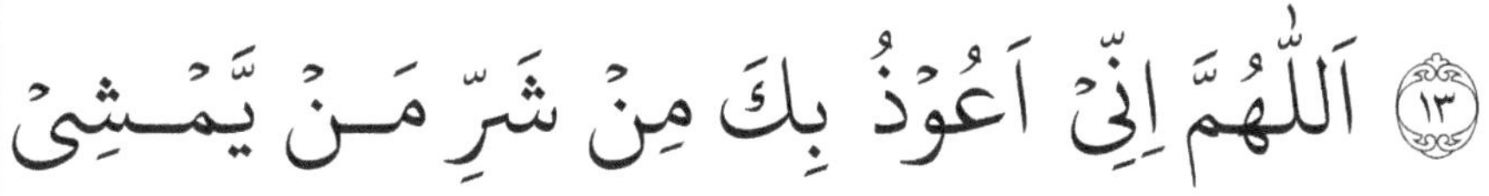

اَللّٰهُمَّ اِنِّىْ اَعُوْذُ بِكَ مِنْ شَرِّ مَنْ يَّمْشِىْ

13. O Allah! I seek Your protection from the evil of those (animals) which crawl on

عَلٰى بَطْنِهٖ۔ وَمِنْ شَرِّ مَنْ يَّمْشِىْ عَلٰى رِجْلَيْنِ

their bellies, those animals which walk on two legs and those

وَمِنْ شَرِّ مَنْ يَّمْشِىْ عَلٰى اَرْبَعٍ

which walk on four legs.

اَللّٰهُمَّ اِنِّىْ اَعُوْذُ بِكَ مِنِ امْرَاَةٍ تُشَيِّبُنِىْ قَبْلَ

14. O Allah! I seek Your protection from a wife who makes me old

الْمَشِيْبِ وَاَعُوْذُ بِكَ مِنْ وَّلَدٍ يَّكُوْنُ عَلَىَّ

before my time, from children who become

13. Kanzul Ummaal # 379   14. Musnad Al-Firdaus # 5974

وَبَالًا وَاَعُوْذُ بِكَ مِنْ مَّالٍ يَّكُوْنُ عَلَىَّ عَذَابًا

a nuisance to me, from wealth which becomes a punishment for me

وَاَعُوْذُ بِكَ مِنْ صَاحِبٍ خَدِيْعَةٍ اِنْ رَّأَى

and from a disloyal friend who conceals my good

حَسَنَةً دَفَنَهَا وَاِنْ رَّأَى سَيِّئَةً اَفْشَاهَا

and discloses my faults far and wide.

﴿١٥﴾ اَللّٰهُمَّ اِنَّكَ تَعْلَمُ سِرِّىْ وَعَلَانِيَتِىْ فَاقْبَلْ

15. O Allah! You know well what I conceal and what I reveal so please accept

مَعْذِرَتِىْ. وَتَعْلَمُ حَاجَتِىْ فَاَعْطِنِىْ سُؤْلِىْ

my repentance. (O Allah) You know my needs so please bless me with what I am begging for

15. Mu'jamul Awsat # 5974

وَتَعْلَمُ مَا فِىْ نَفْسِىْ فَاغْفِرْلِىْ ذُنُوْبِىْ۔ اَللّٰهُمَّ

and You know what is in my heart so please forgive my sins. O Allah!

اِنِّىْ اَسْاَلُكَ اِيْمَانًا يُّبَاشِرُ قَلْبِىْ وَيَقِيْنًا صَادِقًا

I beg of You to bless me with such Imaan that penetrates my heart and the proper (yaqeen) conviction

حَتّٰى اَعْلَمَ اَنَّهٗ لَايُصِيْبُنِىْ اِلَّا مَا كَتَبْتَ لِىْ

which will enable me to realise that whatever befalls me was already predestined by You for me.

وَرِضًا بِمَا قَسَمْتَ لِىْ اِنَّكَ عَلٰى كُلِّ شَىْءٍ قَدِيْرٌ

Allow me to be pleased with whatever You have apportioned for me. Verily You have power over everything.

اَللّٰهُمَّ لَكَ الْحَمْدُ حَمْدًا دَآئِمًا مَّعَ دَوَامِكَ ﴿١٦﴾

16. O Allah! You alone are worthy of such praise which remains eternal with Your eternity.

16. Kanzul Ummaal # 3854

وَلَكَ الْحَمْدُ حَمْدًا خَالِدًا مَّعَ خُلُوْدِكَ وَلَكَ

You alone are worthy of praise which is continuous with Your continuity. You alone

الْحَمْدُ حَمْدًا لَّامُنْتَـهَى لَهُ دُوْنَ مَـشِيْئَتِكَ

are worthy of praise which will not end except by Your will.

وَلَكَ الْحَمْدُ حَمْدًا دَآئِمًا لَّايُرِيْدُ قَآئِلُهُ اِلَّا

You alone are worthy of eternal praise, in a manner in which the one praising You desires nothing but

رِضَاكَ وَلَكَ الْحَمْدُ حَمْـدًا عِنْـدَ كُلِّ طَرْفَـةِ

Your pleasure. You alone are worthy of praise at every blink of the eye,

عَيْنٍ وَّتَنَفُّسٍ كُلِّ نَفَسٍ

and at every breath.

اَللّٰهُمَّ اَقْبِلْ بِقَلْبِيْ اِلٰى دِيْنِكَ وَاحْفَظْ مِنْ

17. O Allah! Turn my heart towards Your Deen and guard us from

وَرَآءِنَا بِرَحْمَتِكَ

behind through Your Mercy.

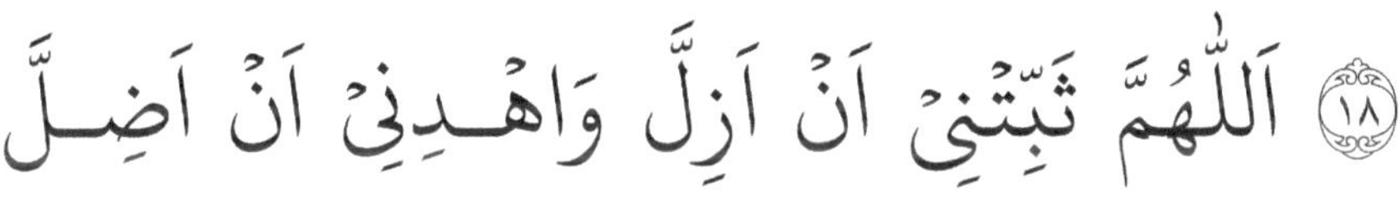

اَللّٰهُمَّ ثَبِّتْنِيْ اَنْ اَزِلَّ وَاهْـدِنِيْ اَنْ اَضِـلَّ

18. O Allah! Keep me firm lest I should slip (from the right path) and continue to guide me lest I should be misguided.

اَللّٰهُمَّ كَمَا حُلْتَ بَيْنِيْ وَبَيْنَ قَلْبِيْ فَحُلْ بَيْنِيْ

O Allah! As You have intervened between me and my heart, intervene between me

وَبَيْنَ الشَّيْطَانِ وَعَمَلِهٖ

and shaytaan and his evil doings.

17. Musnad Abi Ya'la # 3485	18. Ma'rifatus Sahaabah # 10

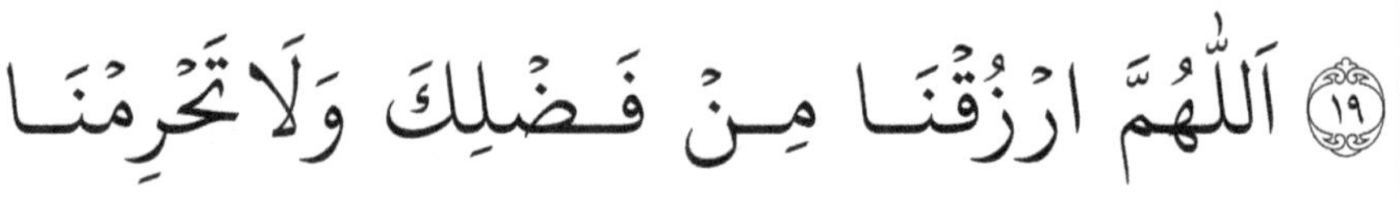

19. O Allah! Grant us (rizq) sustenance by Your Grace, do not deprive us

of Your sustenance, add barkat (blessings) to the sustenance You grant us, favour us

with the wealth of contentment and grant us a passion for that which is

with You (i.e. spiritual blessings).

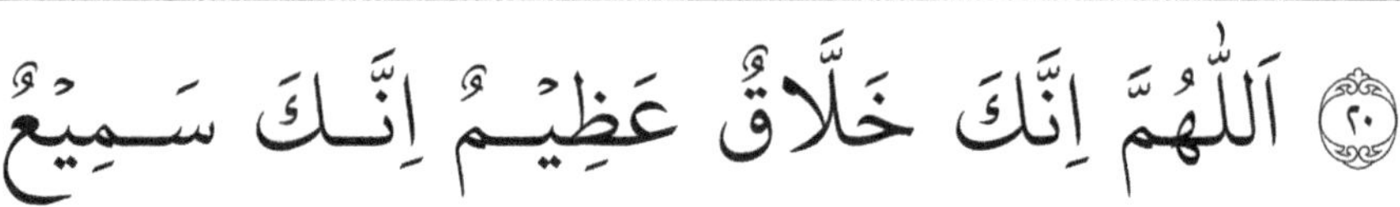

20. O Allah! You are the Creator, full of greatness. You hear

19. Kanzul Ummaal # 38	20. Kanzul Ummaal # 5111

عَلِيْمٌ اِنَّكَ غَفُوْرٌ رَّحِيْمٌ اِنَّكَ رَبُّ الْعَرْشِ

and know everything. You are Forgiving and Merciful and You are indeed the Rabb of the

الْعَظِيْمِ. اَللّٰهُمَّ اِنَّكَ الْبَرُّ الْجَوَّادُ الْكَرِيْمُ

Great Throne. O Allah! You are extremely Compassionate, Generous and Kind.

اِغْفِرْلِيْ وَارْحَمْنِيْ وَعَافِنِيْ وَارْزُقْنِيْ وَاسْتُرْنِيْ

Please forgive me and have mercy on me. Grant me ease and sustenance, cover my faults,

وَاجْبُرْنِيْ وَارْفَعْنِيْ وَاهْدِنِيْ وَلَا تُضِلَّنِيْ

restore my losses, elevate me, guide me, do not let me go astray

وَاَدْخِلْنِيَ الْجَنَّةَ بِرَحْمَتِكَ يَآ اَرْحَمَ

and admit me to Jannah through Your Mercy, O Most

الرَّاحِمِيْنَ.

Merciful of those who show mercy.

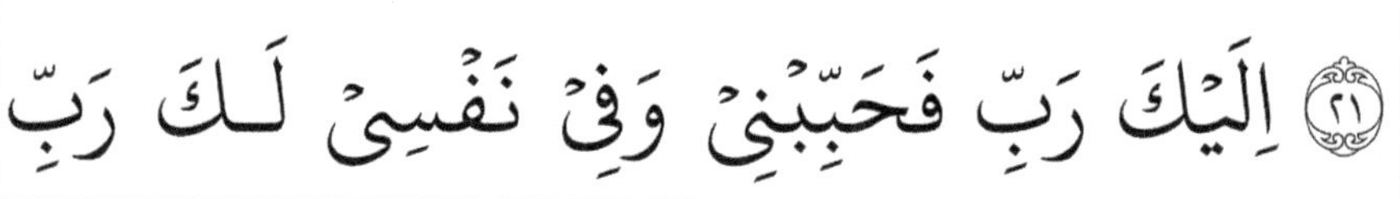

21. O Allah! Make me beloved to You, place in my heart submission towards You

فَذَلِّلْنِيْ وَفِيْ اَعْيُنِ النَّاسِ فَعَظِّمْنِيْ وَمِنْ

and grant me honour in the eyes of the people and save me from

سَيِّئِ الْاَخْلَاقِ فَجَنِّبْنِيْ

evil manners.

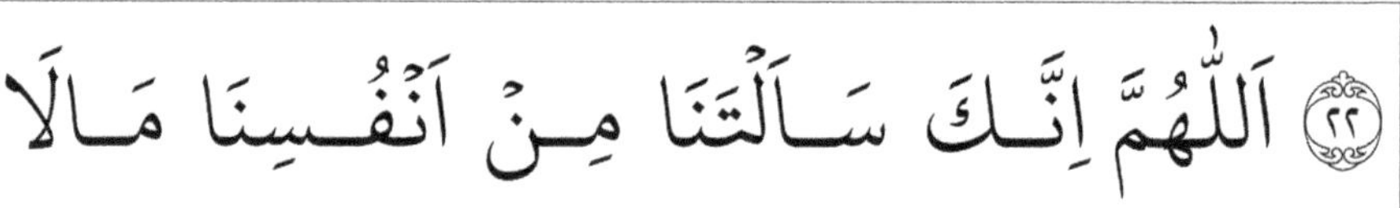

22. O Allah! You have asked us to do things which we are not able to do except

---

21. Kanzul Ummaal # 5087   22. Jaami'us Sagheer # 1459

نَمْلِكُهٗ اِلَّا بِكَ فَاَعْطِنَا مِنْهَا مَا يُرْضِيْكَ عَنَّا

with Your help (i.e. righteous deeds and sincere ibaadat) so grant us the ability to do such deeds which will please You.

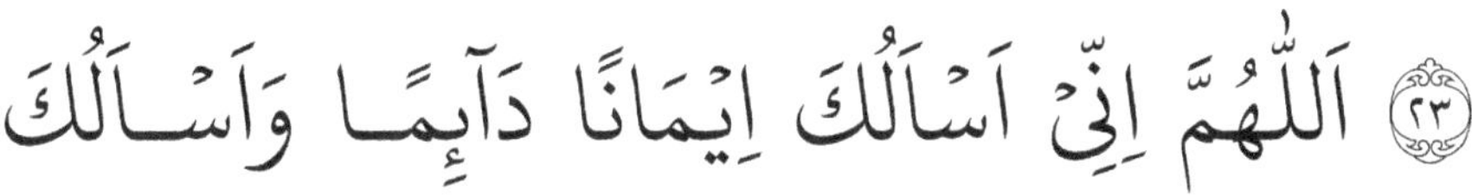

اَللّٰهُمَّ اِنِّیْ اَسْاَلُكَ اِيْمَانًا دَآئِمًا وَاَسْاَلُكَ

23. O Allah! I beg of You (to bless me with) Imaan which remains forever, and I ask You

قَلْبًا خَاشِعًا وَاَسْاَلُكَ يَقِيْنًا صَادِقًا وَاَسْاَلُكَ

for a submissive heart and true conviction. I ask You

دِيْنًا قَيِّمًا وَاَسْاَلُكَ الْعَافِيَةَ مِنْ كُلِّ بَلِيَّةٍ.

for firmness in Deen and I beg You for safety from all mishaps.

وَاَسْاَلُكَ دَوَامَ الْعَافِيَةِ وَاَسْاَلُكَ الشُّكْرَ عَلَى

I beg You for continuous *aafiyat* (ease, safety), I beg You to make me grateful for the

23. Kanzul Ummaal # 5055

اَلْعَافِيَةِ. وَاَسْاَلُكَ الْغِنٰى عَنِ النَّاسِ

aafiyat (ease) You have granted to me and make me independent of people.

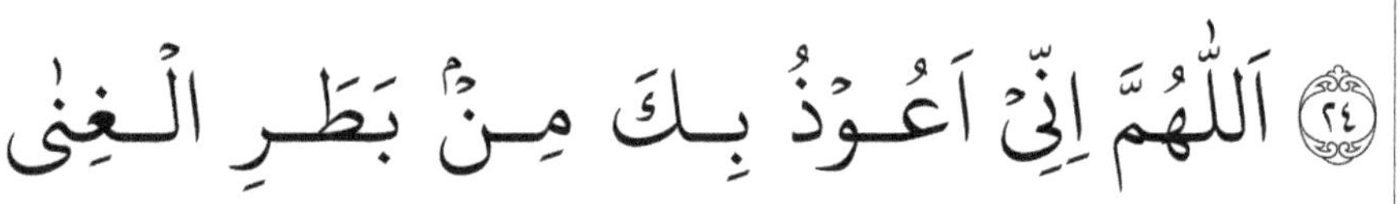

(٢٤) اَللّٰهُمَّ اِنِّىْ اَعُوْذُ بِكَ مِنْ بَطَرِ الْغِنٰى

24. O Allah! I seek Your protection from arrogance due to wealth

وَمَذَلَّةِ الْفَقْرِ يَا مَنْ وَّعَدَ فَوَفٰى. وَاَوْعَدَ فَعَفَا.

and disgrace due to poverty. O The One who fulfils His promises, Who warned us of punishment but instead forgave us,

اِغْفِرْ لِمَنْ ظَلَمَ وَاَسٰى. يَا مَنْ يَّسُرُّهٗ طَاعَتِىْ

please forgive the one who has committed injustice and acted wrongly. O The One to Whom my obedience brings pleasure

وَلَا تَضُرُّهٗ مَعْصِيَتِىْ. هَبْ لِىْ مَا يَسُرُّكَ

and my sins cause Him no harm, grant me what is pleasing to You

24. Musnad al-Firdaus # 460

وَاغْفِرْلِي مَا لَا يَضُرُّكَ

and forgive me, from that which causes You no harm.

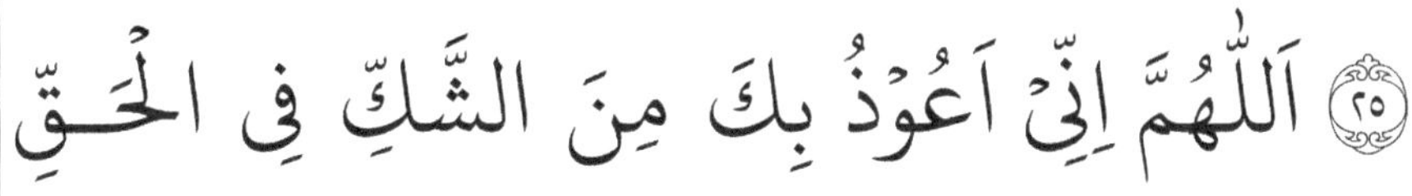

اَللّٰهُمَّ اِنِّيْ اَعُوْذُ بِكَ مِنَ الشَّكِّ فِى الْحَقِّ ۲۵

25. O Allah! I seek Your protection from having doubts in the truth

بَعْدَ الْيَقِيْنِ. وَاَعُوْذُ بِكَ مِنَ الشَّيْطَانِ

after being convinced. I seek Your protection from the

الرَّجِيْمِ. وَاَعُوْذُ بِكَ مِنْ شَرِّ يَوْمِ الدِّيْنِ

accursed devil and I seek Your protection from the evil of the Day of Judgement.

اَللّٰهُمَّ اِنِّيْ اَسْتَغْفِرُكَ لِمَا تُبْتُ اِلَيْكَ مِنْهُ ۲۶

26. O Allah! I beg Your forgiveness for sins which I have committed after having repented for them.

25. Kanzul Ummaal # 3817	26. Kanzul Ummaal# 5124

ثُمَّ عُدْتُ فِيهِ وَاَسْتَغْفِرُكَ لِمَا اَعْطَيْتُكَ مِـنْ

I beg Your forgiveness for all the promises which I made to You

نَفْسِيْ ثُمَّ لَمْ اُوْفِ لَكَ بِهٖ وَاَسْتَغْفِرُكَ

but failed to fulfil them. I beg Your forgiveness

لِلنِّعَمِ الَّتِيْ تَقَوَّيْتُ بِهَا عَلٰى مَعْصِيَتِكَ.

for having used Your favours to commit sins against You.

وَاَسْتَغْفِرُكَ لِكُلِّ خَيْرٍ اَرَدْتُ بِهٖ وَجْهَـكَ

I beg Your forgiveness for all such actions which I intended to do purely for Your sake but

فَخَالَطَنِيْ فِيهِ مَالَيْسَ لَكَ. اَللّٰهُـمَّ لَا تُخْـزِنِيْ

thereafter mixed them with something which was not solely for Your pleasure. O Allah! Do not disgrace me

even though You know everything about me and do not punish me even though You have full power over me.

27. O Allah! Make me from amongst those who placed their trust in You

and then found You to be sufficient. (Make me from those) who sought guidance from You and were then guided and (make me

from those) who asked You for help and then You helped them.

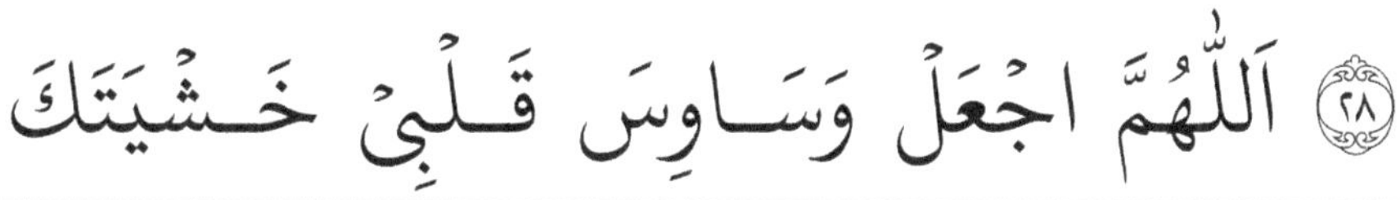

28. O Allah! Change the stray thoughts of my heart into fear for You

27. Kanzul Ummaal # 5106   28. Musnad al-Firdaus # 474

وَذِكْرَكَ وَاجْعَلْ هِمَّتِيْ وَهَـوَاىَ فِيْمَا تُحِبُّ

and remembrance of You, and O Allah! Divert my courage and desires to do such deeds

وَتَرْضٰى. اَللّٰهُمَّ وَمَا ابْتَلَيْتَنِيْ بِهٖ مِـنْ رَّخَآءٍ

which will please You. O Allah! In whichever way You may test me, whether with mildness

وَشِـدَّةٍ فَمَـسِّكْنِيْ بِسُنَّةِ الْحَـقِّ وَشَرِيْعَـةِ

or difficulty, make it such that I remain firm on the path of truth and upon the commandments

الْاِسْلَامِ

of Islam.

اَللّٰهُمَّ اِنِّيْ اَسْاَلُكَ تَمَامَ النِّعْمَةِ فِى الْاَشْيَآءِ ۝

29. O Allah! I beg of You to bless me with complete blessings in all matters

29. Kanzul Ummaal # 5034

كُلِّهَا وَالشُّكْرَ لَكَ عَلَيْهَا حَتَّى تَرْضَى وَبَعْدَ

and I beg You to allow me to be grateful over them until You are pleased and after

الرِّضَا الْخِيَرَةَ فِي جَمِيعِ مَا يَكُونُ فِيهِ الْخِيَرَةُ

being pleased choose for me all those things which are to be chosen and O Allah!

وَبِجَمِيعِ مَيْسُورِ الْأُمُورِ كُلِّهَا لَا بِمَعْسُورِهَا

Most Gracious I ask You for ease in all my tasks not that You make

يَا كَرِيْمُ

it difficult for me, O The Most Kind.

اَللّٰهُمَّ فَالِقَ الْاِصْبَاح وَجَاعِلَ اللَّيْلِ ۩

30. O Allah! The One Who brings out the morning and has made the night

30. Ibnu Abi Shaybah # 26

سَكَنًا وَالشَّمْسَ وَالْقَمَرَ حُسْبَانًا اِقْضِ عَنِّيْ

a time of rest, and the sun and the moon a means of calculating (time), pay out my

الدَّيْنَ وَاَغْنِنِيْ مِنَ الْفَقْرِ وَقَوِّنِيْ عَلَى الْجِهَادِ

debts, free me from poverty and give me the strength to make jihaad

فِيْ سَبِيْلِكَ

in Your path.

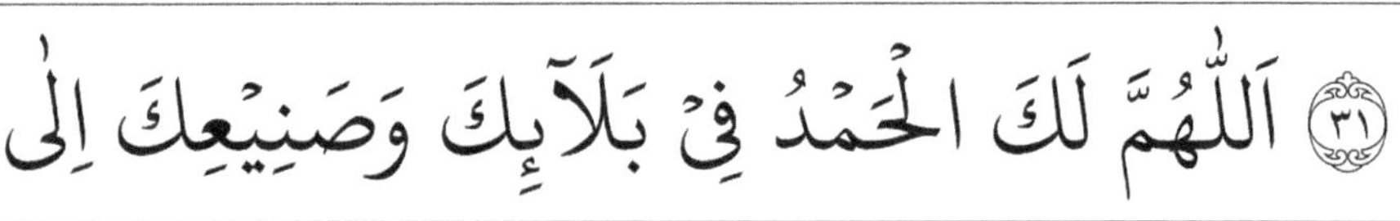

31. O Allah! All praises are due to You in Your tests and doings with

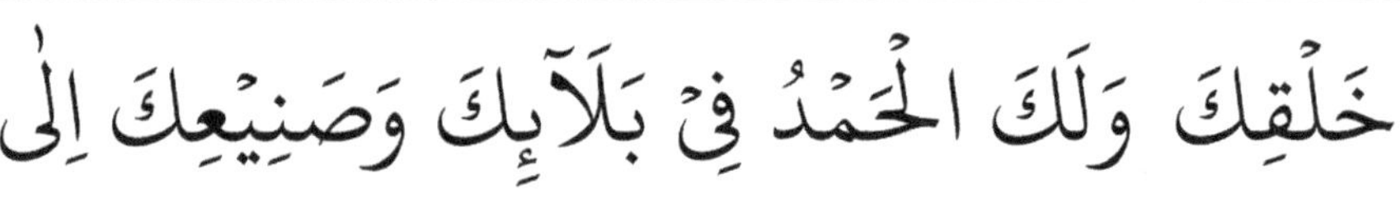

Your creation. All praises are due to You with Your tests and doings with

31. Kanzul Ummaal # 5100

اَهْلِ بُيُوْتِنَا وَلَكَ الْحَمْدُ فِيْ بَلَاۤئِكَ وَصَنِيْعِكَ

our household. All praises are due to You in Your tests and doings

اِلٰۤى اَنْفُسِنَا خَاصَّةً وَّلَكَ الْحَمْدُ بِمَا هَدَيْتَنَا

specifically with our lives. All Praise is due to You for having guided us.

وَلَكَ الْحَمْدُ بِمَاۤ اَكْرَمْتَنَا وَلَكَ الْحَمْدُ بِمَا

Praise is due to You for having honoured us. Praise is due to You for

سَتَرْتَنَا وَلَكَ الْحَمْدُ بِالْقُرْاٰنِ وَلَكَ الْحَمْدُ

covering our faults. Praise is due to You on account of the Qur-aan shareef and praise is due to You

بِالْاَهْلِ وَالْمَالِ وَلَكَ الْحَمْدُ بِالْمُعَافَـاةِ وَلَكَ

for the family and wealth (You bestowed on us). Praise is due to You for having granted us ease

اَلْحَمْدُ حَتّٰى تَرْضٰى وَلَكَ الْحَمْدُ اِذَا رَضِيتَ يَآ

and praise be to You until You are pleased. Praises be upon You when You become pleased, O The

اَهْلَ التَّقْوٰى وَاَهْلَ الْمَغْفِرَةِ

One Who ought to be feared and The One Who is worthy of forgiving (sins).

٣٢ اَللّٰهُمَّ وَفِّقْنِيْ لِمَا تُحِبُّ وَتَرْضٰى مِنَ الْقَوْلِ

32. O Allah! Bless me with the *taufeeq* (ability) to say such words,

وَالْعَمَلِ وَالْفِعْلِ وَالنِّيَّةِ وَالْهُدٰى اِنَّكَ عَلٰى كُلِّ

And do such actions, intentions and acts of guidance that will lead to earning Your pleasure and happiness. Verily You have

شَىْءٍ قَدِيْرٌ

power over everything.

32. Kanzul Ummaal # 3797

٣٣ اَللّٰهُمَّ رَبَّ السَّمٰوَاتِ السَّبْعِ وَرَبَّ الْعَرْشِ

33. O Allah! The Rabb of the seven heavens and The Rabb of the Great

الْعَظِيْمِ. اَللّٰهُمَّ اكْفِنِيْ كُلَّ مُهِمٍّ مِّنْ حَيْثُ

Throne (Arsh). O Allah! Be sufficient for me in every important matter as

شِئْتَ وَمِنْ اَيْنَ شِئْتَ

You wish and from wherever You wish.

٣٤ حَسْبِيَ اللّٰهُ لِدِيْنِيْ حَسْبِيَ اللّٰهُ لِمَا اَهَمَّنِيْ

34. Allah is enough for me for my Deen. Allah is enough for me whenever I am worried

حَسْبِيَ اللّٰهُ لِمَنْ بَغٰى عَلَيَّ حَسْبِيَ اللّٰهُ لِمَنْ

Allah is enough for when I am victimised by anybody, Allah is enough for me

33. Kanzul Ummaal # 3433   34. Kanzul Ummaal # 3558

حَسَدَنِيْ حَسْبِيَ اللهُ لِمَنْ كَادَنِيْ بِسُوْءٍ حَسْبِيَ

when someone is jealous of me or when anybody plans to harm me. Allah is enough for me

اللهُ عِنْدَ الْمَوْتِ حَسْبِيَ اللهُ عِنْدَ الْمَسْأَلَةِ فِي

during the pangs of death. Allah is enough for me at the time of questioning

الْقَبْرِ حَسْبِيَ اللهُ عِنْدَ الْمِيْزَانِ حَسْبِيَ اللهُ

in the grave. Allah is enough for me when my actions will be weighed on the scales on the Day of Qiyaamah. Allah is enough for

عِنْدَ الصِّرَاطِ حَسْبِيَ اللهُ لَآ اِلٰهَ اِلَّا هُوَ عَلَيْهِ

me at the time when I have to pass over the Bridge. Allah is enough for me. There is no supreme being besides Him, on Him

تَوَكَّلْتُ وَهُوَ رَبُّ الْعَرْشِ الْعَظِيْمِ

have I placed my trust and He is the Rabb of the Great Throne.

35. O Allah! Make death beloved to all those who believe

that our Nabi Muhammad ﷺ is Your Messenger.

36. O Allah! You are the Mighty Rabb. Nothing created by You

can encompass You. You see everything, yet You cannot be seen. You are

at a very lofty position. To You belongs the hereafter and this world.

35. Jaami'us Sagheer # 1474	36. Kanzul Ummaal # 3782

الْمَمَاتُ وَالْمَحْيَا وَاِلَيْكَ الْمُنْتَهٰى وَالرُّجْعٰى

Life and death are dedicated to You. You are the ultimate end and goal. All things will return to You.

نَعُوْذُ بِكَ اَنْ نَّذِلَّ وَنَخْزٰى.

We seek refuge in You against disgrace and humiliation.

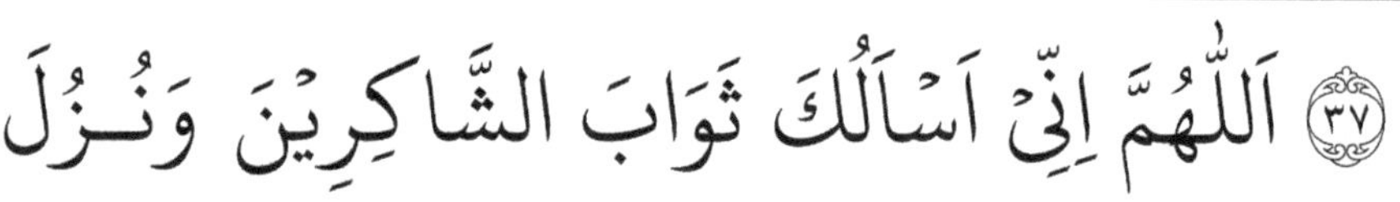

اَللّٰهُمَّ اِنِّيْ اَسْاَلُكَ ثَوَابَ الشَّاكِرِيْنَ وَنُـزُلَ

37. O Allah! I ask of You to bless me with the reward of the Shaakireen (Those who are grateful to You),

الْمُقَرَّبِيْنَ وَمُرَافَقَةَ النَّبِيِّيْنَ وَيَقِيْنَ

the respect granted to those who are very close to You, the company of the Ambiyaa عَلَيْهِمُ السَّلَامُ, the *yaqeen* (conviction)

الصِّدِّيْقِيْنَ وَذِلَّةَ الْمُتَّقِيْنَ وَاِخْبَاتَ الْمُـوْقِنِيْنَ

of the Awliyaa, the humility of the pious and the submission of those who have *Yaqeen* (complete conviction).

---

37. Kanzul Ummaal # 4945

حَتّٰى تَوَفَّانِيْ عَلٰى ذٰلِكَ يَآ اَرْحَمَ الرَّاحِمِيْنَ.

O The Most Merciful and Compassionate, bless me with all of this till my death.

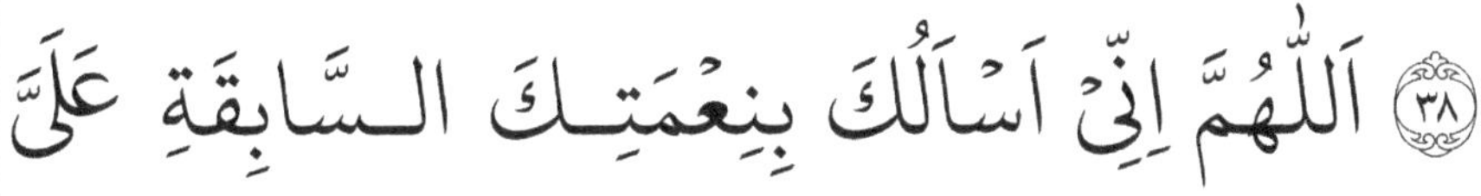

اَللّٰهُمَّ اِنِّيْ اَسْاَلُكَ بِنِعْمَتِكَ السَّابِقَةِ عَلَيَّ

38. O Allah, I beg of You through the past favours which You have blessed me with

وَبَلَآئِكَ الْحَسَنِ الَّذِى ابْتَلَيْتَنِيْ بِهٖ.

and through the good tests which You have put me through

وَفَضْلِكَ الَّذِىْ فَضَّلْتَ عَلَيَّ اَنْ تُدْخِلَنِيَ الْجَنَّةَ

and by the bounties which You rain upon me that You admit me into Jannah

بِمَنِّكَ وَفَضْلِكَ وَرَحْمَتِكَ.

by Your grace, kindness and mercy.

38. Kanzul Ummaal # 3784

39. O Allah! I beg of You by Your Kind Personality

and Your Supreme Command that You save me from the Fire, from disbelief and

from poverty.

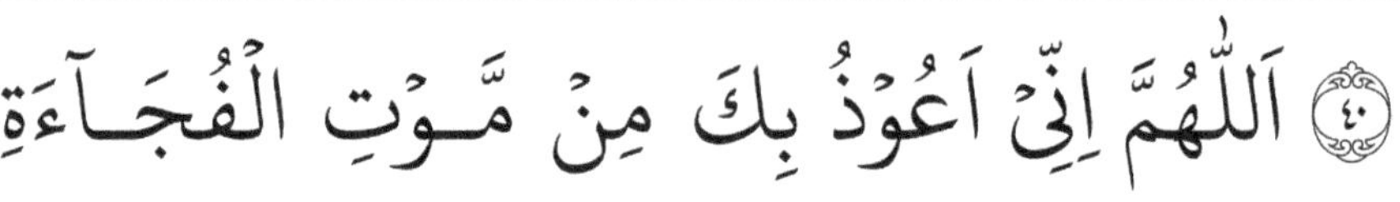

40. O Allah! I seek Your protection from sudden death,

from being bitten by a snake, or being attacked by a beast, from being drowned

39. Kanzul Ummaal # 3785   40. Kanzul Ummaal # 3786

وَمِنَ الْحَرَقِ وَمِنْ اَنْ اَخِرَّ عَلٰى شَىْءٍ وَمِنَ

or burnt to death, or that I should fall down upon anything and from

الْقَتْلِ عِنْدَ فِرَارِ الزَّحْفِ

being killed whilst I'm running away from the battle field.

﴿٤١﴾ اَللّٰهُمَّ اِنِّىْ اَسْاَلُكَ اِيْمَانًا دَائِمًا وَهُدًى

41. O Allah! I beg of You for Imaan that is unshakable, correct guidance

قَيِّمًا وَعِلْمًا نَّافِعًا

and beneficial knowledge.

﴿٤٢﴾ اَللّٰهُمَّ لَا تَجْعَلْ لِفَاجِرٍ عِنْدِىْ نِعْمَةً

42. O Allah! do not let me be obligated to an immoral person whom I may have to

أُكَافِيهِ بِهَا فِى الدُّنْيَا وَالْأَخِرَةِ

pay him back in this world or the hereafter.

43. O Allah! Forgive my sins, expand for me my character (make me big hearted),

وَطَيِّبْ لِى كَسْبِى وَقَنِّعْنِى بِمَارَزَقْتَنِى

provide me with halaal sustenance, grant me contentment in my earnings

وَلَاتُذْهِبْ طَلَبِى اِلَى شَىْءٍ صَرَّفْتَهُ عَنِّى

and don't incline my heart towards something which You have not ordained for me.

اَللّٰهُ اَكْبَرُ اللّٰهُ اَكْبَرُ اللّٰهُ اَكْبَرُ بِسْمِ

44. Allah is The Greatest, Allah is The Greatest, Allah is The Greatest. I invoke the blessings of Allah's name

43. Kazul Ummaal # 5061　　44. Kanzul Ummaal # 3850

اَللهِ عَلٰى نَفْسِىْ وَدِيْنِىْ بِسْمِ اللهِ عَلٰى اَهْلِىْ

upon my soul, my Deen, my family, my wealth

وَمَالِىْ بِسْمِ اللهِ عَلٰى كُلِّ شَىْءٍ اَعْطَانِىْ رَبِّىْ

and whatever my Rabb has gifted to me. I begin with the name of Allah

بِسْمِ اللهِ خَيْرِ الْاَسْمَآءِ بِسْمِ اللهِ رَبِّ الْاَرْضِ

which is the best of names, who is the Rabb of the heavens and the earth.

وَالسَّمَآءِ بِسْمِ اللهِ الَّذِىْ لَا يَضُرُّ مَعَ اسْمِهٖ دَآءٌ

I begin with the name of Allah by virtue of which no disease can harm me.

بِسْمِ اللهِ اِفْتَتَحْتُ وَعَلَى اللهِ تَوَكَّلْتُ اَللهُ اَللهُ

I begin with the name of Allah and my reliance is totally upon Him.

رَبِّيْ لَا اُشْرِكُ بِهٖ اَحَدًا اَسْاَلُكَ اللّٰهُمَّ بِخَيْرِكَ

Allah, verily Allah is my Rabb and I do not join any partners with Him. O Allah! I beg of You

مِنْ خَيْرِكَ الَّذِىْ لَا يُعْطِيْهِ غَيْرُكَ عَزَّ جَارُكَ

through Your goodness, which You alone bestow, respected is Your protection

وَجَلَّ ثَنَآئُكَ وَلَاۤ اِلٰهَ اِلَّا اَنْتَ اِجْعَلْنِيْ فِيْ

and lofty is Your praise, there is no deity besides You; to keep me

عِيَاذِكَ وَجِوَارِكَ مِنْ كُلِّ سُوْءٍ وَّمِنَ الشَّيْطَانِ

in Your protection against all evils and the

الرَّجِيْمِ اَللّٰهُمَّ اِنِّيْ اَسْتَجِيْرُكَ مِنْ جَمِيْعِ كُلِّ

accursed shaytaan. O Allah! I seek refuge in You from everything

شَىْءٍ خَلَقْتَ وَاحْتَرِسُ بِـكَ مِنْهُنَّ وَاُقَـدِّمُ

that You have created and I seek Your protection from their evil.

بَيْنَ يَدَىَّ بِسْمِ اللهِ الرَّحْمٰنِ الرَّحِيْمِ

I place in front of me the following Surah of the Qur-aan Shareef: In the name of Allah, Most Merciful, Most Gracious.

قُلْ هُوَ اللهُ اَحَدٌ اَللهُ الصَّمَدُ لَمْ يَلِدْ

Say: Allah is One. Allah is absolutely independent. He did not give birth to anyone

وَلَمْ يُوْلَدْ وَلَمْ يَكُنْ لَّهٗ كُفُوًا اَحَدٌ مِنْ اَمَامِىْ

neither did anyone give birth to Him and nor is anyone equal to Him." In front of me,

وَمِنْ خَلْفِىْ وَعَنْ يَّمِيْنِىْ وَعَنْ شِــمَالِىْ وَمِنْ

behind me, on my right and left,

فَوْقِيْ وَمِنْ تَحْتِيْ

above me and beneath me.

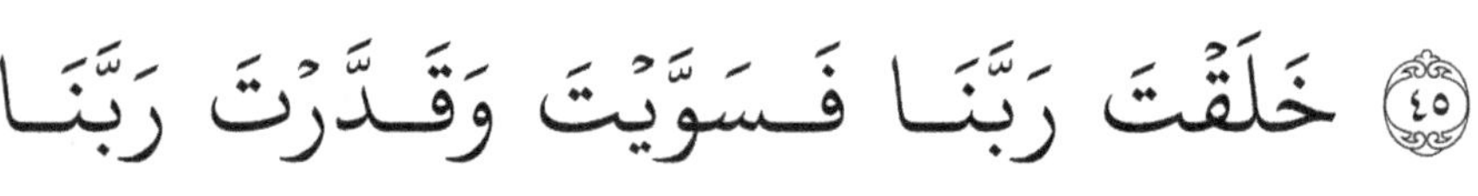

﴿٤٥﴾ خَلَقْتَ رَبَّنَا فَسَوَّيْتَ وَقَدَّرْتَ رَبَّنَا

45. Our Rabb, You created and perfected all creation. Our Rabb, You had destined (predetermined everything)

فَقَضَيْتَ وَعَلٰى عَرْشِكَ اِسْتَوَيْتَ وَاَمَتَّ

and accordingly Your decree was fulfilled. You established Yourself on Your throne (in a manner that is befitting Your

فَاَحْيَيْتَ وَاَطْعَمْتَ فَاَشْبَعْتَ وَاَسْقَيْتَ

majesty). You give death and thereafter You give life again. You provide food and satisfy the appetite. You provide water

فَاَرْوَيْتَ وَحَمَّلْتَ فِيْ بَرِّكَ وَبَحْرِكَ عَلٰى فُلْكِكَ

and quench the thirst. You transport us across the land and sea with Your boats

45. Kanzul Ummaal # 3855

وَعَلٰى دَوَآبِّكَ وَعَلٰٓى اَنْعَامِكَ فَاجْعَلْ لِّيْ عِنْدَكَ

and animals. Enter me into

وَلِيْجَةً وَّاجْعَلْ لِّيْ عِنْدَكَ زُلْفٰى وَحُسْنَ مَاٰبٍ

the secrets of Your heavenly court, draw me in closeness to You and grant me an excellent abode.

وَاجْعَلْنِيْ مِمَّنْ يَّخَافُ مَقَامَكَ وَوَعِيْدَكَ

(O Allah) make me from those who fear standing before You, fear Your warnings

وَيَرْجُوْ لِقَآئَكَ وَاجْعَلْنِيْ مِمَّنْ يَّتُوْبُ اِلَيْكَ

and are desirous of meeting You. Make me from those who offer

تَوْبَةً نَّصُوْحًا وَّاَسْاَلُكَ عَمَلًا مَّتَقَبَّلًا وَّعِلْمًا

sincere repentance to You and I beg of You to bless me with actions that are accepted by You, and knowledge, which is

نَّجِيحًا وَّسَعْيًا مَّشْكُوْرًا وَّتِجَارَةً لَّنْ تَبُوْرَ ۚ

sound and an effort which earns Your appreciation and a trade which never suffers a loss.

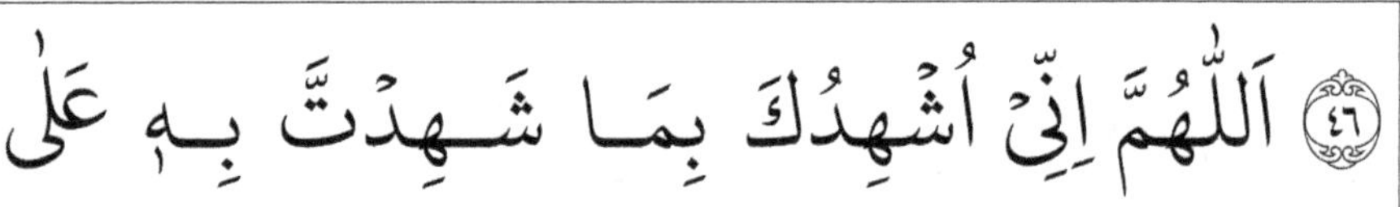

اَللّٰهُمَّ اِنِّيْ اُشْهِدُكَ بِمَا شَهِدْتَّ بِهٖ عَلٰى

46. O Allah! I make You a witness to what You have already bore testimony to,

نَفْسِكَ وَشَهِدَتْ بِهٖ مَلَآئِكَتُكَ وَاَنْبِيَآئُكَ

regarding Yourself. Your angels, Your Messengers,

وَاُولُوا الْعِلْمِ وَمَنْ لَّمْ يَشْهَدْ بِمَا شَهِدْتَّ بِهٖ

the learned Ulama have also testified to it, and if anyone has not testified to what You have testified to,

فَاكْتُبْ شَهَادَتِيْ مَكَانَ شَهَادَتِهٖ اَنْتَ السَّلَامُ

then write down my testimony in his place. You are "As Salaam" (Full of peace),

46. Kanzul Ummaal # 4966

وَمِنْكَ السَّلَامُ تَبَارَكْتَ يَاذَا الْجَلَالِ

peace comes from You and You are full of blessings, O Most Magnificent and

وَالْاِكْرَامِ. اَللّٰهُمَّ اِنِّيْ اَسْاَلُكَ فِكَاكَ رَقَبَتِيْ مِنَ

Most Kind. O Allah! I beg of You to free my neck from the

النَّارِ

fire of Hell.

اَللّٰهُمَّ اَعِنِّيْ عَلٰى غَمَرَاتِ الْمَوْتِ ۝٤٧

47. O Allah! Please help me during the pangs

وَسَكَرَاتِ الْمَوْتِ

and pains of death.

47. Tirmizi # 978

﴿٤٨﴾ وَاٰخِرُ دُعَائِهٖ صَلَّى اللهُ عَلَيْهِ وَسَلَّمَ۔ اَللّٰهُمَّ

48. The last dua that Rasulullah ﷺ made was as follows: "O Allah!

اغْفِرْلِيْ وَارْحَمْنِيْ وَاَلْحِقْنِيْ بِالرَّفِيْقِ الْاَعْلٰى

Forgive me, have mercy upon me and join me with the Highest Companion." (i.e. join me with You O Allah!)

﴿٤٩﴾ سُبْحٰنَ رَبِّكَ رَبِّ الْعِزَّةِ عَمَّا يَصِفُوْنَ

49. Glorified is Your Rabb, The Rabb of Honour and Power. He is free from what the unbelievers say about Him.

وَسَلٰمٌ عَلَى الْمُرْسَلِيْنَ وَالْحَمْدُ لِلّٰهِ رَبِّ

Peace be upon the Messengers and all praise is due to Allah, the Cherisher

الْعٰلَمِيْنَ

of the worlds.

---

48. Bukhaari # 5674   49. Saaffaat # 180 - 182

FRIDAY

اَللّٰهُمَّ صَلِّ عَلٰى مُحَمَّدٍ وَّعَلٰى اٰلِ مُحَمَّدٍ كَمَا

1.   O Allah! Bestow Your special mercy on our Noble leader, Muhammad ﷺ and on his family

صَلَّيْتَ عَلٰى اِبْرَاهِيْمَ وَعَلٰى اٰلِ اِبْرَاهِيْمَ اِنَّكَ

just as You bestowed mercy on Ibraahim عَلَيْهِ السَّلَام and his family.

حَمِيْدٌ مَّجِيْدٌ۔ اَللّٰهُمَّ بَارِكْ عَلٰى مُحَمَّدٍ وَّعَلٰى

Verily You are the Praiseworthy and the Glorious. O Allah! Pour Your blessings on our Noble Master, Muhammad ﷺ and on

اٰلِ مُحَمَّدٍ كَمَا بَارَكْتَ عَلٰى اِبْرَاهِيْمَ وَعَلٰى اٰلِ

the family of our Noble Master, Nabi Muhammad ﷺ just as You blessed Ibraahim عَلَيْهِ السَّلَام and his family.

1. Bukhaari # 319

اِبْرَاهِيْمَ اِنَّكَ حَمِيْدٌ مَّجِيْدٌ

Verily You are worthy of all praise and the Glorious.

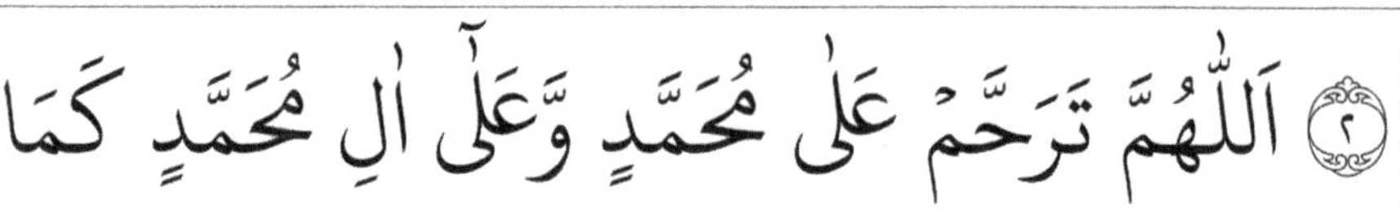

2. O Allah! Show your special compassion to our Noble Master, Nabi Muhammad ﷺ and his family

تَرَحَّمْتَ عَلٰى اِبْرَاهِيْمَ وَعَلٰى اٰلِ اِبْرَاهِيْمَ اِنَّكَ

just as You showed your special compassion to Ibraahim عَلَيْهِ السَّلَام and his family.

حَمِيْدٌ مَجِيْدٌ۔ اَللّٰهُمَّ تَحَنَّنْ عَلٰى مُحَمَّدٍ وَّعَلٰى اٰلِ

Verily You are worthy of all praise and the Glorious. O Allah! Be compassionate towards our Noble Master, Nabi Muhammad

مُحَمَّدٍ كَمَا تَحَنَّنْتَ عَلٰى اِبْرَاهِيْمَ وَعَلٰى اٰلِ

ﷺ and his family just as You showed compassion towards Ibraahim عَلَيْهِ السَّلَام and his family.

2. Kanzul Ummaal # 3991

اِبْرَاهِيْمَ اِنَّكَ حَمِيْدٌ مَّجِيْدٌ.

Verily You are worthy of all praise and the Glorious.

اَللّٰهُمَّ سَلِّمْ عَلٰى مُحَمَّدٍ وَّعَلٰى اٰلِ مُحَمَّدٍ كَمَا

O Allah! Grant peace to our Noble Master, Nabi Muhammad ﷺ and his family just as

سَلَّمْتَ عَلٰى اِبْرَاهِيْمَ وَعَلٰى اٰلِ اِبْرَاهِيْمَ اِنَّكَ

You granted peace to Ibraahim عَلَيْهِ السَّلَامُ and his family. Verily You are

حَمِيْدٌ مَّجِيْدٌ

the Praiseworthy and the Glorious.

(٣) اَللّٰهُمَّ صَلِّ عَلٰى مُحَمَّدٍ النَّبِيِّ (الْاُمِّيِّ)

3. O Allah! Bestow Your special mercy on our Noble Master, Nabi Muhammad ﷺ, (the unlettered Prophet),

3. Abu Dawood Page 141

وَاَزْوَاجِهٖ اُمَّهَاتِ الْمُؤْمِنِيْنَ وَذُرِّيَّتِهٖ وَاَهْلِ

on his wives, the spiritual mothers of the Muslims, his children and

بَيْتِهٖ كَمَا صَلَّيْتَ عَلٰى اِبْرَاهِيْمَ وَعَلٰى اٰلِ

his household just as You bestowed mercy on Ibraahim عَلَيْهِ السَّلَامُ and his family.

اِبْرَاهِيْمَ وَبَارِكْ عَلٰى مُحَمَّدِ النَّبِيِّ الْاُمِّيِّ وَعَلٰى

Bless our Noble Master, Nabi Muhammad صَلَّى اللهُ عَلَيْهِ وَسَلَّمَ the unlettered prophet,

اٰلِ مُحَمَّدٍ وَّاَزْوَاجِهٖ وَاَهْلِ بَيْتِهٖ وَذُرِّيَّتِهٖ كَمَا

his wives, his household and children

بَارَكْتَ عَلٰى اِبْرَاهِيْمَ وَعَلٰى اٰلِ اِبْرَاهِيْمَ فِي

just as You blessed Ibraahim عَلَيْهِ السَّلَامُ and his family amongst all the

الْعَالَمِيْنَ اِنَّكَ حَمِيْدٌ مَّجِيْدٌ

inhabitants of the world. Verily You are worthy of all praise and
the Glorious.

اَللّٰهُمَّ اَنْزِلْهُ الْمَقْعَدَ الْمُقَرَّبَ عِنْدَكَ يَوْمَ

4. O Allah! Grant him (Nabi Muhammad ﷺ) a place of
nearness to You in Your Court

الْقِيَامَةِ.

on the Day of Judgement.

اَللّٰهُمَّ اجْعَلْ صَلَوَاتِكَ وَرَحْمَتَكَ وَبَرَكَاتِكَ

5. O Allah! Bestow Your special mercy, blessings and grace on the

عَلٰى سَيِّدِ الْمُرْسَلِيْنَ وَاِمَامِ الْمُتَّقِيْنَ وَخَـاتَـمِ

leader of all the Messengers, leader of the pious, the last of

4. Musnad Ahmad #16543	5. Ibnu Majah # 906

النَّبِيِّيْنَ مُحَمَّدٍ صَلَّى اللهُ عَلَيْهِ وسَلَّمَ عَبْدِكَ

all prophets, our Noble Master, Nabi Muhammad ﷺ, Your servant

وَرَسُوْلِكَ اِمَامِ الْخَيْرِ وَقَآئِدِ الْخَيْرِ رَسُوْلِ

and messenger, a guide towards good and a leader in virtue; The Rasool

الرَّحْمَةِ. اَللّٰهُمَّ ابْعَثْهُ مَقَامًا مَّحْمُوْدًا يَّغْبِطُهٗ

of mercy. O Allah! Raise him to that praiseworthy position where he will be envied by

بِهِ الْاَوَّلُوْنَ وَالْاٰخِرُوْنَ

the first and the last of the entire mankind.

٦ اَللّٰهُمَّ اجْعَلْ صَلَوَاتِكَ وَبَرَكَاتِكَ وَرَحْمَتَكَ

6. O Allah! Bless our Noble Master, Nabi Muhammad ﷺ with Your special blessings, mercy and grace

---

6. Musnad Ahmad # 22479

عَلٰى مُحَمَّدٍ وَّعَلٰٓى اٰلِ مُحَمَّدٍ صَلَّى اللهُ عَلَيْهِ

and bless the family of Nabi Muhammad ﷺ

وَسَلَّمَ كَمَا جَعَلْتَهَا عَلٰى اِبْرَاهِيْمَ وَعَلٰى اٰلِ

just as You blessed Ibraahim عَلَيْهِ السَّلَام and his family.

اِبْرَاهِيْمَ اِنَّكَ حَمِيْدٌ مَّجِيْدٌ.

Verily, You are the Praiseworthy and the Glorious.

٧ اَللّٰهُمَّ صَلِّ عَلٰى مُحَمَّدٍ صَلَّى اللهُ عَلَيْهِ

7. O Allah! Bestow Your special mercy on our Noble Master, Muhammad ﷺ

وَسَلَّمَ وَاَبْلِغْهُ الْوَسِيْلَةَ وَالدَّرَجَةَ الرَّفِيْعَةَ

and raise him to the position of Waseelah and to the highest position

7. Al Qawlul Badee. Page: 106

مِنَ الْجَنَّةِ اَللّٰهُمَّ اجْعَلْ فِى الْمُصْطَفَيْنَ

in Jannah. O Allah! Grant Your chosen ones his love and (grant) to those near to You,

مَحَبَّتَهٗ وَفِى الْمُقَرَّبِيْنَ مَوَدَّتَهٗ وَفِى الْاَعْلَيْنَ

his friendship and manifest his name on the lips of the highest ranking personalities.

ذِكْرَهٗ وَالسَّلَامُ عَلَيْهِ وَرَحْمَةُ اللهِ وَبَرَكَاتُهٗ

May peace and Allah's mercy and blessings be upon him.

﴿٨﴾ اَللّٰهُمَّ دَاحِىَ الْمَدْحُوَّاتِ وَبَارِئَ

8. O Allah! The being who levelled the earth, creator

الْمَسْمُوْكَاتِ وَجَبَّارَ الْقُلُوْبِ عَلٰى فِطْرَتِهَا

of the high skies. O Master of the hearts which have been moulded on their natural disposition

8. Kanzul Ummaal # 3989

شَقِيّهَا وَسَعِيدِهَا اِجْعَلْ شَرَآئِفَ صَلَوَاتِكَ

good or bad. Grant your honourable mercies

وَنَوَامِى بَرَكَاتِكَ وَرَأفَةَ تَحَنُّنِكَ عَلَى مُحَمَّدٍ

Your fruitful blessing and most lavish kindness to Muhammad ﷺ

صَلَّى اللهُ عَلَيْهِ وَسَلَّمَ عَبْدِكَ وَرَسُوْلِكَ الْخَاتِمِ

may the peace and blessings of Allah Ta'ala be upon him, your servant and messenger; the one who has (perfected) and sealed

لِمَا سَبَقَ وَالْفَاتِح لِمَا أُغْلِقَ وَالْمُعْلِنِ الْحَقَّ

nubuwwat which continued before him, the opener of (avenues of spiritual perfection) which has been closed, the one who has

بِالْحَقِّ وَالدَّامِغ لِجَيْشَاتِ الْأَبَاطِيْلِ كَمَا

announced true deen with honesty, the conqueror of the armies of falsehood. As he was

حُمِّلَ فَاضْطَلَعَ بِاَمْرِكَ لِطَاعَتِكَ مُسْتَوْفِزًا فِيْ

entrusted with this responsibility, he got ready to obey you as per your command, enthusiastic to acquire

مَرْضَاتِكَ بِغَيْرِ نِكْلٍ عَنْ قَدَمٍ وَّلَا وَهْنٍ فِيْ

Your pleasure without hesitating and without the least dullness in

عَزْمٍ وَّاعِيًا لِّوَحْيِكَ حَافِظًا لِّعَهْدِكَ مَاضِيًا

resolve, the one who safeguarded your revelations. And fully observed the promises made to you, one who worked (tirelessly)

عَلٰى نَفَاذِ اَمْرِكَ حَتّٰى اَوْرٰى قَبَسًا لِّقَابِسٍ

to execute Your commandments until he kindled the light for the one seeking light.

اٰلَآءُ اللهِ تَصِلُ بِاَهْلِهِ اَسْبَابَهٗ بِهٖ هُدِيَتِ

The favours of Allah Ta'ala convey the seekers of light to the enlightened path. Through him ﷺ the hearts

الْقُلُوْبُ بَعْدَ خَوْضَاتِ الْفِتَنِ وَالْاِثْمِ وَاَبْهَجَ

were enabled to be guided after being submerged in trials and sins
and through him ﷺ Allah Ta'ala exposed

مُوْضِحَاتِ الْاَعْلَامِ وَمُنِيْرَاتِ الْاِسْلَامِ

the clear signs. and the radiant light of Islam

وَنَآئِرَاتِ الْاَحْكَامِ فَهُوَ اَمِيْنُكَ الْمَأْمُوْنُ

and its bright practices. So he is the trusted one on whom you
have full confidence

وَخَازِنُ عِلْمِكَ الْمَخْزُوْنِ وَشَهِيْدُكَ يَوْمَ

and the custodian of Your treasure of knowledge and Your witness
on the day of

الدِّيْنِ وَبَعِيْثُكَ نِعْمَةً وَّرَسُوْلُكَ بِالْحَقِّ رَحْمَةً.

Judgement, he is the one who you have blessed with nubuwwat
out of Your sheer grace, the one who, You, out of your mercy has

اَللّٰهُمَّ افْسَحْ لَهٗ مَفْسَحًا فِيْ عَدْنِكَ وَاجْزِهٖ

charged to be Your true messenger. O Allah Ta'ala! Widen for his spacious residence in your eternal paradise.

مُضَاعَفَاتِ الْخَيْرِ مِنْ فَضْلِكَ مُهَنَّئَاتٍ لَّهٗ

and by Your grace reward him with multiplied virtues i.e. Your special abundant reward

غَيْرَ مُكَدَّرَاتٍ مِّنْ وُّفُوْرِثَوَابِكَ الْمَضْنُوْنِ

and Your immense treasure of gifts which will prove to be

وَجَزِيْلِ عَطَآئِكَ الْمَخْزُوْنِ. اَللّٰهُمَّ اَعْلِ عَلٰى

a source of happiness for him and not a source of displeasing him. O Allah Ta'ala! Raise his structure

بِنَآءِ الْبَانِيْنَ بِنَآئَهٗ وَاَكْرِمْ مَّثْوَاهُ لَدَيْكَ

Above the structures of others and honour his presence in Your court and afford him

وَنُزُلَهُۥ ۚ وَاَتْمِمْ لَهُۥ نُوْرَهُۥ وَاجْزِهٖ مِنِ انْبِعَاثِكَ

the best hospitality. And perfect for him his light. And honour him to rise in the plains of Hashr,

لَهُۥ مَقْبُوْلَ الشَّهَادَةِ وَمَرْضِيَّ الْمَقَالَةِ ذَا مَنْطِقٍ

With his testimony, earning Your approval, his speech conforming to Your pleasure, his word being

عَدْلٍ وَّخُطَّةٍ فَصْلٍ وَّحُجَّةٍ وَّبُرْهَانٍ عَظِيْمٍ

just, his line of action being the decisive factor between right and wrong, his argument being triumphant and strong.

صَلَّى اللهُ عَلَيْهِ وَسَلَّمَ

May the peace and blessings of Allah Ta'ala be upon him.

﴿٩﴾ اَللّٰهُمَّ اجْعَلْنَا سَامِعِيْنَ مُطِيْعِيْنَ وَاَوْلِيَآءَ

9. O Allah! Make us submissive and obedient to Your commands and make us sincere friends

مُخْلِصِيْنَ وَرُفَقَآءَ مُصَاحِبِيْنَ. اَللّٰهُمَّ اَبْلِغْهُ

and pleasant companions. O Allah! Convey our salaam to Rasulullah ﷺ

مِنَّا السَّلَامَ وَارْدُدْ عَلَيْنَا مِنْهُ السَّلَامَ

and favour us with a salaam from him.

﴿١٠﴾ اَللّٰهُمَّ صَلِّ عَلٰى مُحَمَّدٍ النَّبِيِّ عَدَدَ مَنْ

10. O Allah! Bestow Your special mercy on our Noble Master Muhammad ﷺ, the Prophet, as many times as those

صَلَّى عَلَيْهِ مِنْ خَلْقِكَ وَصَلِّ عَلٰى مُحَمَّدٍ النَّبِيِّ

among Your creatures have uttered their greetings to him and bestow Your special mercy on our Noble Master Muhammad

كَمَا يَنْبَغِيْ لَنَا اَنْ نُّصَلِّيَ عَلَيْهِ وَصَلِّ عَلٰى

ﷺ, the Prophet, in proportion to the obligation we are under to send greetings upon him; and bestow Your special mercy

10. Kanzul Ummaal # 3981

مُحَمَّدِ النَّبِيِّ كَمَا اَمَرْتَنَا اَنْ نُصَلِّيَ عَلَيْهِ

on our Noble Master Muhammad ﷺ, the Nabi, as You have commanded us to offer greetings to him.

اَللّٰهُمَّ صَلِّ عَلٰى مُحَمَّدٍ صَلَّى اللهُ عَلَيْهِ ⑪

11. O Allah! Bestow Your special mercy on our Noble Master Muhammad ﷺ

وَسَلَّمَ حَتّٰى لَا يَبْقٰى مِنْ صَلَوَاتِكَ شَيْءٌ.

to the extent of Your unlimited mercy and

وَبَارِكْ عَلٰى مُحَمَّدٍ صَلَّى اللهُ عَلَيْهِ وَسَلَّمَ حَتّٰى

bless our Noble Master Muhammad ﷺ to the extent of Your unlimited blessings

لَا يَبْقٰى مِنْ بَرَكَاتِكَ شَيْءٌ . وَسَلِّمْ عَلٰى مُحَمَّدٍ

and send peace upon our Noble Master Muhammad ﷺ,

11. Kanzul Ummaal # 4004

صَلَّى اللهُ عَلَيْهِ وَسَلَّمَ حَتَّى لَا يَبْقَى مِنْ سَلَامِكَ

as much peace that is in Your possession

شَيْءٌ. وَارْحَمْ مُحَمَّدًا صَلَّى اللهُ عَلَيْهِ وَسَلَّمَ

(and have mercy on our Noble Master Muhammad ﷺ

حَتَّى لَا يَبْقَى مِنْ رَّحْمَتِكَ شَيْءٌ

to the extent of Your unlimited mercy.)

جَزَى اللهُ عَنَّا مُحَمَّدًا صَلَّى اللهُ عَلَيْهِ ﴿١٢﴾

12. O Allah! Grant our Noble Master Muhammad ﷺ a

وَسَلَّمَ بِمَا هُوَ اَهْلُهُ

suitable reward on our behalf

12. Kanzul Ummaal # 3900

(١٣) اَللّٰهُمَّ صَلِّ عَلٰى رُوْحِ مُحَمَّدٍ فِي الْاَرْوَاحِ

13. O Allah! Bestow Your special mercy on the soul of our Noble Master Muhammad ﷺ among all souls,

وَصَلِّ عَلٰى جَسَدِ مُحَمَّدٍ فِي الْاَجْسَادِ وَصَلِّ

bestow Your special mercy on the body of our Noble Master Muhammad ﷺ, among all bodies, bestow Your special

عَلٰى قَبْرِ مُحَمَّدٍ فِي الْقُبُوْرِ

mercy on the grave of our Noble Master Muhammad ﷺ among all the graves.

(١٤) اِنَّ اللّٰهَ وَمَلٰئِكَتَهٗ يُصَلُّوْنَ عَلَى النَّبِيِّ يَآاَيُّهَا

14. Verily, Allah Ta'ala and His angels send durood upon Nabi ﷺ. O you

الَّذِيْنَ اٰمَنُوْا صَلُّوْا عَلَيْهِ وَسَلِّمُوْا تَسْلِيْمًا

who believe, send durood and salaams upon him.

لَبَّيْكَ اَللّٰهُمَّ رَبِّيْ وَسَعْدَيْكَ صَلَوَاتُ اللهِ الْبَرِّ

O Allah! My Rabb, I am present and of Your service. May the mercy of Allah, The Kind and Compassionate, be showered on our Noble

الرَّحِيْمِ وَالْمَلَآئِكَةِ الْمُقَرَّبِيْنَ وَالنَّبِيِّيْنَ

Master Muhammad ﷺ and similarly the greetings of His angels, His chosen ones, the Messengers,

وَالصِّدِّيْقِيْنَ وَالشُّهَدَآءِ وَالصَّالِحِيْنَ وَمَا

the awliyaa, the martyrs and the righteous people

سَبَّحَ لَكَ مِنْ شَىْءٍ يَّارَبَّ الْعَالَمِيْنَ عَلٰى مُحَمَّدِ

and all things which glorify Allah, be offered to our Noble Master Muhammad ﷺ

بْنِ عَبْدِ اللهِ خَاتَمِ النَّبِيِّيْنَ وَسَيِّدِ

the son of Abdullah, the last Nabi and the head of all

الْمُرْسَلِيْنَ وَاِمَامِ الْمُتَّقِيْنَ وَرَسُوْلِ رَبِّ

the Ambiyaa, the leader of the pious, the messenger of the Rabb of

الْعَالَمِيْنَ الشَّاهِدِ الْبَشِيْرِ الدَّاعِيْ اِلَيْكَ

the worlds, who will be a witness (on the Day of Judgement). He is the giver of glad tidings, and he invites to You with Your

بِاِذْنِكَ السِّرَاجِ الْمُنِيْرِ وَعَلَيْهِ السَّلَامُ

permission and he spreads the light (like an illuminating lamp), so peace be upon him.

١٥ اَللّٰهُمَّ تَقَبَّلْ شَفَاعَةَ مُحَمَّدِ الْكُبْرٰى وَارْفَعْ

15. O Allah! Accept the intercession of our Noble Master Muhammad ﷺ which is most weighty, raise him to the

دَرَجَتَهُ الْعُلْيَا وَاَعْطِهِ سُؤْلَهٗ فِى الْاٰخِرَةِ

highest rank and grant him whatever he has asked for, in this world and in the Hereafter

15. Al Qawlul Badee Page 122

وَالْاُوْلٰى كَمَاۤ اٰتَيْتَ اِبْرَاهِيْمَ وَمُوْسٰى

just as You granted it to Ibraahim ﷺ and Musa ﷺ.

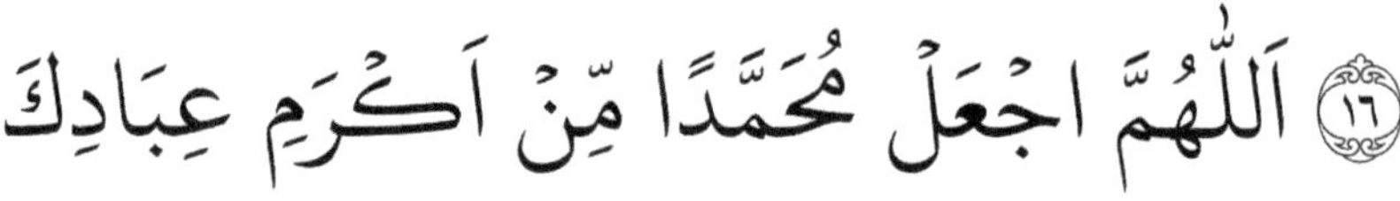

اَللّٰهُمَّ اجْعَلْ مُحَمَّدًا مِّنْ اَكْرَمِ عِبَادِكَ

16. O Allah! Grant our Noble Master Muhammad ﷺ the greatest excellence

عَلَيْكَ كَرَامَةً وَّمِنْ اَرْفَعِهِمْ عِنْدَكَ دَرَجَةً

and the highest rank and honour in Your Court from amongst all Your servants

وَّمِنْ اَعْظَمِهِمْ عِنْدَكَ خَطَرًا وَّمِنْ اَمْكَنِهِمْ

and make his intercession the most acceptable to You.

عِنْدَكَ شَفَاعَةً. اَللّٰهُمَّ اَتْبِعْهُ مِنْ اُمَّتِهٖ

O Allah! Grant him such followers from amongst his people

16. Al Qawlul Badee Page 122

وَذُرِّيَّتِهٖ مَا تَقَرُّ بِهٖ عَيْنُهٗ وَاجْزِهٖ عَنَّا خَيْرَ مَا

and children, that it may become a source of coolness to his eyes. Grant him a reward on our behalf which is better

جَزَيْتَ نَبِيًّا عَنْ اُمَّتِهٖ وَاجْزِ الْاَنْبِيَآءَ كُلَّهُمْ

than what You have granted to any Nabi on behalf of his followers and grant an excellent reward to all the Ambiyaa

خَيْرًا وَّسَلَامٌ عَلَى الْمُرْسَلِيْنَ وَالْحَمْدُ لِلّٰهِ رَبِّ

and may peace be upon all the Messengers and all praise is due to Allah,

الْعَالَمِيْنَ.

the Cherisher of the worlds.

اَللّٰهُمَّ صَلِّ عَلٰى مُحَمَّدٍ وَّعَلٰى اٰلِ مُحَمَّدٍ ⒘

17. O Allah! Bestow Your special mercy on our Noble Master Muhammad ﷺ, his family,

17. Al Qawlul Badee Page 122

وَاَصْحَابِهٖ وَاَوْلَادِهٖ وَاَهْلِ بَيْتِهٖ وَذُرِّيَّتِهٖ

companions, children, his household, his progeny,

وَمُحِبِّيْهِ وَاَتْبَاعِهٖ وَاَشْيَاعِهٖ وَعَلَيْنَا مَعَهُمْ

his lovers, followers, devotees and include us

اَجْمَعِيْنَ يَآ اَرْحَمَ الرَّاحِمِيْنَ۠

along with all of them, O Most Merciful and Most Compassionate.

(١٨) اَللّٰهُمَّ صَلِّ عَلٰى مُحَمَّدٍ مِّلْءَ الدُّنْيَا وَمِلْءَ

18. O Allah! Bestow Your special mercy on our Noble Master Muhammad ﷺ in quantities equal to this world and the

الْاٰخِرَةِ وَبَارِكْ عَلٰى مُحَمَّدٍ مِّلْءَ الدُّنْيَا وَمِلْءَ

Hereafter. Shower Your blessings on our Noble Master Muhammad ﷺ in quantities equal to this world and the

18. Al Qawlul Badee Page 122

الْاٰخِرَةِ وَارْحَمْ مُحَمَّدًا مِّلْءَ الدُّنْيَا وَمِلْءَ

Hereafter and be kind to our Noble Master Muhammad ﷺ in quantities equivalent to this world and the Hereafter. Grant

الْاٰخِرَةِ وَسَلِّمْ عَلٰى مُحَمَّدٍ مِّلْءَ الدُّنْيَا وَمِلْءَ

peace to our noble master Muhammad ﷺ in quantities equal to this world

الْاٰخِرَةِ

and the hereafter.

اَللّٰهُمَّ اِنِّىْ اَسْاَلُكَ يَا اَللّٰهُ يَا رَحْمٰنُ يَا ﴿١٩﴾

19. O Allah! I beg You, O Allah! The Compassionate,

رَحِيْمُ. يَاجَارَ الْمُسْتَجِيْرِيْنَ يَا اَمَانَ

the Merciful, the Giver of protection to those who seek it, the Comforter

19. Al Qawlul Badee Page 123

الْخَآئِفِيْنَ يَا عِمَادَ مَنْ لَّاعِمَادَ لَهٗ يَا سَنَدَ مَنْ

of the fear stricken people, The Helper of the helpless, The Support of one

لَّاسَنَدَ لَهٗ يَا ذُخْرَ مَنْ لَّاذُخْرَ لَهٗ يَا حِرْزَ

who has no support, The Supplier for the one who has no provisions, The Sanctuary

الضُّعَفَآءِ يَا كَنْزَ الْفُقَرَآءِ يَا عَظِيْمَ الرَّجَآءِ يَا

of the weak, The Treasure of the poor, The Greatest Source of hope,

مُنْقِذَ الْهَلْكٰى يَا مُنْجِىَ الْغَرْقٰى يَا مُحْسِنُ يَا

The Saviour of the drowned and doomed ones, The Benefactor,

مُجْمِلُ يَا مُنْعِمُ يَا مُفْضِلُ

The Beneficent, The Gracious, The Bountiful,

يَا عَزِيْزُ يَا جَبَّارُ يَا مُنِيْرُ اَنْتَ الَّذِىْ سَجَدَ

The Almighty, The Overpowering Rabb, The Radiant One before whom

لَكَ سَوَادُ اللَّيْلِ وَضَوْءُ النَّهَارِ وَشُعَاعُ الشَّمْسِ

the darkness of the night, the brightness of the day, the rays of the sun,

وَنُوْرُ الْقَمَرِ وَحَفِيْفُ الشَّجَرِ وَدَوِىُّ الْمَآءِ يَا

The light of the moon, the rustling of the trees and the humming of the streams all make sajdah.

اَللّٰهُ اَنْتَ اللّٰهُ لَاشَرِيْكَ لَكَ اَسْأَلُكَ اَنْ تُصَلِّيَ

O Allah! You are indeed Allah and You have no partner. I beg of You that You bestow Your special mercy on our Noble Master

عَلٰى مُحَمَّدٍ عَبْدِكَ وَرَسُوْلِكَ وَعَلٰى اٰلِ مُحَمَّدٍ.

Muhammad ﷺ, Your servant and messenger, and upon his family.

۞ اَللّٰهُمَّ صَلِّ عَلٰى مُحَمَّدٍ وَّعَلٰى اٰلِ مُحَمَّدٍ فِى

20. O Allah! Bestow Your special mercy on our Noble Master Muhammad 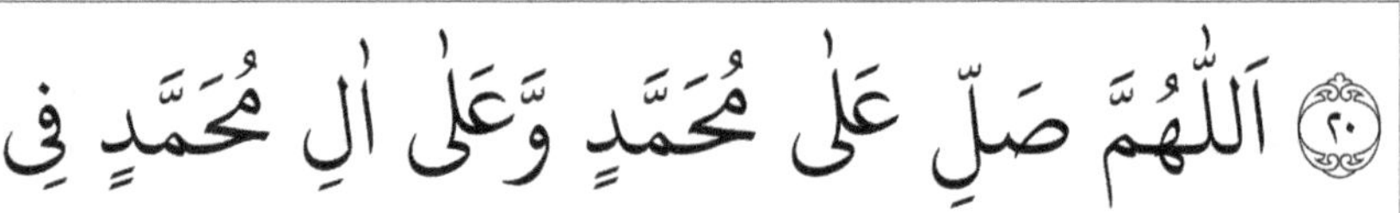 and his progeny from the first to the last

الْاَوَّلِيْنَ وَالْاٰخِرِيْنَ وَفِى الْمَلَاءِ الْاَعْلٰى اِلٰى يَوْمِ

among human beings and the high-ranking angels, till the Day

الدِّيْنِ

of Qiyaamah

۞ اَللّٰهُمَّ صَلِّ عَلٰى مُحَمَّدٍ وَّعَلٰى اٰلِ مُحَمَّدٍ كَمَا

21. O Allah! Bestow Your special mercy on our Noble Master Muhammad and his family

تُحِبُّ وَتَرْضٰى لَهٗ

as much as You would love and be pleased with.

20. Al Qawlul Badee Page 124	21. Al Qawlul Badee Page 125

اَللّٰهُمَّ صَلِّ عَلٰى مُحَمَّدٍ وَّعَلٰى اٰلِ مُحَمَّدٍ

22. O Allah! Bestow Your special mercy on our Noble Master Muhammad ﷺ and his family,

صَلٰوةً تَكُوْنُ لَكَ رِضًا وَّلِحَقِّهٖ اَدَآءً. وَاَعْطِهِ

a mercy which pleases You, and fulfils his right towards You and grant him

الْوَسِيْلَةَ وَالْمَقَامَ الْمَحْمُوْدَ الَّذِیْ وَعَدْتَّهٗ

the position of Waseelah and Maqaam-e-Mahmood (Special positions in Jannah) which You have promised.

وَاجْزِهٖ عَنَّا مَا هُوَ اَهْلُهٗ وَاجْزِهٖ عَنَّا اَفْضَلَ مَا

And grant him a befitting reward on our behalf, the best of rewards which You have ever

جَزَيْتَ نَبِيًّا عَنْ اُمَّتِهٖ وَصَلِّ عَلٰى جَمِيْع

granted to any Nabi on behalf of his people. And bestow Your special mercy on all

22. Al Qawlul Badee Page 125

اِخْوَانِهٖ مِنَ النَّبِيِّيْنَ وَالصَّالِحِيْنَ يَآ اَرْحَمَ

his brethren from the Ambiyaa and the righteous servants, O The Most Merciful

الرَّاحِمِيْنَ

of those who show mercy.

(٢٣) اَللّٰهُمَّ صَلِّ عَلٰى مُحَمَّدٍ فِى الْاَوَّلِيْنَ. وَصَلِّ

23. O Allah! Bestow Your special mercy on our Noble Master Muhammad ﷺ among those that came first. Bestow Your

عَلٰى مُحَمَّدٍ فِى الْاٰخِرِيْنَ وَصَلِّ عَلٰى مُحَمَّدٍ فِى

special mercy on him among those that came last. Bestow Your special mercy on him

النَّبِيِّيْنَ. وَصَلِّ عَلٰى مُحَمَّدٍ فِى الْمُرْسَلِيْنَ وَصَلِّ

amongst the prophets. Bestow Your special mercy on him amongst the Messengers

---

23. Al Qawlul Badee Page 127

عَلٰى مُحَمَّدٍ فِى الْمَلَاءِ الْاَعْلٰى اِلٰى يَوْمِ الدِّيْنِ

and bestow Your special mercy on him, till the Day of Judgement, amongst the high ranking angels.

اَللّٰهُمَّ صَلِّ عَلٰى مُحَمَّدٍ حَتّٰى تَرْضٰى وَصَلِّ عَلٰى

O Allah! Continue sending durood upon our Noble Master Muhammad ﷺ until you are pleased

مُحَمَّدٍ بَعْدَ الرِّضَا وَصَلِّ عَلٰى مُحَمَّدٍ اَبَدًا اَبَدًا

and continue sending blessings upon him even after You are pleased and bless him forever and ever.

اَللّٰهُمَّ صَلِّ عَلٰى مُحَمَّدٍ كَمَا اَمَرْتَ بِالصَّلٰوةِ

O Allah! Bestow Your special mercy on our Noble Master Muhammad ﷺ as

عَلَيْهِ وَصَلِّ عَلٰى مُحَمَّدٍ كَمَا تُحِبُّ اَنْ يُّصَلّٰى

You have commanded us to offer salutations to him; send salutations upon him in the manner, You would be pleased that

عَلَيْهِ. وَصَلِّ عَلٰى مُحَمَّدٍ كَمَا اَرَدْتَّ اَنْ يُّصَلّٰى

durood is sent upon him. And send salutations upon Nabi Muhammad ﷺ as much as You desire to be sent

عَلَيْهِ.

upon him.

اَللّٰهُمَّ صَلِّ عَلٰى مُحَمَّدٍ عَدَدَ خَلْقِكَ وَصَلِّ عَلٰى

O Allah! Grant Your special mercy to our Noble Master, Nabi Muhammad ﷺ equal to the number of Your creation and

مُحَمَّدٍ رِضَآءَ نَفْسِكَ. وَصَلِّ عَلٰى مُحَمَّدٍ زِنَةَ

to the extent of Your pleasure. Send salutations upon Nabi Muhammad ﷺ equal to the weight of

عَرْشِكَ وَصَلِّ عَلٰى مُحَمَّدٍ مِّدَادَ كَلِمَاتِكَ

Your Throne and send salutations equal to the ink used to write Your words

اَلَّتِيْ لَا تَنْفَدُ. اَللّٰهُمَّ اَعْطِ مُحَمَّدَ الْوَسِيْـلَـةَ

which never end. O Allah! Grant our Noble Master, Nabi Muhammad ﷺ the position of Waseela and

وَالْفَضْلَ وَالْفَضِيْلَةَ وَالدَّرَجَةَ الرَّفِيْعَةَ

grant him excellence and a very high rank.

اَللّٰهُمَّ عَظِّمْ بُرْهَانَهٗ وَاَفْلِجْ حُجَّتَهٗ وَاَبْـلِـغْـهُ

O Allah! Honour his testimony to prophet-hood (with acceptance), strengthen his testimony and fulfil his wishes regarding his

مَاۡمُوْلَهٗ فِيْ اَهْلِ بَيْتِهٖ وَاُمَّتِهٖ.

household and his followers.

اَللّٰهُمَّ اجْعَلْ صَلَوَاتِكَ وَبَـرَكَاتِـكَ وَرَاۡفَـتَـكَ

O Allah! Shower Your blessings, mercy and kindness on our Noble Master,

 وَرَحْمَتَكَ عَلٰى مُحَمَّدٍ حَبِيْبِكَ وَصَفِيِّكَ وَعَلٰى

Nabi Muhammad ﷺ who is Your beloved and chosen one and shower your blessings on

اَهْلِ بَيْتِهِ الطَّيِّبِيْنَ الطَّاهِرِيْنَ

the members of his family who are completely purified and pure.

اَللّٰهُمَّ صَلِّ عَلٰى مُحَمَّدٍ بِاَفْضَلِ مَا صَلَّيْتَ عَلٰى

O Allah! From all the grace and bounties You have bestowed upon anyone of Your creation, bestow Your best salawaat (salutation)

اَحَدٍ مِّنْ خَلْقِكَ وَبَارِكْ عَلٰى مُحَمَّدٍ مِّثْلَ ذٰلِكَ

on our Noble Master, Nabi Muhammad ﷺ. Bless him and

وَارْحَمْ مُحَمَّدًا مِّثْلَ ذٰلِكَ. اَللّٰهُمَّ صَلِّ عَلٰى

have mercy upon him in the same manner. O Allah! Shower Your mercy on our Noble Master,

مُحَمَّدٍ فِى اللَّيْلِ اِذَا يَغْشَى وَصَلِّ عَلَى مُحَمَّدٍ

Nabi Muhammad ﷺ during the night when its darkness covers all things and

فِى النَّهَارِ اِذَا تَجَلَّى. وَصَلِّ عَلَى مُحَمَّدٍ فِى

during the day when everything is brighten and shower Your mercy upon him

الْاٰخِرَةِ وَالْاُوْلَى. اَللّٰهُمَّ صَلِّ عَلَى مُحَمَّدٍ

in this world and the Hereafter. O Allah! Bestow Your

الصَّلٰوةَ التَّآمَّةَ وَبَارِكْ عَلَى مُحَمَّدٍ الْبَرَكَةَ

complete mercy, blessings and peace on our Noble Master,

التَّآمَّةَ وَسَلِّمْ عَلَى مُحَمَّدٍ السَّلَامَ التَّآمَّ

Nabi Muhammad ﷺ.

اَللّٰهُمَّ صَلِّ عَلٰى مُحَمَّدٍ اِمَامِ الْخَيْرِ وَقَآئِدِ

O Allah! Bestow Your special mercy on our Noble Master Muhammad ﷺ who is a guide to goodness, the leader of

الْخَيْرِ وَرَسُوْلِ الرَّحْمَةِ. اَللّٰهُمَّ صَلِّ عَلٰى

virtue and a Rasool of mercy. O Allah! Shower Your special mercy on our Noble Master, Nabi Muhammad ﷺ

مُحَمَّدٍ اَبَدَ الْاٰبِدِيْنَ وَصَلِّ عَلٰى مُحَمَّدٍ دَهْرَ

for ever and ever and for all times.

الدَّاهِرِيْنَ. اَللّٰهُمَّ صَلِّ عَلٰى مُحَمَّدِ النَّبِيِّ

O Allah! Bestow Your special mercy on our Noble Master, Nabi Muhammad ﷺ the unlettered Arab Nabi,

الْاُمِّيِّ الْعَرَبِيِّ الْقُرَشِيِّ الْهَاشِمِيِّ الْاَبْطَحِيِّ

who is Quraishi and Haashmi by descent, hailing from the areas Bathaa, Tihaamah and holy city of Makkah Mukarramah

التِّهَامِيِّ الْمَكِّيِّ صَاحِبِ التَّاجِ وَالْهِرَاوَةِ

the possessor of the crown (leadership) and the staff (discipline),

وَالْجِهَادِ وَالْكَرَامَةِ وَالْمَغْنَمِ وَالْمَقْسَمِ

one who is blessed with Jihaad (striving in the path of Allah), and honour, spoils of war and the distributor of it.

صَاحِبِ الْخَيْرِ وَالْمَيْرِ صَاحِبِ السَّرَايَا

One who imparts virtue and benefits, has armies under his command,

وَالْعَطَايَا وَالْآيَاتِ الْمُعْجِزَاتِ وَالْعَلَامَاتِ

is a generous giver, possess of miraculous signs and special symbols and

الْبَاهِرَاتِ وَالْمَقَامِ الْمَشْهُودِ وَالْحَوْضِ

is predestined to occupy the highest pedestal in the Hereafter. The one who is in charge of the Haudh-e-Kausar (Pond of water) which

اَلْمَوْرُوْدِ وَالشَّفَاعَةِ وَالسُّجُوْدِ لِرَبِّ الْمَحْمُوْدِ

will be visited by all the thirsty, and to intercede on behalf of all the creatures by performing sajdah before Allah Ta'ala the

اَللّٰهُمَّ صَلِّ عَلٰى مُحَمَّدٍ بِعَدَدِ مَنْ صَلّٰى عَلَيْهِ

Praiseworthy. O Allah! Bestow Your special mercy on our Noble Master, Nabi Muhammad ﷺ equal to the number of times

وَصَلِّ عَلٰى مُحَمَّدٍ بِعَدَدِ مَنْ لَّمْ يُصَلِّ عَلَيْهِ

people have offered their salaams to him as well as the number of those who have not sent salaams upon him.

(٢٤) اَللّٰهُمَّ صَلِّ عَلٰى سَيِّدِنَا مُحَمَّدِ الَّذِىْ

24. O Allah! Bless our Noble Master, Nabi Muhammad ﷺ who,

اَشْرَقَتْ بِنُوْرِهِ الظُّلَمُ ۚ اَللّٰهُمَّ صَلِّ عَلٰى سَيِّدِنَا

with his noor, turned darkness into light. O Allah! Bless our Noble Master,

24. Al Qawlul Badee Page 129

مُحَمَّدِ الْمَبْعُوثِ رَحْمَةً لِّكُلِّ الْأُمَمِ.

Nabi Muhammad ﷺ who was sent as a mercy for all the people of the worlds.

اَللّٰهُمَّ صَلِّ عَلٰى سَيِّدِنَا مُحَمَّدِ الْمُخْتَارِ

O Allah! Bless our Noble Master, Nabi Muhammad ﷺ who had been chosen

لِلسِّيَادَةِ وَالرِّسَالَةِ قَبْلَ خَلْقِ اللَّوْحِ وَالْقَلَمِ.

For leadership and prophethood even before the plate and the pen were created.

اَللّٰهُمَّ صَلِّ عَلٰى سَيِّدِنَا مُحَمَّدِ الْمَوْصُوفِ

O Allah! Bestow Your special mercy on our Noble Master, Nabi Muhammad ﷺ who was

بِأَفْضَلِ الْأَخْلَاقِ وَالشِّيَمِ. اَللّٰهُمَّ صَلِّ عَلٰى

the best in morals and habits. O Allah! Bestow Your special mercy

سَيِّدِنَا مُحَمَّدِ الْمَخْصُوْصِ بِجَوَامِعِ الْكَلِمِ

on our Noble Master, Nabi Muhammad ﷺ who is unique with comprehensive speech

وَخَوَآصِّ الْحِكَمِ. اَللّٰهُمَّ صَلِّ عَلٰى سَيِّدِنَا

and blessed with deep wisdom. O Allah! Bless our Noble Master,

مُحَمَّدِ الَّذِىْ كَانَ لَا تُنْتَهَكُ فِىْ مَجَالِسِهِ

Nabi Muhammad ﷺ in whose presence no one was ever insulted

الْحُرَمُ وَلَا يُغْضٰى عَنْ مَّنْ ظَلَمَ

nor was the slightest form of injustice, done by anyone, overlooked.

اَللّٰهُمَّ صَلِّ عَلٰى سَيِّدِنَا مُحَمَّدِ الَّذِىْ كَانَ اِذَا

O Allah! Bestow Your special mercy on our Noble Master, Nabi Muhammad ﷺ who

مَشٰى تُظِلُّهُ الْغَمَامَةُ حَيْثُ مَا يَمَّمَ

used to be shaded by a cloud whenever he would travel in any direction.

اَللّٰهُمَّ صَلِّ عَلٰى سَيِّدِنَا مُحَمَّدِ الَّذِىْ اِنْشَقَّ

O Allah! Bless our Noble Master, Nabi Muhammad ﷺ for whom

لَهُ الْقَمَرُ وَكَلَّمَهُ الْحَجَرُ وَاَقَرَّ بِرِسَالَتِهٖ

the moon was split into two pieces, stones talked to him and testified to his prophet-hood

وَصَمَّمَ. اَللّٰهُمَّ صَلِّ عَلٰى سَيِّدِنَا مُحَمَّدِ الَّذِىْ

and supported it. O Allah! Bless our Noble Master, Nabi Muhammad ﷺ who

اَثْنٰى عَلَيْهِ رَبُّ الْعِزَّةِ رِضًا فِىْ سَالِفِ الْقِدَمِ

was praised by Allah Ta'ala Himself having been pleased with him since eternity.

اَللّٰهُمَّ صَلِّ عَلٰى سَيِّدِنَا مُحَمَّدِ الَّذِىْ صَلَّى

O Allah! Bestow Your special mercy on our Noble Master, Nabi Muhammad ﷺ

عَلَيْهِ رَبُّنَا فِىْ مُحْكَمِ كِتَابِهٖ وَاَمَرَ اَنْ يُّصَلَّى

who has been blessed by our Rabb in His Divine Book and we have been commanded therein to send

عَلَيْهِ وَيُسَلِّمَ صَلَّى اللهُ عَـلَـيْـهِ وَعَلٰى اٰلِهٖ

salaat and salaam upon him. Hence we ask You, O Allah! To be pleased with him and to shower Your special mercy on him, his

وَاَصْحَابِهٖ وَاَزْوَاجِهٖ مَا انْهَلَّتِ الدِّيَمُ وَمَـا

family, companions and wives for as long as the rains continue

جُرَّتْ عَلَى الْمُذْنِبِيْنَ اَذْيَالُ الْكَرَمِ وَسَـلَّـمَ

to pour and the sails of forgiveness are extended over the sinners and

تَسْلِيمًا وَّشَرَفَ وَكَرَّمَ

(O Allah) grant him peace, excellence and honour.

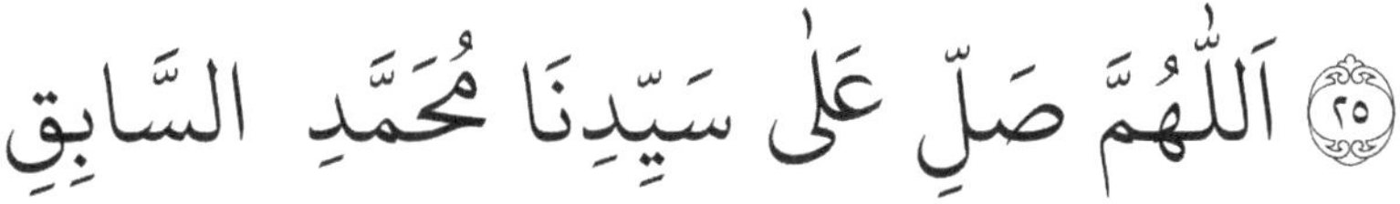

اَللّٰهُمَّ صَلِّ عَلٰى سَيِّدِنَا مُحَمَّدِ السَّابِقِ

25. O Allah! Bestow Your special mercy on our Noble Master, Nabi Muhammad ﷺ

لِلْخَلْقِ نُوْرُهُ وَالرَّحْمَةِ لِلْعَالَمِينَ ظُهُورُهُ. عَدَدَ

whose noor (light) preceded the entire creation and whose arrival became a mercy unto all the worlds.

مَنْ مَّضَى مِنْ خَلْقِكَ وَمَنْ بَقِيَ وَمَنْ سَعِدَ

let Your special mercy be repeated as many times as the number of Your creatures, past, present and future, as well as the number

مِنْهُمْ وَمَنْ شَقِيَ صَلٰوةً تَسْتَغْرِقُ الْعَدَّ

of fortunate and doomed among them. Rather, a mercy which exceeds all mathematical figures

25. Al Qawlul Badee Page 130

وَتُحِيْطُ بِالْحَدِّ صَلَاةً لَّا غَايَةَ لَهَا وَلَا اِنْتِهَآءَ

and whose limits know no end. Such salawaat which is

وَلَا اَمَدَ لَهَا وَلَا اِنْقِضَآءَ صَلَاةً دَآئِمَةً

everlasting with Your eternal existence

بِدَوَامِكَ وَعَلَى اٰلِهٖ وَصَحْبِهٖ كَذَالِكَ

and (O Allah) favour the family and companions of our beloved Nabi ﷺ with the same amount of mercy.

وَالْحَمْدُ لِلّٰهِ عَلَى ذٰلِكَ

All praise is due to Allah for all of this.

(٢٦) اَللّٰهُمَّ صَلِّ عَلَى مُحَمَّدٍ عَبْدِكَ وَرَسُوْلِكَ

26. O Allah! Bestow Your special mercy on our Noble Master, Nabi Muhammad ﷺ, Your servant and messenger, and bestow

26. Al Qawlul Badee Page 269

وَصَلِّ عَلَى الْمُؤْمِنِيْنَ وَالْمُؤْمِنَاتِ وَالْمُسْلِمِيْنَ

Your mercy on all the believing men and women and all Muslim men

وَالْمُسْلِمَاتِ

and Muslim women.

اَللّٰهُمَّ صَلِّ عَلٰى مُحَمَّدٍ وَّعَلٰى اٰلِ مُحَمَّدٍ ۲۷

27. O Allah! Bless our Noble Master, Nabi Muhammad ﷺ and his family.

وَهَبْ لَنَا اَللّٰهُمَّ مِنْ رِّزْقِكَ الْحَلَالِ الطَّيِّبِ

O Allah! Bless us with halaal sustenance which is pure blessed,

الْمُبَارَكِ مَا تَصُوْنُ بِهٖ وُجُوْهَنَا عَنِ التَّعَرُّضِ

and full of blessings such that it will save our respect from having to approach

27. Al Qawlul Badee Page 272

اِلٰى اَحَدٍ مِّنْ خَلْقِكَ.

any one of Your creation for help.

اَللّٰهُمَّ اجْعَلْ لَّنَا اِلَيْكَ طَرِيْقًا سَهْلًا مِّنْ غَيْرِ

O Allah! Make for us an easy path towards You which is not

تَعَبٍ وَّلَا نَصَبٍ وَّلَا مِنَّةٍ وَّلَا تَبِعَةٍ وَجَنِّبْنَا

tiresome or painful and has no obligation for us towards others.

اللّٰهُمَّ الْحَرَامَ حَيْثُ كَانَ وَاَيْنَ كَانَ

O Allah! Save us from haraam (unlawful) in whichever form, from whichever place or

وَعِنْدَ مَنْ كَانَ وَحُلْ بَيْنَنَا وَبَيْنَ اَهْلِهٖ

from any person. Please intervene between us and those people who have such (haraam) means.

وَاقْبِضْ عَنَّا اَيْدِيَهُمْ وَاصْرِفْ عَنَّا قُلُوْبَهُمْ

turn away their hands from us and divert their hearts away from us,

حَتّٰى لَانَتَقَلَّبَ اِلَّا فِيْمَا يُرْضِيْكَ وَلَانَسْتَعِيْنَ

so that we become immune from such things and act only in accordance with Your pleasure. (O Allah) enable us to utilise

بِنِعْمَتِكَ اِلَّا عَلٰى مَا تُحِبُّ يَآ اَرْحَمَ الرَّاحِمِيْنَ

Your gifts to do such actions which are pleasing to You, O The Most Merciful of those who show mercy.

اَللّٰهُمَّ اِنِّيْ اَسْاَلُكَ بِاَفْضَلِ مَسْاَلَتِكَ ﴿٢٨﴾

28. O Allah! I beg of You with a request that is the best in Your sight,

وَبِاَحَبِّ اَسْمَآئِكَ اِلَيْكَ وَاَكْرَمِهَا عَلَيْكَ وَبِمَا

(I beg of You) through Your names which are dearest and most exalted to You,

28. Al Qawlul Badee Page 360

مَنَنْتَ بِهٖ عَلَيْنَا بِمُحَمَّدٍ نَّبِيِّنَا صَلَّى اللّٰهُ عَلَيْهِ

through Your greatest favour upon us, i.e. favouring us with Nabi Muhammad ﷺ

وَسَلَّمَ وَاسْتَنْقَذْتَنَا بِهٖ مِنَ الضَّلَالَةِ وَاَمَرْتَنَا

and saving us through him from falling into misguidance. You commanded us

بِالصَّلَاةِ عَلَيْهِ وَجَعَلْتَ صَلَاتَنَا عَلَيْهِ دَرَجَةً

to send salawaat upon him and made the recitation of durood a means of achieving great heights,

وَّكَفَّارَةً وَّلُطْفًا وَّمَنًّا مِّنْ عَطَآئِكَ فَاَدْعُوْكَ

an atonement for our sins and attaining Your kindness and mercy. I beg of You,

تَعْظِيْمًا لِّاَمْرِكَ وَاتِّبَاعًا لِّوَصِيَّتِكَ وَتَنْجِيْزًا

honouring Your command, in compliance with Your order and in fulfilment of the duty

لِمَوْعِدِكَ بِمَا يَجِبُ لِنَبِيِّنَا صَلَّى اللهُ عَلَيْهِ

which we owe to our Nabi ﷺ

وَسَلَّمَ عَلَيْنَا فِيْ اَدَآءِ حَقِّهٖ قِبَلَنَا وَاَمَرْتَ

in an attempt to try and fulfil his rights which we owe to him. You have commanded

الْعِبَادَ بِالصَّلَاةِ عَلَيْهِ فَرِيْضَةً افْتَرَضْتَهَا

Your servants that they offer salawaat upon him; an obligation which you have made compulsory

عَلَيْهِمْ فَنَسْاَلُكَ بِجَلَالِ وَجْهِكَ وَنُوْرِ

on them I also beg of You by the Majesty of Your countenance and the light of

عَظَمَتِكَ اَنْ تُصَلِّيَ اَنْتَ وَمَلَآئِكَتُكَ عَلَى

Your Greatness that You, O Allah! Along with Your angels send the best greetings and bestow the best mercy upon

مُحَمَّدٍ عَبْدِكَ وَرَسُوْلِكَ وَنَبِيِّكَ وَصَفِيِّكَ

our Noble Master, Nabi Muhammad ﷺ, Your servant, your prophet, your messenger and your chosen one.

اَفْضَلَ مَا صَلَّيْتَ بِهٖ عَلٰى اَحَدٍ مِّنْ خَلْقِكَ اِنَّكَ

More then you bestowed to any of your creation, verily You are the

حَمِيْدٌ مَّجِيْدٌ اَللّٰهُمَّ ارْفَعْ دَرَجَتَهٗ. وَاَكْرِمْ

Praiseworthy and the Glorious. O Allah! Grant him a high rank, an honourable

مَّقَامَهٗ وَثَقِّلْ مِيْزَانَهٗ وَاَجْزِلْ ثَوَابَهٗ

position, make his scales weighty, grant him his reward in abundance,

وَاَفْلِجْ حُجَّتَهٗ. وَاَظْهِرْ مِلَّتَهٗ. وَاَضِئْ نُوْرَهٗ.

strengthen his testimony, allow his Deen to prevail and intensify his light,

وَاَدِمْ كَرَامَتَهُ مِنْ ذُرِّيَّتِهٖ وَاَهْلِ بَيْتِهٖ مَا تَقَرُّ

continue his excellence and nobility through his children and family who may become a source of coolness

بِهٖ عَيْنُهُ وَعَظِّمْهُ فِى النَّبِيِّيْنَ الَّذِيْنَ خَلَوْا

to his eyes and grant him superiority over all the Ambiyaa عَلَيْهِمُ السَّلَامُ that preceded him.

قَبْلَهٗ. اَللّٰهُمَّ اجْعَلْ مُحَمَّدًا اَكْثَرَ النَّبِيِّيْنَ

O Allah! Grant superiority to our Noble Master, Nabi Muhammad صَلَّى اللّٰهُ عَلَيْهِ وَسَلَّمَ over all other Ambiyaa

تَبَعًا وَّاَكْثَرَهُمْ اَزْرًا وَّاَفْضَلَهُمْ كَرَامَةً وَّنُوْرًا

in as far as the number of his followers and supporters are concerned, in excellence,

وَاَعْلَاهُمْ دَرَجَةً وَّاَفْسَحَهُمْ فِى الْجَنَّةِ مَنْزِلًا.

splendour and rank, grant him the most spacious abodes in paradise,

وَاَزِيْدَهُمْ ثَوَابًا وَاَقْرَبَهُمْ مَّجْلِسًا وَاَثْبَتَهُمْ

the most amount of reward, the closest to You in Your presence,

مَّقَامًا وَاَصْوَبَهُمْ كَلَامًا

most firmness in position, most correctness in speech,

وَاَنْجَحَهُمْ مَّسْاَلَةً وَاَوْفَرَهُمْ لَدَيْكَ نَصِيْبًا

most success in having his duas answered, the most fortunate in Your Court,

وَاَقْوَاهُمْ فِيْمَا عِنْدَكَ رَغْبَةً وَاَنْزِلْهُ فِىْ اَعْلٰى

the most desirous for what is with You and (O Allah) grant him the highest abode in

غُرَفِ الْفِرْدَوْسِ مِنَ الدَّرَجَاتِ الْعُلٰى.

Jannah tul firdous to live therein forever.

اَللّٰهُمَّ اجْعَلْ مُحَمَّدًا اَصْدَقَ قَآئِلٍ وَاَنْجَحَ

O Allah! Make our Noble Master, Nabi Muhammad ﷺ the most truthful in speech, most successful

سَآئِلٍ وَاَوَّلَ شَافِعٍ وَاَفْضَلَ مُشَفَّعٍ وَشَفِّعْهُ فِى

in his duas, the first to intercede (on the Day of Judgement), the most privileged amongst the intercessors and accept his

اُمَّتِهٖ شَفَاعَةً يَّغْبِطُهٗ بِهَا الْاَوَّلُوْنَ وَالْاٰخِرُوْنَ

intercession on behalf of his ummat to the extent which may be enviable to all Ambiyaa, the first and the last

وَاِذَا مَيَّزْتَ بَيْنَ عِبَادِكَ لِفَصْلِ الْقَضَآءِ

and (O Allah) when You give Your final verdict (on the Day of Judgement), assigning different positions to Your servants,

فَاجْعَلْ مُحَمَّدًا فِى الْاَصْدَقِيْنَ قِيْلًا وَّفِى

then place our Noble Master, Nabi Muhammad ﷺ in the category of those who are the most truthful in expression,

الْاَحْسَنِيْنَ عَمَلًا وَفِي الْمَهْدِيِّيْنَ سَبِيْلًا

most virtuous in deeds and the best guided as far as treading the path is concerned.

اَللّٰهُمَّ اجْعَلْ نَبِيَّنَا لَنَا فَرَطًا وَّحَوْضَهٗ لَنَا

O Allah! Make our Nabi ﷺ our forerunner (pre - arranger in the here after) and make his pond (Haudh-e-Kausar) a place for

مَوْرِدًا اَللّٰهُمَّ احْشُرْنَا فِيْ زُمْرَتِهٖ. وَاسْتَعْمِلْنَا

quenching our thirst. O Allah! Raise us (on the Day of Judgement) amongst his assembly, enable us to follow

بِسُنَّتِهٖ. وَتَوَفَّنَا عَلٰى مِلَّتِهٖ. وَاجْعَلْنَا فِيْ زُمْرَتِهٖ

his Sunnah, cause us to die adhering to his religion and raise us from amongst his group.

وَحِزْبِهٖ اَللّٰهُمَّ اجْمَعْ بَيْنَنَا وَبَيْنَهٗ كَمَا اٰمَنَّا

O Allah! Unite us with him as we have believed in him

بِهٖ وَلَمْ نَرَهٗ وَلَاتُفَرِّقْ بَيْنَنَا وَبَيْنَهٗ حَتّٰى

without having seen him and make it such that we may not be separated from him to the extent

تُدْخِلَنَا مُدْخَلَهٗ. وَتَجْعَلَنَا مِنْ رُّفَقَآئِهٖ مَعَ

that we enter into Jannah with him and (O Allah) include us amongst his companions along with

النَّبِيِّيْنَ وَالصِّدِّيْقِيْنَ وَالشُّهَدَآءِ

the Ambiyaa, Awliyaa, the martyrs

وَالصَّالِحِيْنَ وَحَسُنَ أُولٰئِكَ رَفِيْقًا

and the righteous. And What a blessed company that will be!

اَللّٰهُمَّ صَلِّ عَلٰى مُحَمَّدٍ نُوْرِ الْهُدٰى وَالْقَآئِدِ

O Allah! Bestow Your special mercy on our Noble Master, Nabi Muhammad ﷺ who is the light of guidance, who leads

اِلَى الْخَيْرِ وَالدَّاعِىٰ اِلَى الرُّشْدِ نَبِيّ الرَّحْمَةِ

people towards virtue, calls them to righteousness, The Nabi of Mercy,

(وَكَاشِفِ الْغُمَّةِ) وَاِمَامِ الْمُتَّقِيْنَ وَرَسُوْلِ رَبِّ

who soothes all grief, is the head of all the pious and the messenger of the Rabb

الْعَالَمِيْنَ كَمَا بَلَّغَ رِسَالَاتِكَ وَتَلَا اٰيَاتِكَ

of the worlds. (O Allah bestow Your special mercy on him) as he conveyed Your message, recited Your aayaat,

وَنَصَحَ لِعِبَادِكَ وَاَقَامَ حُدُوْدَكَ وَوَفّٰى

advised Your servants, established Your laws (limits), fulfilled

بِعَهْدِكَ وَاَنْفَذَ حُكْمَكَ وَاَمَرَ بِطَاعَتِكَ

his promises to You, carried out Your commandments, enjoined obedience to You,

وَنَهٰى عَنْ مَّعَاصِيْكَ وَوَالٰى وَلِيَّكَ الَّذِىْ

prohibited Your disobedience, befriended those whom You

تُحِبُّ اَنْ تُوَالِيَهٗ. وَعَادٰى عَدُوَّكَ الَّذِىْ تُحِبُّ

liked to be befriended, showed enmity towards Your enemies whom You were pleased that they be treated such.

اَنْ تُعَادِيَهٗ. وَصَلَّى اللهُ عَلٰى مُحَمَّدٍ وَّسَلَّمَ

May Allah's blessings be showered on our Noble Master, Nabi Muhammad ﷺ.

اَللّٰهُمَّ صَلِّ عَلٰى جَسَدِهٖ فِى الْاَجْسَادِ وَعَلٰى

O Allah! Bestow Your special mercy on his body among all other bodies,

رُوْحِهٖ فِى الْاَرْوَاحِ وَعَلٰى مَوْقِفِهٖ فِى الْمَوَاقِفِ

on his soul among all other souls, on his abode among all other abodes,

وَعَلٰى مَشْهَدِهٖ فِي الْمَشَاهِدِ وَعَلٰى ذِكْرِهٖ اِذَا

on his position among all other positions and (O Allah) wherever there is mention of his name

ذُكِرَ. صَلٰوةً مِّنَّا عَلٰى نَبِيِّنَا صَلَّى اللهُ عَلَيْهِ وَسَلَّمَ

let it be supplemented by our durood to our Nabi ﷺ.

اَللّٰهُمَّ اَبْلِغْهُ مِنَّا السَّلَامَ كُلَّمَا ذُكِرَ وَالسَّلَامُ

O Allah! Convey our salaams to him whenever there is mention of it and may peace

عَلَى النَّبِيِّ وَرَحْمَةُ اللهِ وَبَرَكَاتُهٗ

and Allah's blessings and mercy be upon Nabi ﷺ.

اَللّٰهُمَّ صَلِّ عَلٰى مَلَآئِكَتِكَ الْمُقَرَّبِيْنَ وَعَلٰى

O Allah! Bestow Your special mercy on Your special close angels,

اَنْبِيَآئِكَ الْمُطَهَّرِيْنَ وَعَلٰى رُسُلِكَ

all the pure Ambiyaa and messengers sent by You,

الْمُرْسَلِيْنَ وَعَلٰى حَمَلَةِ عَرْشِكَ اَجْمَعِيْنَ وَعَلٰى

on all the carriers of Your Throne,

جِبْرِيْلَ وَمِيْكَائِيْلَ وَاِسْرَافِيْلَ وَمَلَكِ الْمَوْتِ

on Jibraeel عَلَيْهِ السَّلَامُ Mikaeel عَلَيْهِ السَّلَامُ, Israfeel عَلَيْهِ السَّلَامُ, the angel of death,

وَرِضْوَانَ وَمَالِكٍ وَصَلِّ عَلَى الْكِرَامِ الْكَاتِبِيْنَ

Ridwaan (the angels guarding Jannah), Maalik (the angel guarding Jahannam), on Kiraaman Kaatibeen (the angels who record good

وَعَلٰى اَهْلِ بَيْتِ نَبِيِّكَ صَلَّى اللهُ عَلَيْهِ وَسَلَّمَ

and bad deeds) and (O Allah) send Your choicest blessings upon the family of our Nabi's صَلَّى اللهُ عَلَيْهِ وَسَلَّمَ

اَفْضَلَ مَاۤ اٰتَيْتَ اَحَدًا مِّنْ اَهْلِ بُيُوْتِ

household compared to the inmates of the households

الْمُرْسَلِيْنَ وَاجْزِ اَصْحَابَ نَبِيِّكَ صَلَّى اللّٰهُ

of all the other Messengers and the best reward to the companions of Your

عَلَيْهِ وَسَلَّمَ اَفْضَلَ مَا جَزَيْتَ اَحَدًا مِّنْ

Nabi ﷺ as compared to all the companions

اَصْحَابِ الْمُرْسَلِيْنَ

of the other Messengers.

اَللّٰهُمَّ اغْفِرْ لِلْمُؤْمِنِيْنَ وَالْمُؤْمِنَاتِ

O Allah! Forgive all the believing men and women,

وَالْمُسْلِمِيْنَ وَالْمُسْلِمَاتِ اَلْاَحْيَآءِ مِنْهُمْ

all the Muslim men and women including those who are alive and those

وَالْاَمْوَاتِ وَلِاِخْوَانِنَا الَّذِيْنَ سَبَقُوْنَا

who have passed away and our Muslim brothers who brought Imaan before us, and

بِالْاِيْمَانِ وَلَا تَجْعَلْ فِيْ قُلُوْبِنَا غِلًّا لِّلَّذِيْنَ

(O Allah) do not leave any ill-feelings in our hearts towards the

اٰمَنُوْا رَبَّنَآ اِنَّكَ رَءُوْفٌ رَّحِيْمٌ

Muslims. Verily You are Most Kind and all Merciful.

﴿٢٩﴾ اَللّٰهُمَّ صَلِّ عَلٰى مُحَمَّدٍ عَبْدِكَ وَنَبِيِّكَ

29. O Allah! Bestow Your special mercy on our Noble Master, Nabi Muhammad ﷺ, Your servant, Your messenger,

29. Al Qawlul Badee Page 378

وَرَسُوْلِكَ النَّبِيِّ الْأُمِّيِّ (وَعَلٰى اٰلِهٖ وَاَصْحَابِهٖ وَسَلِّمْ)

And a Nabi who is unlettered and upon all his family members and companions. Peace be upon them all.

اَللّٰهُمَّ صَلِّ عَلٰى مُحَمَّدٍ كُلَّمَا ذَكَرَهُ ۝٣٠

30. O Allah! Bestow Your special mercy on our Noble Master, Nabi Muhammad ﷺ whenever people

الذَّاكِرُوْنَ وَصَلِّ عَلٰى مُحَمَّدٍ كُلَّمَا غَفَلَ عَنْ

remember and mention his name and bestow Your special mercy on our Noble Master, Nabi Muhammad ﷺ whenever

ذِكْرِهِ الْغَافِلُوْنَ

heedless people fail to remember and mention him.

اَللّٰهُمَّ صَلِّ عَلٰى مُحَمَّدٍ عَبْدِكَ وَرَسُوْلِكَ ۝٣١

31. O Allah! Bestow Your special mercy on our Noble Master, Nabi Muhammad ﷺ Your servant, Your messenger

30. Al Qawlul Badee Page # 466

النَّبِيِّ الْاُمِّيِّ الَّذِىْ اٰمَنَ بِكَ وَبِكِتَابِكَ

and the unlettered nabi, who has believed in You and Your Book

وَاَعْطِهٖ اَفْضَلَ رَحْمَتِكَ. وَاٰتِهِ الشَّرَفَ عَلٰى

and (O Allah), favour him with Your special mercy, elevate him over all

خَلْقِكَ يَوْمَ الْقِيَامَةِ وَاجْزِهٖ خَيْرَ الْجَزَآءِ

Your creatures (for all time) up to the Day of Judgement and grant Him the best reward.

وَالسَّلَامُ عَلَيْهِ وَرَحْمَةُ اللهِ وَبَرَكَاتُهٗ

May peace and Allah's mercy and blessings be upon him.

سُبْحٰنَ رَبِّكَ رَبِّ الْعِزَّةِ عَمَّا يَصِفُوْنَ وَسَلٰمٌ ۝

32. Your Rabb who is Most Honoured, is unblemished and far above what the unbelievers say (about Him). Peace be upon all the

32. S: Saafaat V: 180-182

عَلَى الْمُرْسَلِيْنَ وَالْحَمْدُ لِلّٰهِ رَبِّ الْعٰلَمِيْنَ

Messengers and all praise is due to Allah, the Cherisher of the worlds.

SALAAT
&
SALAAM

بِسْمِ اللهِ الرَّحْمٰنِ الرَّحِيْمِ

سَلَامٌ عَلٰى عِبَادِهِ الَّذِيْنَ اصْطَفٰى، سَلَامٌ عَلٰى

الْمُرْسَلِيْنَ.

(١) أَللّٰهُمَّ صَلِّ عَلٰى مُحَمَّدٍ وَّعَلٰى اٰلِ مُحَمَّدٍ وَّأَنْزِلْهُ

الْمَقْعَدَ الْمُقَرَّبَ عِنْدَكَ

(٢) أَللّٰهُمَّ رَبَّ هٰذِهِ الدَّعْوَةِ الْقَآئِمَةِ وَالصَّلٰوةِ

النَّافِعَةِ صَلِّ عَلٰى مُحَمَّدٍ وَّارْضَ عَنِّيْ رِضًا

| Qur-aan | 1. Tabraani | 2. Musnad-e-Ahmad |

لَا تَسْخَطْ بَعْدَهُ أَبَدًا

۞٣ اَللّٰهُمَّ صَلِّ عَلٰى مُحَمَّدٍ عَبْدِكَ وَرَسُوْلِكَ وَصَلِّ

عَلَى الْمُؤْمِنِيْنَ وَالْمُؤْمِنَاتِ وَالْمُسْلِمِيْنَ

وَالْمُسْلِمَاتِ

۞٤ اَللّٰهُمَّ صَلِّ عَلٰى مُحَمَّدٍ وَّعَلٰى اٰلِ مُحَمَّدٍ وَّبَارِكْ

عَلٰى مُحَمَّدٍ وَّعَلٰى اٰلِ مُحَمَّدٍ وَّارْحَمْ مُحَمَّدًا وَّاٰلَ

مُحَمَّدٍ كَمَا صَلَّيْتَ وَبَارَكْتَ وَرَحِمْتَ عَلٰى

اِبْرَاهِيْمَ وَعَلٰى اٰلِ اِبْرَاهِيْمَ اِنَّكَ حَمِيْدٌ مَّجِيْدٌ

۞٥ اَللّٰهُمَّ صَلِّ عَلٰى مُحَمَّدٍ وَّعَلٰى اٰلِ مُحَمَّدٍ كَمَا

3. Ibn Hibbaan	4. Bayhaqi	5. Bukhaari Shareef

صَلَّيْتَ عَلٰى اٰلِ اِبْرَاهِيْمَ، اِنَّكَ حَمِيْدٌ مَّجِيْدٌ. اَللّٰهُمَّ

بَارِكْ عَلٰى مُحَمَّدٍ وَّعَلٰى اٰلِ مُحَمَّدٍ كَمَا بَارَكْتَ عَلٰى

اٰلِ اِبْرَاهِيْمَ اِنَّكَ حَمِيْدٌ مَّجِيْدٌ

٦ اَللّٰهُمَّ صَلِّ عَلٰى مُحَمَّدٍ وَّعَلٰى اٰلِ مُحَمَّدٍ كَمَا

صَلَّيْتَ عَلٰى اٰلِ اِبْرَاهِيْمَ اِنَّكَ حَمِيْدٌ مَّجِيْدٌ. وَبَارِكْ

عَلٰى مُحَمَّدٍ وَّعَلٰى اٰلِ مُحَمَّدٍ كَمَا بَارَكْتَ عَلٰى اٰلِ

اِبْرَاهِيْمَ، اِنَّكَ حَمِيْدٌ مَّجِيْدٌ

٧ اَللّٰهُمَّ صَلِّ عَلٰى مُحَمَّدٍ وَّعَلٰى اٰلِ مُحَمَّدٍ كَمَا

صَلَّيْتَ عَلٰى اِبْرَاهِيْمَ اِنَّكَ حَمِيْدٌ مَّجِيْدٌ. اَللّٰهُمَّ

6. Muslim Shareef	7. Ibn Maajah

بَارِكْ عَلٰى مُحَمَّدٍ وَّعَلٰى اٰلِ مُحَمَّدٍ كَمَا بَارَكْتَ عَلٰى

اِبْرَاهِيْمَ اِنَّكَ حَمِيْدٌ مَّجِيْدٌ

٨ اَللّٰهُمَّ صَلِّ عَلٰى مُحَمَّدٍ وَّعَلٰى اٰلِ مُحَمَّدٍ كَمَا

صَلَّيْتَ عَلٰى اِبْرَاهِيْمَ وَعَلٰى اٰلِ اِبْرَاهِيْمَ اِنَّكَ حَمِيْدٌ

مَّجِيْدٌ وَّبَارِكْ عَلٰى مُحَمَّدٍ وَّعَلٰى اٰلِ مُحَمَّدٍ كَمَا

بَارَكْتَ عَلٰى اِبْرَاهِيْمَ اِنَّكَ حَمِيْدٌ مَّجِيْدٌ

٩ اَللّٰهُمَّ صَلِّ عَلٰى مُحَمَّدٍ وَّعَلٰى اٰلِ مُحَمَّدٍ كَمَا

صَلَّيْتَ عَلٰى اِبْرَاهِيْمَ وَبَارِكْ عَلٰى مُحَمَّدٍ وَّعَلٰى اٰلِ

مُحَمَّدٍ كَمَا بَارَكْتَ عَلٰى اِبْرَاهِيْمَ اِنَّكَ حَمِيْدٌ مَّجِيْدٌ

---

8. Nasai	9. Abu Dawood

(١٠) اَللّٰهُمَّ صَلِّ عَلٰى مُحَمَّدٍ وَّعَلٰى اٰلِ مُحَمَّدٍ كَمَا

صَلَّيْتَ عَلٰى إِبْرَاهِيْمَ اِنَّكَ حَمِيْدٌ مَّجِيْدٌ۔ اَللّٰهُمَّ

بَارِكْ عَلٰى مُحَمَّدٍ وَّعَلٰى اٰلِ مُحَمَّدٍ كَمَا بَارَكْتَ عَلٰى

اٰلِ اِبْرَاهِيْمَ اِنَّكَ حَمِيْدٌ مَّجِيْدٌ

(١١) اَللّٰهُمَّ صَلِّ عَلٰى مُحَمَّدٍ وَّعَلٰى اٰلِ مُحَمَّدٍ كَمَا

صَلَّيْتَ عَلٰى اٰلِ اِبْرَاهِيْمَ وَبَارِكْ عَلٰى مُحَمَّدٍ وَّعَلٰى

اٰلِ مُحَمَّدٍ كَمَا بَارَكْتَ عَلٰى اٰلِ اِبْرَاهِيْمَ فِى

الْعَالَمِيْنَ اِنَّكَ حَمِيْدٌ مَّجِيْدٌ

(١٢) اَللّٰهُمَّ صَلِّ عَلٰى مُحَمَّدٍ وَّاَزْوَاجِهٖ وَذُرِّيَّتِهٖ كَمَا

| 10. Abu Dawood | 11. Muslim Shareef | 12. Abu Dawood |

صَلَّيْتَ عَلٰى اٰلِ اِبْرَاهِيْمَ، وَبَارِكْ عَلٰى مُحَمَّدٍ

وَّاَزْوَاجِهٖ وَذُرِّيَّتِهٖ كَمَا بَارَكْتَ عَلٰى اٰلِ اِبْرَاهِيْمَ

اِنَّكَ حَمِيْدٌ مَّجِيْدٌ

(١٣) اَللّٰهُمَّ صَلِّ عَلٰى مُحَمَّدٍ وَّعَلٰٓى اَزْوَاجِهٖ وَذُرِّيَّتِهٖ

كَمَا صَلَّيْتَ عَلٰى اٰلِ اِبْرَاهِيْمَ وَ بَارِكْ عَلٰى مُحَمَّدٍ

وَّعَلٰٓى اَزْوَاجِهٖ وَذُرِّيَّتِهٖ كَمَا بَارَكْتَ عَلٰى اٰلِ

اِبْرَاهِيْمَ اِنَّكَ حَمِيْدٌ مَّجِيْدٌ.

(١٤) اَللّٰهُمَّ صَلِّ عَلٰى مُحَمَّدٍ النَّبِيِّ وَاَزْوَاجِهٖ اُمَّهَاتِ

الْمُؤْمِنِيْنَ وَذُرِّيَّتِهٖ وَاَهْلِ بَيْتِهٖ كَمَا صَلَّيْتَ عَلٰى

| 13. Muslim Shareef | 14. Abu Dawood |

اِبْرَاهِيْمَ اِنَّكَ حَمِيْدٌ مَّجِيْدٌ.

(١٥) اَللّٰهُمَّ صَلِّ عَلٰى مُحَمَّدٍ وَّعَلٰى اٰلِ مُحَمَّدٍ كَمَا

صَلَّيْتَ عَلٰى اِبْرَاهِيْمَ وَعَلٰى اٰلِ اِبْرَاهِيْمَ وَبَارِكْ عَلٰى

مُحَمَّدٍ وَّعَلٰى اٰلِ مُحَمَّدٍ كَمَا بَارَكْتَ عَلٰى اِبْرَاهِيْمَ وَ

تَرَحَّمْ عَلٰى مُحَمَّدٍ وَّعَلٰى اٰلِ مُحَمَّدٍ كَمَا تَرَحَّمْتَ عَلٰى

اِبْرَاهِيْمَ وَعَلٰى اٰلِ اِبْرَاهِيْمَ.

(١٦) اَللّٰهُمَّ صَلِّ عَلٰى مُحَمَّدٍ وَّعَلٰى اٰلِ مُحَمَّدٍ كَمَا

صَلَّيْتَ عَلٰى اِبْرَاهِيْمَ وَعَلٰى اٰلِ اِبْرَاهِيْمَ اِنَّكَ حَمِيْدٌ

مَّجِيْدٌ. اَللّٰهُمَّ بَارِكْ عَلٰى مُحَمَّدٍ وَّعَلٰى اٰلِ مُحَمَّدٍ

15. Tabri | 16. Si'aayah

كَمَا بَارَكْتَ عَلٰى اِبْرَاهِيْمَ وَعَلٰى اٰلِ اِبْرَاهِيْمَ اِنَّكَ

حَمِيْدٌ مَّجِيْدٌ۔ اَللّٰهُمَّ تَرَحَّمْ عَلٰى مُحَمَّدٍ وَّعَلٰى اٰلِ

مُحَمَّدٍ كَمَا تَرَحَّمْتَ عَلٰى اِبْرَاهِيْمَ وَعَلٰى اٰلِ

اِبْرَاهِيْمَ، اِنَّكَ حَمِيْدٌ مَّجِيْدٌ۔ اَللّٰهُمَّ تَحَنَّنْ عَلٰى مُحَمَّدٍ

وَّعَلٰى اٰلِ مُحَمَّدٍ كَمَا تَحَنَّنْتَ عَلٰى اِبْرَاهِيْمَ وَعَلٰى اٰلِ

اِبْرَاهِيْمَ اِنَّكَ حَمِيْدٌ مَّجِيْدٌ۔ اَللّٰهُمَّ سَلِّمْ عَلٰى مُحَمَّدٍ

وَّعَلٰى اٰلِ مُحَمَّدٍ كَمَا سَلَّمْتَ عَلٰى اِبْرَاهِيْمَ وَعَلٰى اٰلِ

اِبْرَاهِيْمَ اِنَّكَ حَمِيْدٌ مَّجِيْدٌ

(۱۷) اَللّٰهُمَّ صَلِّ عَلٰى مُحَمَّدٍ وَّعَلٰى اٰلِ مُحَمَّدٍ وَّبَارِكْ

17. Si'aayah

وَسَلِّمْ عَلٰى مُحَمَّدٍ وَّعَلٰى اٰلِ مُحَمَّدٍ وَّارْحَمْ مُحَمَّدًا

وَّاٰلَ مُحَمَّدٍ كَمَا صَلَّيْتَ وَبَارَكْتَ وَتَرَحَّمْتَ عَلٰى

اِبْرَاهِيْمَ وَعَلٰى اٰلِ اِبْرَاهِيْمَ فِى الْعَالَمِيْنَ اِنَّكَ حَمِيْدٌ

مَّجِيْدٌ

اَللّٰهُمَّ صَلِّ عَلٰى مُحَمَّدٍ وَّعَلٰى اٰلِ مُحَمَّدٍ كَمَا ﴿١٨﴾

صَلَّيْتَ عَلٰى اِبْرَاهِيْمَ وَعَلٰى اٰلِ اِبْرَاهِيْمَ اِنَّكَ حَمِيْدٌ

مَّجِيْدٌ. اَللّٰهُمَّ بَارِكْ عَلٰى مُحَمَّدٍ وَّعَلٰى اٰلِ مُحَمَّدٍ كَمَا

بَارَكْتَ عَلٰى اِبْرَاهِيْمَ وَعَلٰى اٰلِ اِبْرَاهِيْمَ اِنَّكَ حَمِيْدٌ

مَّجِيْدٌ

18. Sihah Sitta

﴿۱۹﴾ اَللّٰهُمَّ صَلِّ عَلٰى مُحَمَّدٍ عَبْدِكَ وَرَسُوْلِكَ كَمَا

صَلَّيْتَ عَلٰى اٰلِ إِبْرَاهِيْمَ وَ بَارِكْ عَلٰى مُحَمَّدٍ وَّعَلٰى

اٰلِ مُحَمَّدٍ كَمَا بَارَكْتَ عَلٰى اٰلِ اِبْرَاهِيْمَ

﴿۲۰﴾ اَللّٰهُمَّ صَلِّ عَلٰى مُحَمَّدٍ النَّبِيِّ الْأُمِّيِّ وَعَلٰى اٰلِ

مُحَمَّدٍ كَمَا صَلَّيْتَ عَلٰى اِبْرَاهِيْمَ وَبَارِكْ عَلٰى

مُحَمَّدٍ النَّبِيِّ الْأُمِّيِّ كَمَا بَارَكْتَ عَلٰى اِبْرَاهِيْمَ

اِنَّكَ حَمِيْدٌ مَّجِيْدٌ

﴿۲۱﴾ اَللّٰهُمَّ صَلِّ عَلٰى مُحَمَّدٍ عَبْدِكَ وَرَسُوْلِكَ النَّبِيِّ

الْأُمِّيِّ وَعَلٰى اٰلِ مُحَمَّدٍ. اَللّٰهُمَّ صَلِّ عَلٰى مُحَمَّدٍ وَّعَلٰى

| 19. Nasai, Ibn Maajah | 20. Nasai | 21. Al-Qawlul Badee |

اَلِ مُحَمَّدٍ صَلوةً تَكُوْنُ لَكَ رِضًى وَّلَهُ جَزَآءً،

وَّلِحَقِّهٖ اَدَآءً وَّاَعْطِهِ الْوَسِيْلَةَ وَالْفَضِيْلَةَ وَالْمَقَامَ

الْمَحْمُوْدَ الَّذِىْ وَعَدْتَّهٗ وَاجْزِهٖ عَنَّا مَا هُوَ اَهْلُهٗ

وَاجْزِهٖ اَفْضَلَ مَا جَازَيْتَ نَبِيًّا عَنْ قَوْمِهٖ وَ

رَسُوْلًا عَنْ اُمَّتِهٖ وَصَلِّ عَلٰى جَمِيْعِ اِخْوَانِهٖ مِنَ

النَّبِيِّيْنَ وَالصَّالِحِيْنَ يَا اَرْحَمَ الرَّاحِمِيْنَ

۞ ٢٢ اَللّٰهُمَّ صَلِّ عَلٰى مُحَمَّدٍ النَّبِيِّ الْاُمِّيِّ وَعَلٰى اٰلِ

مُحَمَّدٍ كَمَا صَلَّيْتَ عَلٰى اِبْرَاهِيْمَ وَعَلٰى اٰلِ اِبْرَاهِيْمَ

وَبَارِكْ عَلٰى مُحَمَّدٍ النَّبِيِّ الْاُمِّيِّ وَعَلٰى اٰلِ مُحَمَّدٍ

---

22. Bayhaqi, Musnad-e-Ahmad, Mustadrak

كَمَا بَارَكْتَ عَلَى إِبْرَاهِيمَ وَعَلَى أَلِ اِبْرَاهِيمَ اِنَّكَ

حَمِيدٌ مَّجِيدٌ

(۲۳) اَللّٰهُمَّ صَلِّ عَلَى مُحَمَّدٍ وَّعَلَى اَهْلِ بَيْتِهِ كَمَا

صَلَّيْتَ عَلَى اِبْرَاهِيمَ اِنَّكَ حَمِيدٌ مَّجِيدٌ اَللّٰهُمَّ صَلِّ

عَلَيْنَا مَعَهُمْ۔ اَللّٰهُمَّ بَارِكْ عَلَى مُحَمَّدٍ وَّعَلَى اَهْلِ

بَيْتِهِ كَمَا بَارَكْتَ عَلَى اِبْرَاهِيمَ اِنَّكَ حَمِيدٌ مَّجِيدٌ۔

اَللّٰهُمَّ بَارِكْ عَلَيْنَا مَعَهُمْ صَلَوَاتُ اللهِ وَ صَلَوَاتُ

الْمُؤْمِنِينَ عَلَى مُحَمَّدِ النَّبِيِّ الْأُمِّيِّ

(۲٤) اَللّٰهُمَّ اجْعَلْ صَلَوَاتِكَ وَرَحْمَتَكَ وَبَرَكَاتِكَ عَلَى

23. Daara Qutni

مُحَمَّدٍ وَّعَلٰى اٰلِ مُحَمَّدٍ كَمَا جَعَلْتَهَا عَلٰى اٰلِ

اِبْرَاهِيْمَ اِنَّكَ حَمِيْدٌ مَّجِيْدٌ وَبَارِكْ عَلٰى مُحَمَّدٍ وَّعَلٰى

اٰلِ مُحَمَّدٍ كَمَا بَارَكْتَ عَلٰى اِبْرَاهِيْمَ وَعَلٰى اٰلِ

اِبْرَاهِيْمَ اِنَّكَ حَمِيْدٌ مَّجِيْدٌ

(٢٥) وَصَلَّى اللهُ عَلَى النَّبِيِّ الْأُمِّيِّ

(٢٦) اَلتَّحِيَّاتُ لِلّٰهِ وَالصَّلَوَاتُ وَالطَّيِّبَاتُ اَلسَّلَامُ

عَلَيْكَ اَيُّهَا النَّبِيُّ وَرَحْمَةُ اللهِ وَ بَرَكَاتُهٗ اَلسَّلَامُ

عَلَيْنَا وَعَلٰى عِبَادِ اللهِ الصَّالِحِيْنَ اَشْهَدُ اَنْ لَّاۤ اِلٰهَ

اِلَّا اللهُ وَاَشْهَدُ اَنَّ مُحَمَّدًا عَبْدُهٗ وَرَسُوْلُهٗ

| 24. Ibn Abi Aasim | 25. Nasai | 26. Bukhaari Shareef, Nasai |

(۲۷) اَلتَّحِيَّاتُ الطَّيِّبَاتُ الصَّلَوَاتُ لِلّٰهِ اَلسَّلَامُ

عَلَيْكَ اَيُّهَا النَّبِيُّ وَرَحْمَةُ اللهِ وَبَرَكَاتُهُ اَلسَّلَامُ

عَلَيْنَا وَ عَلٰى عِبَادِ اللهِ الصَّالِحِينَ، اَشْهَدُ اَنْ لَّا

اِلٰهَ اِلَّا اللهُ وَاَشْهَدُ اَنَّ مُحَمَّدً عَبْدُهُ وَ رَسُوْلُهُ

(۲۸) اَلتَّحِيَّاتُ لِلّٰهِ الطَّيِّبَاتُ الصَّلَوَاتُ لِلّٰهِ اَلسَّلَامُ

عَلَيْكَ اَيُّهَا النَّبِيُّ وَرَحْمَةُ اللهِ وَبَرَكَاتُهُ اَلسَّلَامُ

عَلَيْنَا وَعَلٰى عِبَادِ اللهِ الصَّالِحِينَ، اَشْهَدُ اَنْ لَّا

اِلٰهَ اِلَّا اللهُ وَحْدَهُ لَاشَرِيْكَ لَهُ وَاَشْهَدُ اَنَّ مُحَمَّدَ

عَبْدُهُ وَ رَسُوْلُهُ

27. Muslim Shareef, Nasai	28. Nasai

٢٩ اَلتَّحِيَّاتُ الْمُبَارَكَاتُ الصَّلَوَاتُ الطَّيِّبَاتُ لِلّٰهِ

سَلَامٌ عَلَيْكَ اَيُّهَا النَّبِيُّ وَرَحْمَةُ اللّٰهِ وَبَرَكَاتُهُ

سَلَامٌ عَلَيْنَا وَعَلٰى عِبَادِ اللّٰهِ الصَّالِحِيْنَ اَشْهَدُ اَنْ

لَّآ اِلٰهَ اِلَّا اللّٰهُ وَاَشْهَدُ اَنَّ مُحَمَّدً عَبْدُهُ وَ رَسُوْلُهُ

٣٠ بِسْمِ اللّٰهِ وَبِاللّٰهِ اَلتَّحِيَّاتُ لِلّٰهِ وَالصَّلَوَاتُ

وَالطَّيِّبَاتُ اَلسَّلَامُ عَلَيْكَ اَيُّهَا النَّبِيُّ وَرَحْمَةُ اللّٰهِ

وَبَرَكَاتُهُ اَلسَّلَامُ عَلَيْنَا وَعَلٰى عِبَادِ اللّٰهِ الصَّالِحِيْنَ

اَشْهَدُ اَنْ لَّآ اِلٰهَ اِلَّا اللّٰهُ وَ اَشْهَدُ اَنَّ مُحَمَّدً عَبْدُهُ

وَرَسُوْلُهُ اَسْأَلُ اللّٰهَ الْجَنَّةَ وَاَعُوْذُ بِاللّٰهِ مِنَ النَّارِ

29. Nasai	30. Nasai

(٣١) اَلتَّحِيَّاتُ لِلّٰهِ الزَّاكِيَاتُ لِلّٰهِ الطَّيِّبَاتُ

الصَّلَوَاتُ لِلّٰهِ اَلسَّلَامُ عَلَيْكَ اَيُّهَا النَّبِىُّ وَرَحْمَةُ

اللّٰهِ وَبَرَكَاتُهٗ اَلسَّلَامُ عَلَيْنَا وَعَلٰى عِبَادِ اللّٰهِ

الصَّالِحِينَ اَشْهَدُ اَنْ لَّآ اِلٰهَ اِلَّا اللّٰهُ وَاَشْهَدُ اَنَّ

مُحَمَّدً عَبْدُهٗ وَرَسُولُهٗ

(٣٢) بِسْمِ اللّٰهِ وَبِاللّٰهِ خَيْرِ الْأَسْمَآءِ اَلتَّحِيَّاتُ

الطَّيِّبَاتُ الصَّلَوَاتُ لِلّٰهِ اَشْهَدُ اَنْ لَّآ اِلٰهَ اِلَّا اللّٰهُ

وَحْدَهٗ لَاشَرِيْكَ لَهٗ وَاَشْهَدُ اَنَّ مُحَمَّدً عَبْدُهٗ

وَرَسُولُهٗ اَرْسَلَهٗ بِالْحَقِّ بَشِيْرًا وَّ نَذِيْرًا وَّاَنَّ السَّاعَةَ

---

31. Muwatta | 32. Mu'jam Tabraani

اٰتِيَةٌ لَّا رَيْبَ فِيْهَا اَلسَّلَامُ عَلَيْكَ اَيُّهَا النَّبِيُّ

وَرَحْمَةُ اللهِ وَبَرَكَاتُهٗ اَلسَّلَامُ عَلَيْنَا وَعَلٰى عِبَادِ

اللهِ الصَّالِحِيْنَ، اَللّٰهُمَّ اغْفِرْلِيْ وَاهْدِنِيْ

۳۳ اَلتَّحِيَّاتُ الطَّيِّبَاتُ وَالصَّلَوَاتُ وَالْمُلْكُ لِلّٰهِ

اَلسَّلَامُ عَلَيْكَ اَيُّهَا النَّبِيُّ وَرَحْمَةُ اللهِ وَبَرَكَاتُهٗ

۳٤ بِسْمِ اللهِ اَلتَّحِيَّاتُ لِلّٰهِ الصَّلَوَاتُ لِلّٰهِ

الزَّاكِيَاتُ لِلّٰهِ اَلسَّلَامُ عَلَى النَّبِيِّ وَرَحْمَةُ اللهِ

وَبَرَكَاتُهٗ اَلسَّلَامُ عَلَيْنَا وَعَلٰى عِبَادِ اللهِ الصَّالِحِيْنَ

شَهِدْتُّ اَنْ لَّآ اِلٰهَ اِلَّا اللهُ شَهِدْتُّ اَنَّ مُحَمَّدًا

34. Muwatta	33. Abu Dawood

رَسُوْلُ اللهِ

(٣٥) اَلتَّحِيَّاتُ الطَّيِّبَاتُ الصَّلَوَاتُ الزَّاكِيَاتُ لِلّٰهِ

اَشْهَدُ اَنْ لَّآ اِلٰهَ اِلَّا اللهُ وَحْدَهُ لَاشَرِيْكَ لَهُ وَاَنَّ

مُحَمَّدً عَبْدُهُ وَ رَسُوْلُهُ اَلسَّلَامُ عَلَيْكَ اَيُّهَا النَّبِيُّ

وَ رَحْمَةُ اللهِ وَبَرَكَاتُهُ اَلسَّلَامُ عَلَيْنَا وَ عَلٰى عِبَادِ

اللهِ الصَّالِحِيْنَ

(٣٦) أَلتَّحِيَّاتُ الطَّيِّبَاتُ الصَّلَوَاتُ الزَّاكِيَاتُ لِلّٰهِ

اَشْهَدُ اَنْ لَّآ اِلٰهَ اِلَّا اللهُ وَاَشْهَدُ اَنَّ مُحَمَّدً عَبْد

اللهِ وَرَسُوْلُهُ اَلسَّلَامُ عَلَيْكَ اَيُّهَا النَّبِيُّ وَرَحْمَةُ

35. Muwatta	36. Muwatta

اللهِ وَبَرَكَاتُهُ اَلسَّلَامُ عَلَيْنَا وَعَلَى عِبَادِ اللهِ

الصَّالِحِينَ

٣٧ اَلتَّحِيَّاتُ الصَّلَوَاتُ لِلّٰهِ اَلسَّلَامُ عَلَيْكَ اَيُّهَا

النَّبِيُّ وَرَحْمَةُ اللهِ وَبَرَكَاتُهُ اَلسَّلَامُ عَلَيْنَا وَعَلَى

عِبَادِ اللهِ الصَّالِحِينَ

٣٨ اَلتَّحِيَّاتُ لِلّٰهِ الصَّلَوَاتُ الطَّيِّبَاتُ اَلسَّلَامُ

عَلَيْكَ اَيُّهَا النَّبِيُّ وَرَحْمَةُ اللهِ اَلسَّلَامُ عَلَيْنَا

وَعَلَى عِبَادِ اللهِ الصَّالِحِينَ اَشْهَدُ اَنْ لَّاۤ اِلٰهَ اِلَّا

اللهُ وَ اَشْهَدُ اَنَّ مُحَمَّدًا عَبْدُهُ وَ رَسُوْلُهُ

37. Tahaawi	38. Abu Dawood

(٣٩) اَلتَّحِيَّاتُ الْمُبَارَكَاتُ الصَّلَوَاتُ الطَّيِّبَاتُ لِلّٰهِ

اَلسَّلَامُ عَلَيْكَ اَيُّهَا النَّبِيُّ وَرَحْمَتُ اللّٰهِ وَ بَرَكَاتُهُ

اَلسَّلَامُ عَلَيْنَا وَعَلٰى عِبَادِ اللّٰهِ الصَّالِحِينَ اَشْهَدُ

اَنْ لَّا اِلٰهَ اِلَّا اللّٰهُ وَاَشْهَدُ اَنَّ مُحَمَّدًا رَّسُوْلُ اللّٰهِ

(٤٠) بِسْمِ اللّٰهِ وَالسَّلَامُ عَلٰى رَسُوْلِ اللّٰهِ

37. Tahaawi   38. Abu Dawood

Manzil

بِسْمِ اللهِ الرَّحْمٰنِ الرَّحِيمِ

اَلْحَمْدُ لِلّٰهِ رَبِّ الْعٰلَمِينَ ۝ الرَّحْمٰنِ الرَّحِيمِ ۝ مٰلِكِ يَوْمِ الدِّينِ ۝

اِيَّاكَ نَعْبُدُ وَاِيَّاكَ نَسْتَعِينُ ۝ اِهْدِنَا الصِّرَاطَ الْمُسْتَقِيمَ ۝ صِرَاطَ الَّذِينَ

اَنْعَمْتَ عَلَيْهِمْ ۝ غَيْرِ الْمَغْضُوبِ عَلَيْهِمْ وَلَا الضَّآلِّينَ ۝

بِسْمِ اللهِ الرَّحْمٰنِ الرَّحِيمِ

الٓمّٓ ۝ ذٰلِكَ الْكِتٰبُ لَا رَيْبَ ۚ فِيهِ ۛ هُدًى لِّلْمُتَّقِينَ ۝ الَّذِينَ يُؤْمِنُونَ

بِالْغَيْبِ وَيُقِيمُونَ الصَّلٰوةَ وَمِمَّا رَزَقْنٰهُمْ يُنْفِقُونَ ۝ وَالَّذِينَ يُؤْمِنُونَ بِمَآ

أُنْزِلَ اِلَيْكَ وَمَآ اُنْزِلَ مِنْ قَبْلِكَ وَبِالْاٰخِرَةِ هُمْ يُوقِنُونَ ۝ أُولٰٓئِكَ عَلٰى

هُدًى مِّنْ رَّبِّهِمْ ۖ وَأُولٰٓئِكَ هُمُ الْمُفْلِحُونَ ۝

وَاِلٰهُكُمْ اِلٰهٌ وَّاحِدٌ ۚ لَاۤ اِلٰهَ اِلَّا هُوَ الرَّحْمٰنُ الرَّحِيمُ ۝۱۶۳

اَللّٰهُ لَاۤ اِلٰهَ اِلَّا هُوَ الْحَيُّ الْقَيُّوْمُ ۚ لَا تَأْخُذُهُ سِنَةٌ وَّلَا نَوْمٌ ۚ لَهُ مَا فِى

السَّمٰوٰتِ وَمَا فِى الْاَرْضِ ۗ مَنْ ذَا الَّذِىْ يَشْفَعُ عِنْدَهُ اِلَّا بِاِذْنِهٖ ۚ يَعْلَمُ مَا

بَيْنَ اَيْدِيْهِمْ وَمَا خَلْفَهُمْ ۚ وَلَا يُحِيْطُوْنَ بِشَيْءٍ مِّنْ عِلْمِهٖ اِلَّا بِمَا شَاۤءَ ۚ

وَسِعَ كُرْسِيُّهُ السَّمٰوٰتِ وَالْاَرْضَ ۚ وَلَا يَئُوْدُهُ حِفْظُهُمَا ۚ وَهُوَ الْعَلِيُّ الْعَظِيْمُ

۝۲۵۵ لَاۤ اِكْرَاهَ فِى الدِّيْنِ ۚ قَدْ تَّبَيَّنَ الرُّشْدُ مِنَ الْغَيِّ ۚ فَمَنْ يَّكْفُرْ بِالطَّاغُوْتِ

وَيُؤْمِنْ بِاللّٰهِ فَقَدِ اسْتَمْسَكَ بِالْعُرْوَةِ الْوُثْقٰى لَا انْفِصَامَ لَهَا ۗ وَاللّٰهُ سَمِيْعٌ

عَلِيْمٌ ۝۲۵۶ اَللّٰهُ وَلِيُّ الَّذِيْنَ اٰمَنُوْا يُخْرِجُهُمْ مِّنَ الظُّلُمٰتِ اِلَى النُّوْرِ ۚ وَالَّذِيْنَ

كَفَرُوْۤا اَوْلِيٰٓـئُهُمُ الطَّاغُوْتُ يُخْرِجُوْنَهُمْ مِّنَ النُّوْرِ اِلَى الظُّلُمٰتِ ۗ اُولٰٓئِكَ

اَصْحٰبُ النَّارِ ۚ هُمْ فِيْهَا خٰلِدُوْنَ ۝۲۵۷

لِلّٰهِ مَا فِى السَّمٰوٰتِ وَمَا فِى الْاَرْضِ ۗ وَاِنْ تُبْدُوْا مَا فِىْ اَنْفُسِكُمْ اَوْ تُخْفُوْهُ

يُحَاسِبْكُمْ بِهِ اللّٰهُ ۚ فَيَغْفِرُ لِمَنْ يَّشَاۤءُ وَيُعَذِّبُ مَنْ يَّشَاۤءُ ۗ وَاللّٰهُ عَلٰى كُلِّ

شَىْءٍ قَدِيْرٌ ۞ اٰمَنَ الرَّسُوْلُ بِمَآ اُنْزِلَ اِلَيْهِ مِنْ رَّبِّهٖ وَالْمُؤْمِنُوْنَ كُلٌّ اٰمَنَ

بِاللّٰهِ وَمَلٰٓئِكَتِهٖ وَكُتُبِهٖ وَرُسُلِهٖ لَا نُفَرِّقُ بَيْنَ اَحَدٍ مِّنْ رُّسُلِهٖ وَقَالُوْا

سَمِعْنَا وَاَطَعْنَا غُفْرَانَكَ رَبَّنَا وَاِلَيْكَ الْمَصِيْرُ ۞ لَا يُكَلِّفُ اللّٰهُ نَفْسًا

اِلَّا وُسْعَهَا لَهَا مَا كَسَبَتْ وَعَلَيْهَا مَا اكْتَسَبَتْ رَبَّنَا لَا تُؤَاخِذْنَآ اِنْ

نَّسِيْنَآ اَوْ اَخْطَأْنَا رَبَّنَا وَلَا تَحْمِلْ عَلَيْنَآ اِصْرًا كَمَا حَمَلْتَهٗ عَلَى الَّذِيْنَ مِنْ

قَبْلِنَا رَبَّنَا وَلَا تُحَمِّلْنَا مَا لَا طَاقَةَ لَنَا بِهٖ وَاعْفُ عَنَّا وَاغْفِرْ لَنَا

وَارْحَمْنَآ اَنْتَ مَوْلٰنَا فَانْصُرْنَا عَلَى الْقَوْمِ الْكٰفِرِيْنَ ۞

شَهِدَ اللّٰهُ اَنَّهٗ لَآ اِلٰهَ اِلَّا هُوَ وَالْمَلٰٓئِكَةُ وَاُولُوا الْعِلْمِ قَآئِمًۢا بِالْقِسْطِ لَآ اِلٰهَ

اِلَّا هُوَ الْعَزِيْزُ الْحَكِيْمُ ۞

قُلِ اللّٰهُمَّ مٰلِكَ الْمُلْكِ تُؤْتِى الْمُلْكَ مَنْ تَشَآءُ وَتَنْزِعُ الْمُلْكَ مِمَّنْ تَشَآءُ

وَتُعِزُّ مَنْ تَشَآءُ وَتُذِلُّ مَنْ تَشَآءُ بِيَدِكَ الْخَيْرُ اِنَّكَ عَلٰى كُلِّ شَىْءٍ قَدِيْرٌ

۞ تُوْلِجُ الَّيْلَ فِى النَّهَارِ وَتُوْلِجُ النَّهَارَ فِى الَّيْلِ وَتُخْرِجُ الْحَىَّ مِنَ الْمَيِّتِ

وَتُخْرِجُ الْمَيِّتَ مِنَ الْحَيِّ ۚ وَتَرْزُقُ مَن تَشَآءُ بِغَيْرِ حِسَابٍ ۝

اِنَّ رَبَّكُمُ اللَّهُ الَّذِى خَلَقَ السَّمٰوٰتِ وَالْأَرْضَ فِى سِتَّةِ أَيَّامٍ ثُمَّ اسْتَوٰى عَلَى الْعَرْشِ ۖ يُغْشِى الَّيْلَ النَّهَارَ يَطْلُبُهُ حَثِيثًا وَّالشَّمْسَ وَالْقَمَرَ وَالنُّجُوْمَ مُسَخَّرٰتٍ بِأَمْرِهِ ۗ أَلَا لَهُ الْخَلْقُ وَالْأَمْرُ ۗ تَبَارَكَ اللَّهُ رَبُّ الْعٰلَمِيْنَ ۝

اُدْعُوْا رَبَّكُمْ تَضَرُّعًا وَّخُفْيَةً ۚ إِنَّهُ لَا يُحِبُّ الْمُعْتَدِيْنَ ۝ وَلَا تُفْسِدُوْا فِى الْأَرْضِ بَعْدَ اِصْلٰحِهَا وَادْعُوْهُ خَوْفًا وَّطَمَعًا ۚ إِنَّ رَحْمَتَ اللَّهِ قَرِيْبٌ مِّنَ الْمُحْسِنِيْنَ ۝

قُلِ ادْعُوا اللَّهَ أَوِ ادْعُوا الرَّحْمٰنَ ۖ أَيًّامَّا تَدْعُوْا فَلَهُ الْأَسْمَآءُ الْحُسْنٰى ۚ وَلَا تَجْهَرْ بِصَلَاتِكَ وَلَا تُخَافِتْ بِهَا وَابْتَغِ بَيْنَ ذٰلِكَ سَبِيْلًا ۝ وَقُلِ الْحَمْدُ لِلَّهِ الَّذِى لَمْ يَتَّخِذْ وَلَدًا وَّلَمْ يَكُن لَّهُ شَرِيْكٌ فِى الْمُلْكِ وَلَمْ يَكُن لَّهُ وَلِيٌّ مِّنَ الذُّلِّ ۖ وَكَبِّرْهُ تَكْبِيْرًا ۝

اَفَحَسِبْتُمْ اَنَّمَا خَلَقْنٰكُمْ عَبَثًا وَّاَنَّكُمْ اِلَيْنَا لَا تُرْجَعُوْنَ ۝١١٥ فَتَعٰلَى اللّٰهُ

الْمَلِكُ الْحَقُّ ۚ لَآ اِلٰهَ اِلَّا هُوَ رَبُّ الْعَرْشِ الْكَرِيْمِ ۝١١٦ وَمَنْ يَّدْعُ مَعَ اللّٰهِ

اِلٰهًا اٰخَرَ لَا بُرْهَانَ لَهٗ بِهٖ فَاِنَّمَا حِسَابُهٗ عِنْدَ رَبِّهٖ اِنَّهٗ لَا يُفْلِحُ الْكٰفِرُوْنَ

۝١١٧ وَقُلْ رَّبِّ اغْفِرْ وَارْحَمْ وَاَنْتَ خَيْرُ الرّٰحِمِيْنَ ۝١١٨

بِسْمِ اللّٰهِ الرَّحْمٰنِ الرَّحِيْمِ

وَالصّٰٓفّٰتِ صَفًّا ۝١ فَالزّٰجِرٰتِ زَجْرًا ۝٢ فَالتّٰلِيٰتِ ذِكْرًا ۝٣ اِنَّ اِلٰهَكُمْ

لَوَاحِدٌ ۝٤ رَبُّ السَّمٰوٰتِ وَالْاَرْضِ وَمَا بَيْنَهُمَا وَرَبُّ الْمَشَارِقِ ۝٥ اِنَّا زَيَّنَّا

السَّمَآءَ الدُّنْيَا بِزِيْنَةِ ِۨالْكَوَاكِبِ ۝٦ وَحِفْظًا مِّنْ كُلِّ شَيْطٰنٍ مَّارِدٍ ۝٧ لَا

يَسَّمَّعُوْنَ اِلَى الْمَلَاِ الْاَعْلٰى وَيُقْذَفُوْنَ مِنْ كُلِّ جَانِبٍ ۝٨ دُحُوْرًا وَّلَهُمْ

عَذَابٌ وَّاصِبٌ ۝٩ اِلَّا مَنْ خَطِفَ الْخَطْفَةَ فَاَتْبَعَهٗ شِهَابٌ ثَاقِبٌ ۝١٠

فَاسْتَفْتِهِمْ اَهُمْ اَشَدُّ خَلْقًا اَمْ مَّنْ خَلَقْنَا اِنَّا خَلَقْنٰهُمْ مِّنْ طِيْنٍ لَّازِبٍ ۝١١

يٰمَعْشَرَ الْجِنِّ وَالْاِنْسِ اِنِ اسْتَطَعْتُمْ اَنْ تَنْفُذُوْا مِنْ اَقْطَارِ السَّمٰوٰتِ

وَالْاَرْضِ فَانْفُذُوْا لَا تَنْفُذُوْنَ اِلَّا بِسُلْطٰنٍ ۝ فَبِاَيِّ اٰلَآءِ رَبِّكُمَا

تُكَذِّبٰنِ ۝ يُرْسَلُ عَلَيْكُمَا شُوَاظٌ مِّنْ نَّارٍ وَّنُحَاسٌ فَلَا تَنْتَصِرٰنِ ۝

فَبِاَيِّ اٰلَآءِ رَبِّكُمَا تُكَذِّبٰنِ ۝ فَاِذَا انْشَقَّتِ السَّمَآءُ فَكَانَتْ وَرْدَةً

كَالدِّهَانِ ۝ فَبِاَيِّ اٰلَآءِ رَبِّكُمَا تُكَذِّبٰنِ ۝ فَيَوْمَئِذٍ لَّا يُسْئَلُ عَنْ

ذَنْۢبِهٖ اِنْسٌ وَّلَا جَآنٌّ ۝ فَبِاَيِّ اٰلَآءِ رَبِّكُمَا تُكَذِّبٰنِ ۝

لَوْ اَنْزَلْنَا هٰذَا الْقُرْاٰنَ عَلٰى جَبَلٍ لَّرَاَيْتَهٗ خَاشِعًا مُّتَصَدِّعًا مِّنْ خَشْيَةِ اللهِ

وَتِلْكَ الْاَمْثَالُ نَضْرِبُهَا لِلنَّاسِ لَعَلَّهُمْ يَتَفَكَّرُوْنَ ۝ هُوَ اللهُ الَّذِيْ لَآ اِلٰهَ

اِلَّا هُوَ ۚ عٰلِمُ الْغَيْبِ وَالشَّهَادَةِ ۚ هُوَ الرَّحْمٰنُ الرَّحِيْمُ ۝ هُوَ اللهُ الَّذِيْ لَآ

اِلٰهَ اِلَّا هُوَ ۚ اَلْمَلِكُ الْقُدُّوْسُ السَّلٰمُ الْمُؤْمِنُ الْمُهَيْمِنُ الْعَزِيْزُ الْجَبَّارُ

الْمُتَكَبِّرُ ۚ سُبْحٰنَ اللهِ عَمَّا يُشْرِكُوْنَ ۝ هُوَ اللهُ الْخَالِقُ الْبَارِئُ الْمُصَوِّرُ

لَهُ الْاَسْمَآءُ الْحُسْنٰى ۚ يُسَبِّحُ لَهٗ مَا فِى السَّمٰوٰتِ وَالْاَرْضِ ۚ وَهُوَ الْعَزِيْزُ

الْحَكِيْمُ ۝

بِسْمِ اللهِ الرَّحْمٰنِ الرَّحِيْمِ

قُلْ اُوْحِيَ اِلَيَّ اَنَّهُ اسْتَمَعَ نَفَرٌ مِّنَ الْجِنِّ فَقَالُوْٓا اِنَّا سَمِعْنَا قُرْاٰنًا عَجَبًا ۝

يَّهْدِيْٓ اِلَى الرُّشْدِ فَاٰمَنَّا بِهٖ ۖ وَلَنْ نُّشْرِكَ بِرَبِّنَآ اَحَدًا ۝ وَّاَنَّهٗ تَعٰلٰى جَدُّ

رَبِّنَا مَا اتَّخَذَ صَاحِبَةً وَّلَا وَلَدًا ۝ وَّاَنَّهٗ كَانَ يَقُوْلُ سَفِيْهُنَا عَلَى اللهِ شَطَطًا

بِسْمِ اللهِ الرَّحْمٰنِ الرَّحِيْمِ

قُلْ يٰٓاَيُّهَا الْكٰفِرُوْنَ ۝ لَآ اَعْبُدُ مَا تَعْبُدُوْنَ ۝ وَلَآ اَنْتُمْ عٰبِدُوْنَ مَآ

اَعْبُدُ ۝ وَلَآ اَنَا عَابِدٌ مَّا عَبَدْتُّمْ ۝ وَلَآ اَنْتُمْ عٰبِدُوْنَ مَآ اَعْبُدُ ۝

لَكُمْ دِيْنُكُمْ وَلِيَ دِيْنِ ۝

بِسْمِ اللهِ الرَّحْمٰنِ الرَّحِيْمِ

قُلْ هُوَ اللهُ اَحَدٌ ۝ اَللهُ الصَّمَدُ ۝ لَمْ يَلِدْ وَلَمْ يُوْلَدْ ۝ وَلَمْ يَكُنْ لَّهٗ

كُفُوًا اَحَدٌ ۝

بِسْمِ اللهِ الرَّحْمٰنِ الرَّحِيْمِ

قُلْ اَعُوْذُ بِرَبِّ الْفَلَقِ ۞ مِنْ شَرِّ مَا خَلَقَ ۞ وَمِنْ شَرِّ غَاسِقٍ اِذَا وَقَبَ ۞ وَمِنْ شَرِّ النَّفّٰثٰتِ فِي الْعُقَدِ ۞ وَمِنْ شَرِّ حَاسِدٍ اِذَا حَسَدَ ۞

بِسْمِ اللهِ الرَّحْمٰنِ الرَّحِيْمِ

قُلْ اَعُوْذُ بِرَبِّ النَّاسِ ۞ مَلِكِ النَّاسِ ۞ اِلٰهِ النَّاسِ ۞ مِنْ شَرِّ الْوَسْوَاسِ الْخَنَّاسِ ۞ الَّذِىْ يُوَسْوِسُ فِيْ صُدُوْرِ النَّاسِ ۞ مِنَ الْجِنَّةِ وَالنَّاسِ ۞